Voyage of the *Adventure*

Voyage of the *Adventure*

Retracing the Donelson Party's Journey to the Founding of Nashville

JOHN GUIDER

Vanderbilt University Press
Nashville, Tennessee

Nashville, Tennessee 37235

First printing 2020
First paperback printing 2021
Printed in Canada

This book is printed on acid-free paper.

LIBRARY OF CONGRESS CATALOGING-IN-PUBLICATION DATA

Names: Guider, John, photographer, writer of introduction. | West, Carroll Van, 1955– author. | Williams, Learotha, Jr., author. | Bender, Albert, author. | Sellers, Jeff, writer of foreword.
Title: Voyage of the Adventure : retracing the Donelson party's journey to the founding of Nashville / John Guider ; essays by Jeff Sellers, Albert Bender, Learotha Williams Jr., and Carroll Van West.
Description: Nashville : Vanderbilt University Press, 2020. | Includes bibliographical references. | Summary: "In the fall of 2016, photographer John Guider retraced John Donelson's journey from the present site of Kingsport, Tennessee, to the founding of a settlement now known as Nashville, over 1,000 river miles away. Guider travelled in his hand-built 14 ft. motorless rowing sailboat while photographing the river as it currently exists 240 years later. This photo book contains 150 images from the course of the journey and includes essays providing long-ignored contemporary histories of the Cherokee and the enslaved people who Donelson encountered and brought with him, some of whom did not survive the journey"— Provided by publisher.
Identifiers: LCCN 2020013208 (print) | LCCN 2020013209 (ebook) | ISBN 9780826501097 (hardcover) | ISBN 9780826502520 (paperback) | ISBN 9780826501110 (epub) | ISBN 9780826501127 (pdf)
Subjects: LCSH: Donelson, John, approximately 1718-approximately 1780. | Cherokee Indians—Tennessee—History. | Tennessee—History. | Tennessee—Pictorial works. | Nashville (Tenn.)—History.
Classification: LCC F436 .G84 2020 (print) | LCC F436 (ebook) | DDC 976.8/55—dc23

LC record available at https://lccn.loc.gov/2020013208
LC ebook record available at https://lccn.loc.gov/2020013209

To my wife Mona. She holds the light that always guides me home.

CONTENTS

ACKNOWLEDGMENTS

Even a journey referred to as a solo adventure cannot be completed without the help of so many others, especially in this day and time. The early pioneers would have been lost without the direction of the Native Americans. This project was dependent on the generosity of so many it is hard to list them all: John Harris of Chesapeake Light Craft designed and modified the boat that has carried me thousands of miles across the North American waterways on this as well as many other adventures, while Allen Doty of Cumberland Transit generously helped me outfit for my long travels. Mark Fly, Stacey Irvin, and Andee Rudloff helped with logistics. Bob Tigert's videography helped spark the genesis for the companion Emmy Award–winning documentary, *Voyage of* Adventure, produced by WNPT under the incredible direction of Will Pedigo and his wonderful, talented crew. I'm indebted to Jeffrey Buntin, Varina Willse, David Fox, and Robinson Regen, who used their marketing skills to bring awareness to the importance of the project and encourage donations for the completion of the documentary. Eileen Beehan, Gilbert S. Merit, Justin Wilson, Calvin and Marilyn Lehue, Andrew Donelson Dunn, and Karen Dunn Cochran heard the call and responded with their financial support. Jessica Hopp Bliss and George Walker Jr. of the *Tennessean*, USA Today Network, followed the journey and created a wonderful eight-page feature for their Sunday supplement, written by Jessica and ripe with incredible images created by George. George's portrait of me graces the back cover of the book. Jane Dugger and Charlotte Reynolds of the Rachael Stockley Donelson chapter of the DAR helped bring national attention to the project and were responsible for my being awarded the DAR's 2019 Conservation Award. Unlike Donelson's party, I was fortunate to have friends such as Rob and Gabi Hoffman and Gerald Kirksey reach out to me along the way. I was also enabled by the kindness of strangers such as James Adams, Amy Aldana, James and Gail Kelly, Randy Ashwerth, Tammy Reasons, and Ron Harr, who opened their hearts to me, making my struggles much easier and reconfirming for me the underlying goodness that defines our humanity.

Andrew Maraniss kindly introduced me to the great people at the Vanderbilt University Press, who encouraged the project. Zachary Gresham and Joell Smith-Borne are amazing editors indeed, while Drohan DiSanto did a fabulous job with the design. Thank you to Jeff Sellers, Albert Bender, Learotha Williams Jr, and Carroll Van West for their contributing essays as well.

I also want to thank my family, especially Mona, Matt, and Kelly, for putting up with me and allowing me to go on these extended forays, absent for months at a time where I was able to explore new personal territories and drink in that restorative tonic known as nature. At age seventy-one I feel as strong and as vibrant as ever. I know these journeys and the love of life they provide are a major reason for my well-being.

FOREWORD

JEFF SELLERS
Director of Education & Engagement at the Tennessee State Museum

In my role as the Education Director at the Tennessee State Museum, I am privileged to share the history of our state through exhibits and artifacts. As we say at the museum, "there are three stars and thousands of stories." One of the most well-known stories is the Donelson journey. Children and adults alike are fascinated by the story of Tennessee's settlement. Whether you are a native Tennessean with roots back to the early settlement period or a new transplant to the "It City" of Nashville, the narrative of the founding of Nashville captures your attention and imagination. Why is Nashville situated on the bluff of the Cumberland River? What did the early settlers to Middle Tennessee encounter? Who were those people who left everything they knew and headed west to start over in a largely unknown land? The stories we tell and retell speak to who we are as a society. The one unfolded here is a story that has been retold through many generations. However, there remain many hidden stories and new perspectives that this book will reveal.

Early Tennesseans recognized the significance of those first pioneers. They recorded their stories and collected artifacts that travelled with these early migrants. On display at the museum is a simple iron kettle. It would be like any other cooking kettle of the period except the small brass label affixed on it claims that it belonged to the Robert Cartwright family and was "used by the Cartwrights on [their] trip to Nashville, 1779–80." There is also a white ironstone serving bowl with scalloped edges. Legend has it that this bowl was carried by the Lucas family on the Donelson journey. The most iconic, enduring, and perhaps most analyzed object is a small bound journal that was reported to have been John Donelson's. This paperbound ledger resides at the Tennessee State Library and Archives and provides a first-person account of the journey written by Col. John Donelson himself. On the front cover the old label reads "The Original, Journal of a Voyage intended by God's permission on the good boat Adventure, from Fort Patrick Henry on Holston River to the French Salt Springs on Cumberland River kept by John Donelson, December 22, 1779." The contents of this journal have informed countless histories of the founding of Nashville and the history of Tennessee. My colleagues and I get to use these objects to better understand and interpret the story of Tennessee's early settlement.

Historian Paul Clements has researched the Donelson Journal extensively. He is an expert on the Tennessee frontier and compiled the most comprehensive reference manual for this era, *The Chronicles of the Cumberland Settlements: 1779–1796*. His assessment of the journal casts doubt that the "original" journal was entirely written during the journey itself. Rather, Clements believes that the journal could have been partially completed decades later by Donelson's son John Donelson Jr. He bases this conclusion on the changing writing styles, changing verb tenses from present to past tense, and points of view that could only have been known after the fact in the story. Perhaps most compelling, Clements identified several written accounts created in later years by John Donelson Jr., who wrote a third person version called the "Donalson Journel," which appears in John Haywood's *Civil and Political History of Tennessee*. Nonetheless, Clements concludes that the events that took place on the voyage are credible and supported by other eyewitness accounts. Therefore, the journal of the Donelson voyage should remain a vital and reliable source for understanding the history of Nashville and Tennessee.[1]

As time passed, the first-person accounts eventually ended and the Donelson party's journey was relegated to Tennessee history textbooks. With many intervening years, the journey becomes a brief paragraph in those textbooks. Today, much of the public interpretation is a statue on the river and a replica of Fort Nashborough in downtown Nashville. As Tennesseans moved further from the historic event, the story has become one dimensional, leaving it almost lifeless without the varied nuances that must have been a part of the original journey. For some, however, the story never felt flat or one dimensional. For some Tennesseans, like John Guider, the story takes over their imaginations and leads to a breakthrough in the way we view it, breathing new life into an old story.

I first met John Guider in 2008 while working on an exhibit the museum hosted called *The River Inside*, which chronicled one of Guider's first river adventures. In it he canoed the creek behind his house to the Harpeth River, then to the Cumberland River, which flowed to the Ohio River, on to the Mississippi River, and finally to New Orleans. Guider canoed the entire watershed of the Cumberland River system! Along the way he used his skills as a professional photographer to capture the changing environment and unique river culture of the people who live and work on and around the river. John Guider is a modern-day adventurer who happens to capture his adventures through the lens of his camera.

Guider has been on many river adventures throughout his illustrious photography career but none as significant to Tennessee history as his 2016 adventure where he retraced the river journey of the Donelson party. Through the lens of his camera and on the same route as the Donelson party, Guider's experiences give us an opportunity to reinterpret this old familiar story. Often the story of Nashville's settlement is told from the perspective of the main character himself, John Donelson. Focusing solely on the central characters does not provide twenty-first-century Tennesseans with the full picture of our state's settlement. So many questions come to mind when we truly think about Donelson's journey: What about women? What about the children? What about the people of color that played just as important a role in this journey? What about the Native Americans that watched as their lands were taken from them? What about the changes to the landscape of the area as humans pushed forward to settle it? Common sense tells us that the story is immensely more complex than a paragraph in a textbook; however, the question is how to rethink the familiar story to resonate with modern Tennesseans.

Guider's photographs taken along the Donelson party's route provide us with a fresh perspective on this early settlement story. This book shifts focus from Donelson and the white settlers to others who were just as important to the settlement of Nashville but had always been relegated to a supporting role in the traditional narrative. This book will give a voice to the enslaved settlers who had no choice in making the perilous journey. It will give a voice to the American Indians who saw the expedition not as settlement but as an invasion—a threat to their very existence. Finally, this book will give a voice to the river itself.

How has the river system that John captured in his photographs changed from the rivers traversed by the Donelson party? This diverse perspective offers a more comprehensive story. One that reveals a multidimensional narrative that extends a way for us to better understand the complicated settlement story.

By the 1770s, land speculation was rampant throughout the western frontier, the area west of the Appalachian Mountains and east of the Mississippi

River. Even George Washington sought investment opportunities in western lands. Frontier wars, treaties, and the eroding influence of British law sparked land negotiations in the Trans-Appalachian West. Opportunistic land speculators formed companies to purchase Indian lands with hopes of selling smaller parcels for profit. One of the most active of these speculators was Richard Henderson. A native Virginian who became a North Carolina judge, Henderson had plenty of influence in both colonies. Using his network, Henderson formed the Transylvania Company. In 1775, he negotiated a private land purchase of twenty-seven thousand square miles in central Kentucky and Tennessee from the Cherokee, called the Treaty of Sycamore Shoals, and he recruited some of the best surveyors and frontiersmen to help negotiate, purchase, and settle the western lands. Two of them were John Donelson and James Robertson.

The treaty was immediately controversial. So controversial that a faction of the Cherokee under the leadership of a young leader named Dragging Canoe left in protest. He and his followers moved south along the Tennessee River and founded villages along the lower Tennessee River near today's Chattanooga. Nonetheless, the treaty was negotiated and signed. In it, the Cherokee agreed to give up a vast swath of land, nearly twenty million acres in total. In exchange, the Cherokee elders received wagonloads of goods. With this land purchase in hand, Donelson and Robertson prepared to settle the fertile river bottoms and establish a land office. Here, with their other investors, they could speculate on land sales anticipating the rush of settlers moving west.

A mere month after the land purchase, the battles of Lexington and Concord sparked the American Revolution. Over the next few years, the frontier settlements became embroiled in brutal warfare with the indigenous tribes. In what would become Tennessee, these included the Watauga, Nolichucky, and Holston settlements. The Cherokee under the leadership of Dragging Canoe allied themselves with the British and attacked hastily built American forts, stations, and isolated homesteads. In retaliation, expeditions of American settlers led by John Sevier and Isaac Shelby attacked Cherokee towns, capturing stores of corn and supplies necessary for the winter months. Finally, the Treaty of Long Island in 1777 ended the Cherokee war and resulted in most of modern day upper East Tennessee being ceded to the Americans. With active military campaigns among the Cherokee abated, the land speculators renewed their focus on settling the Cumberland region.

By the fall of 1779, the banks of the Holston River were a flurry of activity with people arriving daily to build flatboats. James Robertson left the settlement with a large group of frontiersmen who travelled to the French Lick over land. It was determined that the long distance and dangerous terrain would be too arduous for the families intent on settling. Instead, John Donelson would lead a flotilla of flatboats with the families on a river journey of over one thousand miles. The plan was for the flotilla to land at Muscle Shoals, where James Robertson would leave a sign communicating whether or not the overland route was safe to attempt.

The humanity of the stories recorded in the original Donelson journal continue to resonate when students take the time to study the recorded events.

On December 22, 1779, Donelson set off on the river journey.

The travelers endured freezing conditions, Indian attacks, treacherous rapids, and lack of food before finally arriving at the French Lick above the Cumberland River to rejoin their families and acquaintances who had gone overland with Robertson. In all, the journey navigated the Holston River, the Tennessee River, upstream on the Ohio River, and upstream of the Cumberland River to arrive at the French Lick. It took them four months. This traditional narrative has been largely informed by the "original" Donelson journal. It recounts navigating the rapids of Muscle Shoals, and the parting of ways of families who decided to float with the current to Natchez rather than stemming the stiff current of the Ohio. These stories help to make the Donelson story compelling and provide a rare example of human emotion in a historical event.

THE HUMANITY OF the stories recorded in the original Donelson journal continue to resonate when students take the time to study the recorded events. One of these enduring stories involves the tragic story of Mrs. Peyton and her infant child.

The day of March 8 was perhaps the most perilous and memorable of the journey for many of the participants. It begins with the river playing a significant role in the story. The Suck was a bend in the Tennessee River where bluffs on both sides squeezed the river into half its size, creating strong currents that whirled the free-floating boats in circles. It was the perfect strategic point of attack for the Chickamauga. The previous night, the party had encamped on the south bank of the river at an abandoned Chickamauga town. There, a young woman, recorded as Mrs. Ephraim Peyton, delivered a baby.

She was traveling in the boat of her parents, the Jennings, because her husband, Ephraim, was on the overland route with James Robertson. Traveling through the treacherous Suck, one of the canoes full of supplies tipped over, dumping all its supplies and cargo. The Jennings' boat stopped on the bank to collect the supplies that could be salvaged. While gathering supplies, the boat became a prime target of a surprise attack from a group of Chickamauga high above them on the opposite bluff.

As shots poured down on the Jennings boat, everyone on the boat franticly attempted to dislodge it from the bank. In their desperation to throw cargo overboard to lighten the draft, the newborn baby of Mrs. Peyton was tossed overboard and drowned.

This dramatic episode was remembered by John Donelson Jr., Elijah Farris, and Mary Donelson. This story has endured over the years because of the human tragedy associated with it. However, other stories that have just as much meaning have remained hidden. Often these stories are of the less prominent, but no less significant, members of the

Donelson Party. One example is the story of a young enslaved man whose name was never recorded. He tragically died from frostbite along the trip. Because he was an enslaved person, his story was not carried forward through time. All of the traveler's stories deserve to be remembered and studied.

AS WE TRAVEL with John Donelson and John Guider on the same route, we are traveling in two very different eras. To help us navigate these sometimes turbulent historical waters, we will look to three prominent historians. First, we compare the two river journeys, the Donelsons' and Guider's. Over eons the rivers have changed the landscape through which they wind. Likewise, it has been humans that have made drastic changes to the rivers over the two and half centuries since the journey. There was the previously described bottleneck called the Suck, also known as "the Whirl," that struck fear in the heart of any navigator. Then there was the great Muscle Shoals region. This area consisted of miles of shallows where the Tennessee River dropped significantly in elevation, causing turbulent rapids. Today those places are long gone. The danger zones have been flooded by the damming and dredging of the river by the Tennessee Valley Authority or US Army Corps of Engineers. To better understand Guider's photographs and Donelson's journal, the Tennessee State Historian and renowned historic preservationist Dr. Carroll Van West will properly frame the journey in its historical context as it relates to the changing rivers. He will bridge the two journeys and help explain the environmental history of these waters.

Guider's photographs allow us to reexamine the human side of the Donelson journey by moving beyond the main characters to explore multiple perspectives of the varied groups of settlers that embarked on the Donelson journey and even those that resisted it. There are in fact many hidden figures on the journey that played significant roles in the settlement of Nashville. First, the reader will meet all of the travelers in the party. Past descriptions of the journey depicted a largely monochromatic cast of characters in the story. The story is often told of intrepid white frontiersmen who braved the treacherous journey, overcoming many hardships to eventually carve out their place in the wilderness and bring civilization to the frontier. Our perspective has centered on the flatboat slowly drifting down the river with Donelson. This book challenges the reader to upend this perspective. Instead of standing on the flatboat peering at the banks of the river, the reader is encouraged to stand with the Chickamauga Cherokee and view their perspective. To contemplate what it must have been like as they watched the flotilla of boats slowly pass their villages. What did they think? What did this mean to them? This book offers a native voice through a Cherokee author, historian, and attorney, Albert Bender. He explains the significance of this journey for his ancestors and includes the context of western settlement for the Cherokee as they faced broken treaties and false promises.

The book will challenge the reader to consider those individuals who were forced into this journey. Some estimates project that almost half of the migrants were enslaved. Mary Donelson, the daughter of John Donelson, recalled that with the Donelson family alone there were fifteen whites and thirty enslaved African Americans. The Cartwright family's boat had room for three families "besides a number of negroes." Two were named Aliph and Susan, fifteen and thirteen years old respectively.[2] These men, women, and children did not choose to go on the journey. What kind of life would they have when they arrived? What kind of life did they leave behind? And more broadly, what did the journey mean in introducing the institution of slavery to a new fertile region poised for large-scale cultivation. Like the many seeds of tobacco, wheat, corn, and cotton, those enslaved African Americans were brought to plant the seeds of the plantation economy in the Trans-Appalachian West. To help understand this perspective, Dr. Learotha Williams, a professor of African American history and public history at Tennessee State University, will provide insight into the enslaved African American experience on the Donelson journey. Dr. Williams will also offer insights into slavery on the frontier.

By reexamining the Donelson journey as a prism, we see many bands of light. From one facet, we can see an environmental history and how people's impact has affected the land for good and bad. Turning the prism we catch glimpses into what the journey and future looked like for those forced to take part in western expansion. And finally, repositioning the prism once again, we are able to understand that this journey is not one story in time but many stories for many audiences and helps to better understand our own times. So to the reader, as you join John Guider on this float down the river and as you reflect on the Donelson party's parallel float in history, ponder the many facets of the story and try to experience this journey through multiple perspectives.

NOTES

1. Paul Clements, "Tennessee Notes: An Analysis of 'The Original' Donelson Journal and Associated Accounts of the Donelson Party Voyage," *Tennessee Historical Quarterly* 64, no. 4 (Winter 2005): 339–48.
2. Paul Clements, *Chronicles of the Cumberland Settlements: 1779–1796* (Nashville: Foundation of William and Jennifer Frist and Paul Clements, 2012), 133.

REFERENCES

Clements, Paul. *The Chronicles of the Cumberland Settlements: 1779-1796*. Nashville: Foundation of William and Jennifer Frist and Paul Clements, 2012.

Clements, Paul. "Tennessee Notes: An Analysis of 'The Original' Donelson Journal and Associated Accounts of the Donelson Party Voyage." *Tennessee Historical Quarterly* 64, no. 4 (Winter 2005).

Folmsbee, Stanley J., Robert E. Corlew, and Enoch L. Mitchell. *History of Tennessee*. New York: Lewis Historical Publishing Company, 1960.

Ray, Kristofer. *Middle Tennessee 1775–1825: Progress and Popular Democracy on the Southwestern Frontier*. Knoxville: University of Tennessee Press, 2007.

INTRODUCTION

I HAD BEEN ON WATER adventures before. In fact, the year before I started this quest I had just finished sailing and rowing a 6,500-mile watercourse around the eastern coast of the United States known as the Great Loop. For seven years I had gone out in my little motorless fourteen-foot watercraft for about two months at a time. I sailed as far south as Key West before heading up to Canada and around the Great Lakes. It was quite an adventure to say the least.

My little cocoon of a boat had become so personal to me that I had a hard time deciding on a name for it. Then one day, years into my project, I was walking around the Metro Nashville Courthouse and read a plaque detailing John Donelson's journey to the founding of Nashville. His boat was named the *Adventure*. That was it. I would name my boat the

Adventure II because I had left on my odyssey from nearly the same spot where Donelson had landed. In a way, I felt like I was continuing the adventure.

But now that my boat had a name, I had something else to think about. Why did Donelson risk it all to make the journey? For me all that was left was to try to find out. As T. S. Eliot once wrote, "If you aren't in over your head, how do you know how tall you are?"

Fascinated by his story, and in love with the water and Tennessee, I decided to retrace Donelson's one-thousand-mile journey down the Holston, Tennessee, Ohio, and Cumberland Rivers in my handmade row/sail boat to get a visceral sense of the adventure and to see firsthand all that has transpired in the intervening years.

Toward the end of the summer of 1779, John Donelson traveled with his family of ten (including twelve-year-old Rachel) and thirty enslaved people from his one-thousand-acre estate in the Commonwealth of Virginia to the outpost Fort Patrick Henry, which sat on the banks of the free-flowing Holston River in what is now the community of Kingsport, Tennessee. He was ill prepared for what awaited him.

I LAUNCHED ON Monday, September 5, 2016, Labor Day, to much fanfare and many clicking shutters.

Of the hundreds of photographs I took along the way, this book contains the most representative of the Tennessee I saw. My lasting impressions are two. The first is that there are two Tennessees, one rural and one urban, and the gulf between them (social, cultural, economic) is more massive than most of us realize. With 20 percent unemployment the norm in the rural counties, some riverside communities go on welfare every winter until the diners go back to full-time hours. Rebel flags and Trump signs dot the rural landscape, and people speak openly about their resentment toward the nearby cities. The Democrats were not going to carry rural Tennessee in the upcoming election the way they had a few decades earlier.

Rampant unemployment and inferior education facilities combined with inadequate healthcare and social services have put the rural communities at risk, causing many to turn to drugs to counteract a feeling of hopelessness. Stories of the out-of-control meth epidemic ran through my journal from beginning to end.

Nature, of course, is at a tipping point as well. The second lasting impression I came away with is that we have done untold damage to our waterways and the wildlife that relies on them. Nature, given the chance, is self-healing. Massive TVA construction sites are not. Though nature has ways to regenerate and purify itself when damage is fairly small-scale, the locks and dams and power plants remain toxic. Most were designed for a work life of fifty years. The infrastructure has reached that limit, and the cost of repairs is constantly increasing. The American Society of Civil Engineers emphatically warns that modern American infrastructure is in a state of crisis. More than two thousand dams are at risk of collapse; combined with highway degradation and structural damage to more than 10 percent of all bridges, the costs of repairs exceed $3.5 trillion. Where will that money come from, especially when 1 percent of the population controls over 90 percent of the wealth? What happens when the TVA runs out of coal, or when the maintenance costs for those dams and power plants override any potential for profit? What happens when the TVA can no longer afford its CEO's $6.5 million salary?

My love is for nature and for the regenerative and restorative powers it brings to my body, mind, and spirit whenever I am in it. The intention for my photographs is to share the beauty that confronts me. Hopefully they will reinforce the message that natural places need to survive. Vincent van Gogh wrote, "Those who love nature can find beauty anywhere." I want my images to evidence his words.

WHAT REMAINED OF the Donelson party landed on Monday, April 24, 1780, with bleak prospects ahead. On Monday, April 24, 1780, Donelson wrote:

> This day we arrived at our journey's end at the Big Salt Lick. Where we all had the pleasure of finding Capt. Robertson & his company. It is a source of satisfaction to us to be enabled to restore to him & others their families and friends, who were entrusted to our care, and who, some time since despaired of ever meeting again. Tho our prospects at present are dreary. We have found a few log cabins which been built on a Cedar Bluff above the Lick by Capt. Robertson and his company.

A modest party of friends welcomed me into port in Nashville on Saturday, October 29, 2016. My home was already there and waiting. My rest was assured.

For Tennesseans new and old, I hope that this book will awaken a sense of our unique waterways and their unusual history, particularly the harrowing journey that led to the founding of Nashville and the new perils that await us, its residents, if we do not act sooner than later.

JOHN GUIDER
Nashville, Tennessee
September 2019

Voyage of the *Adventure*

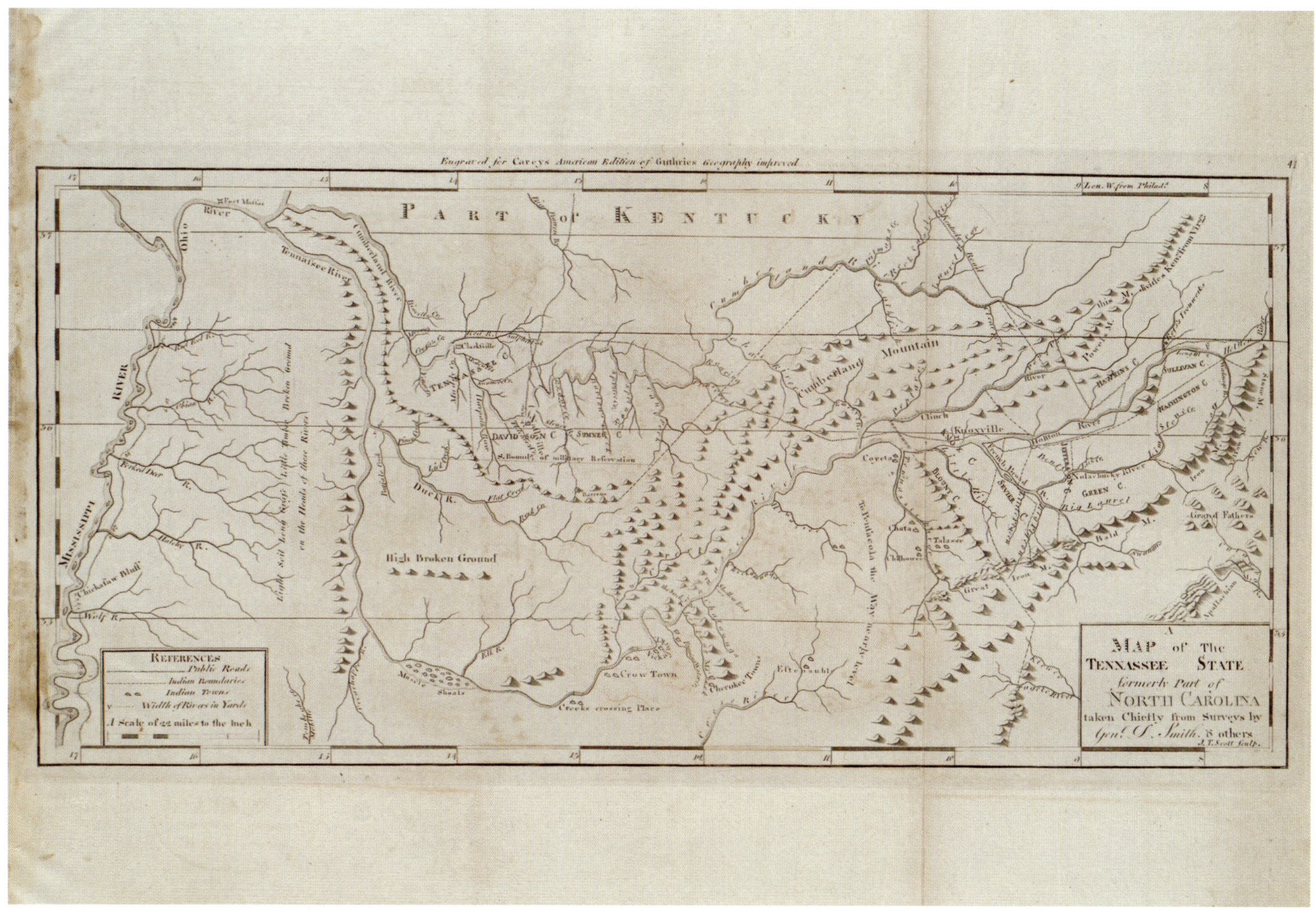

Eighteenth-century survey map illustrating the major river systems in Tennessee.

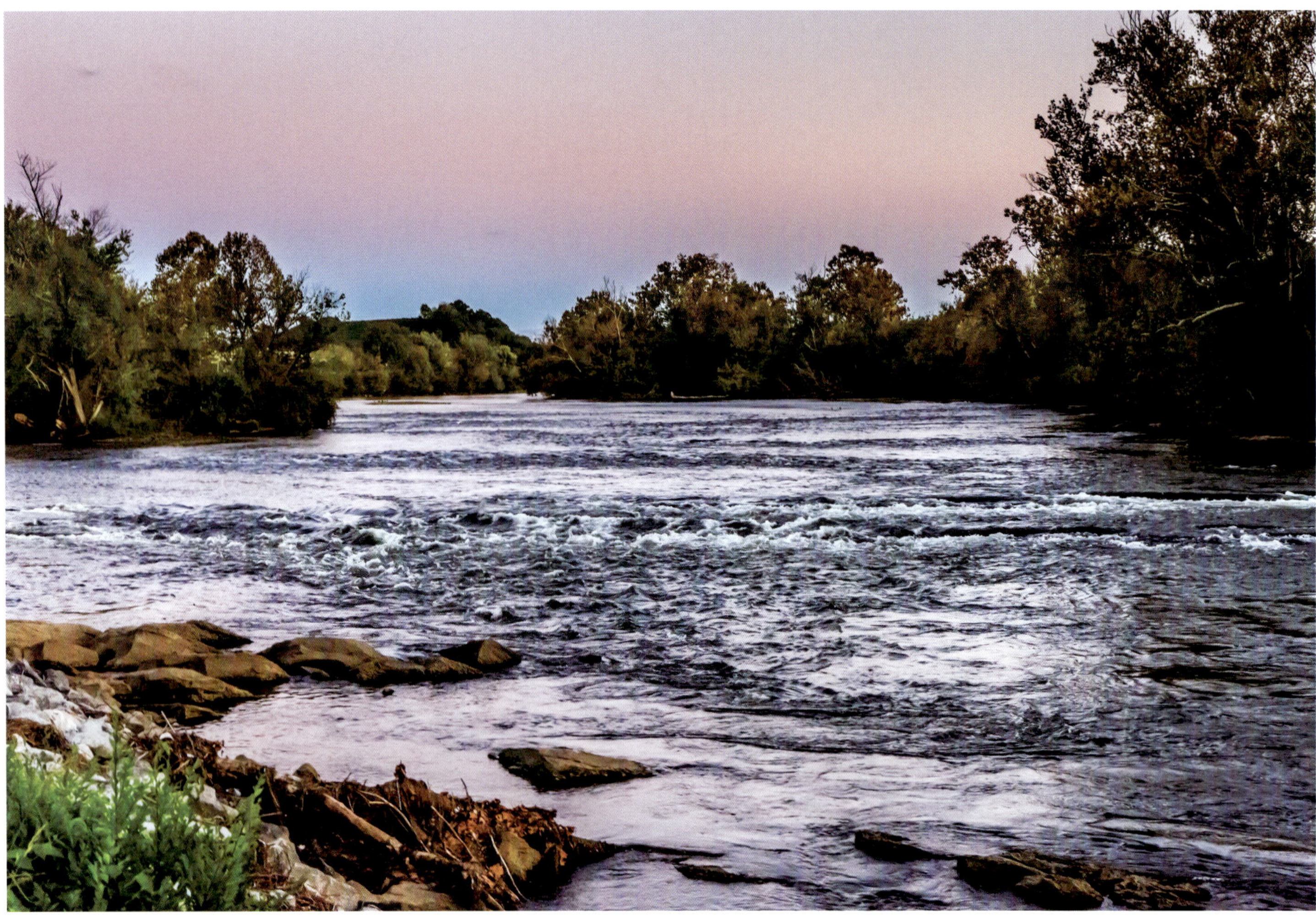

HOLSTON RIVER, KINGSPORT, TENNESSEE, close to where John Donelson constructed and launched his flatboat *Adventure*. The waning light and shadow-infused landscape obscures the industry that lurks behind the trees, offering a glimpse of the river as Donelson may have seen it as he walked the riverbanks.

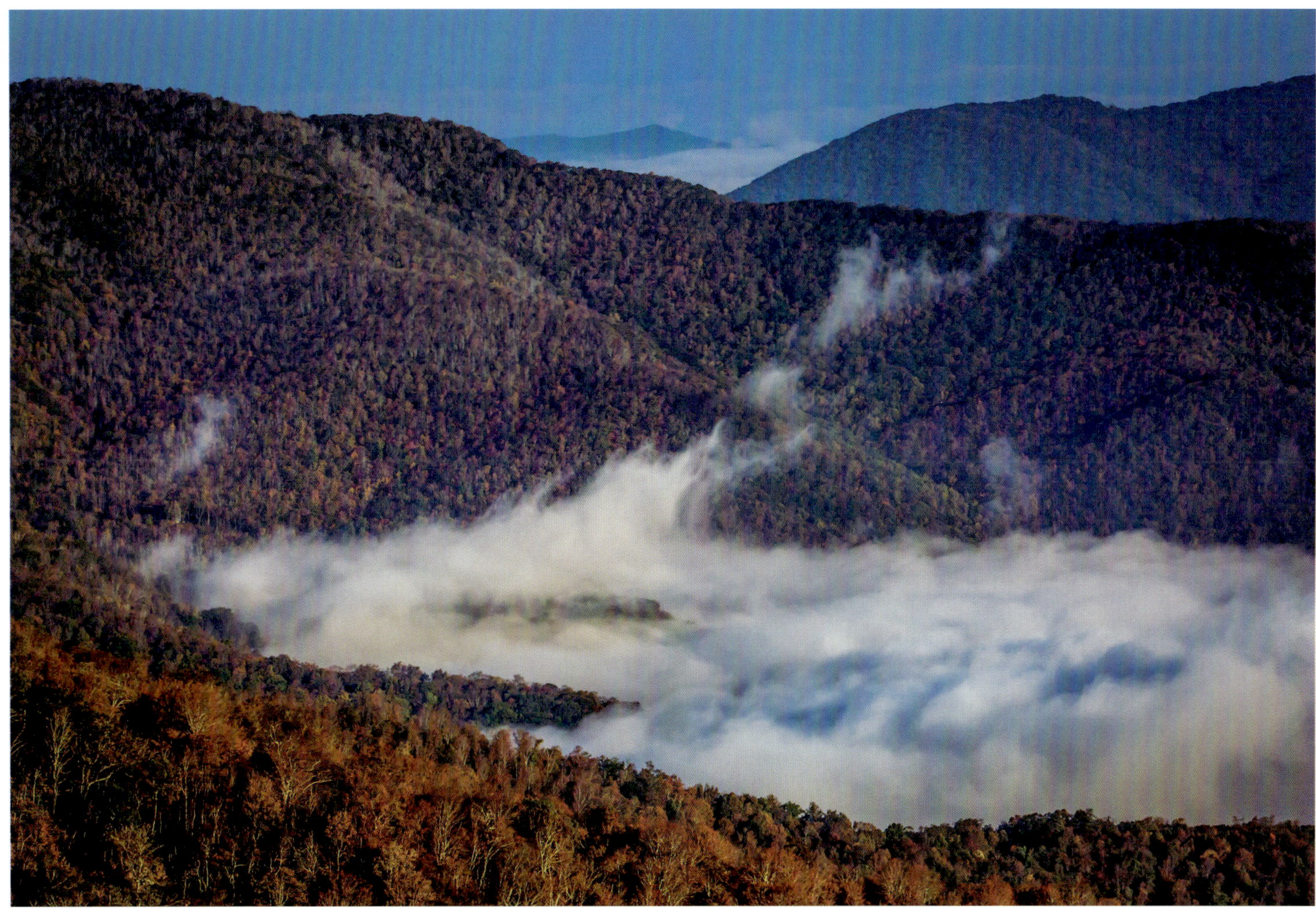

View of the Appalachian Mountains from the top of Roan Mountain, illustrating the great natural divide between the original colonies and the rest of the western continent.

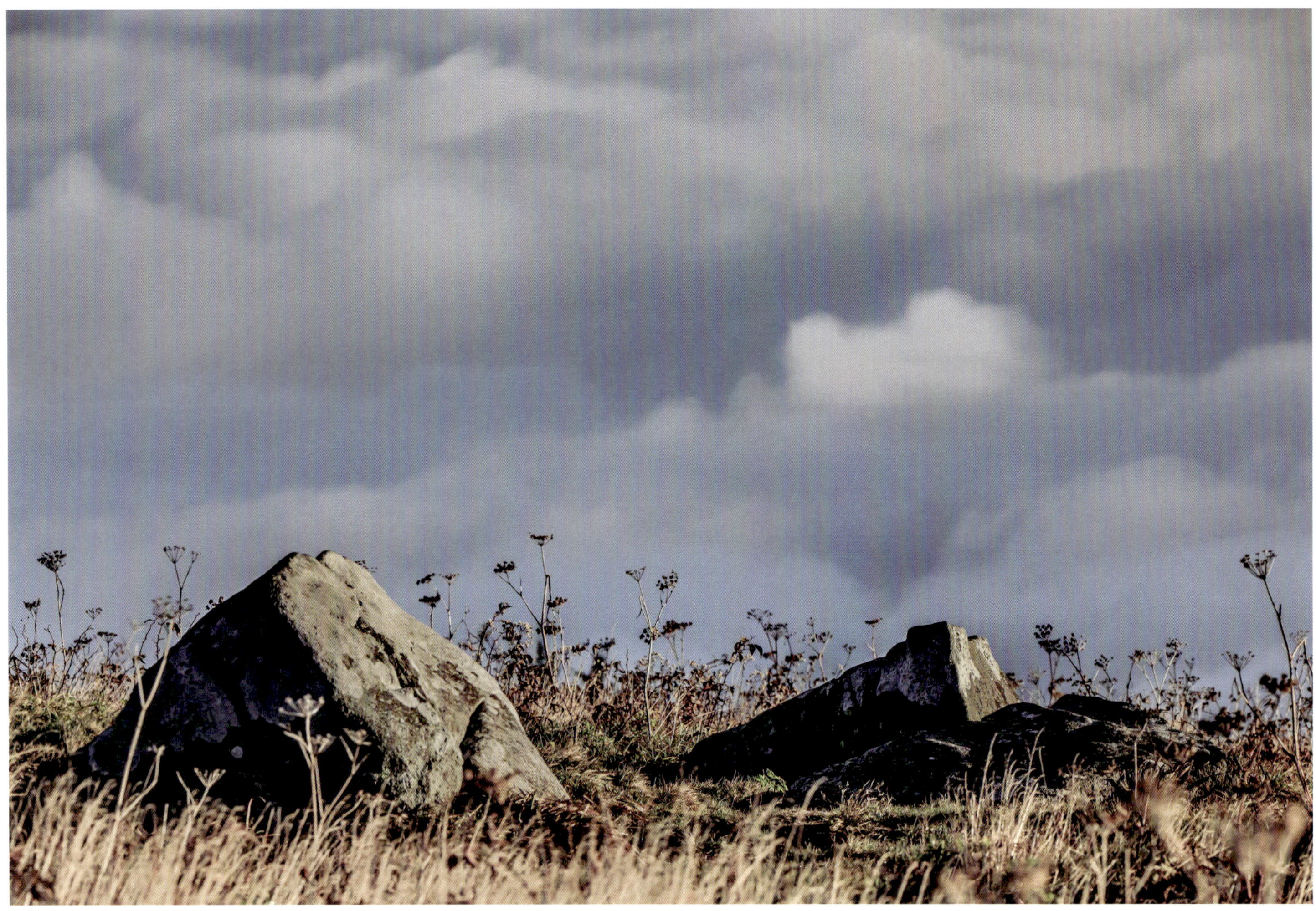

ROAN MOUNTAIN. Rock outcrops so evident in East Tennessee illustrate how difficult cultivation would have been in that region.

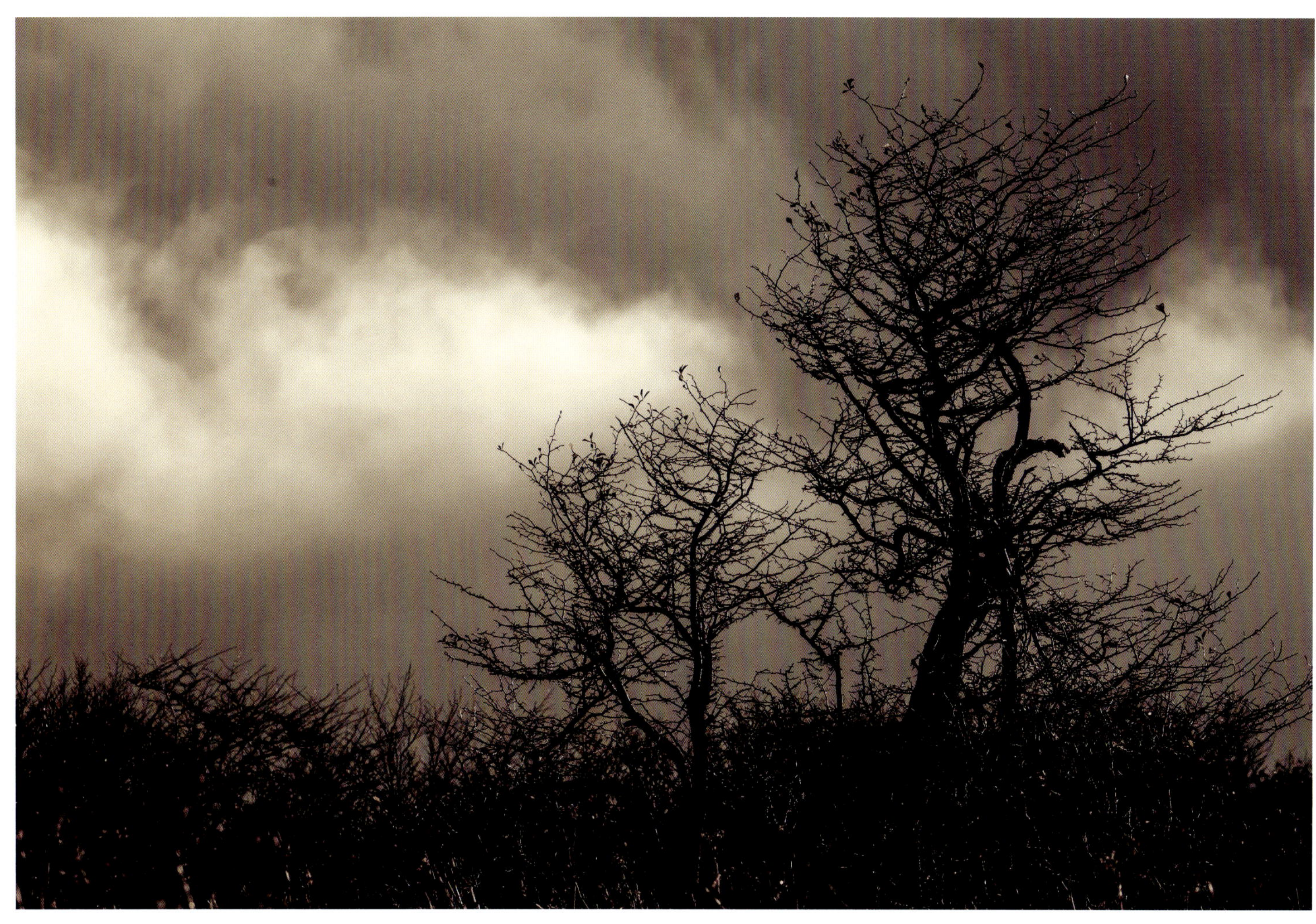

ROAN MOUNTAIN. Barren trees presage the ominous journey that lay ahead.

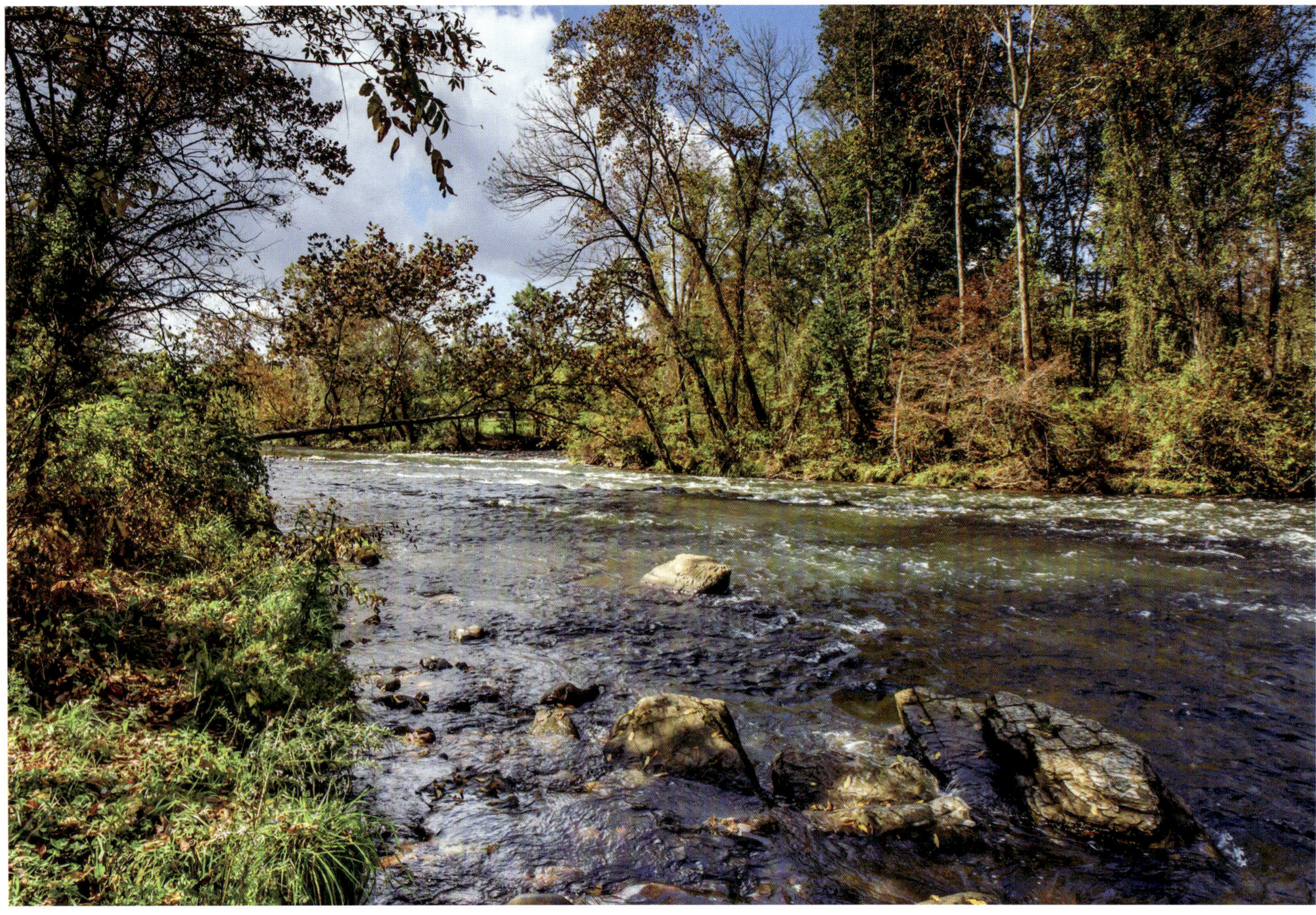

WATAUGA RIVER AT SYCAMORE SHOALS. Site of the first settlement outside of the original colonies; it broke all the rules set by the King of England and encroached on Native American territory.

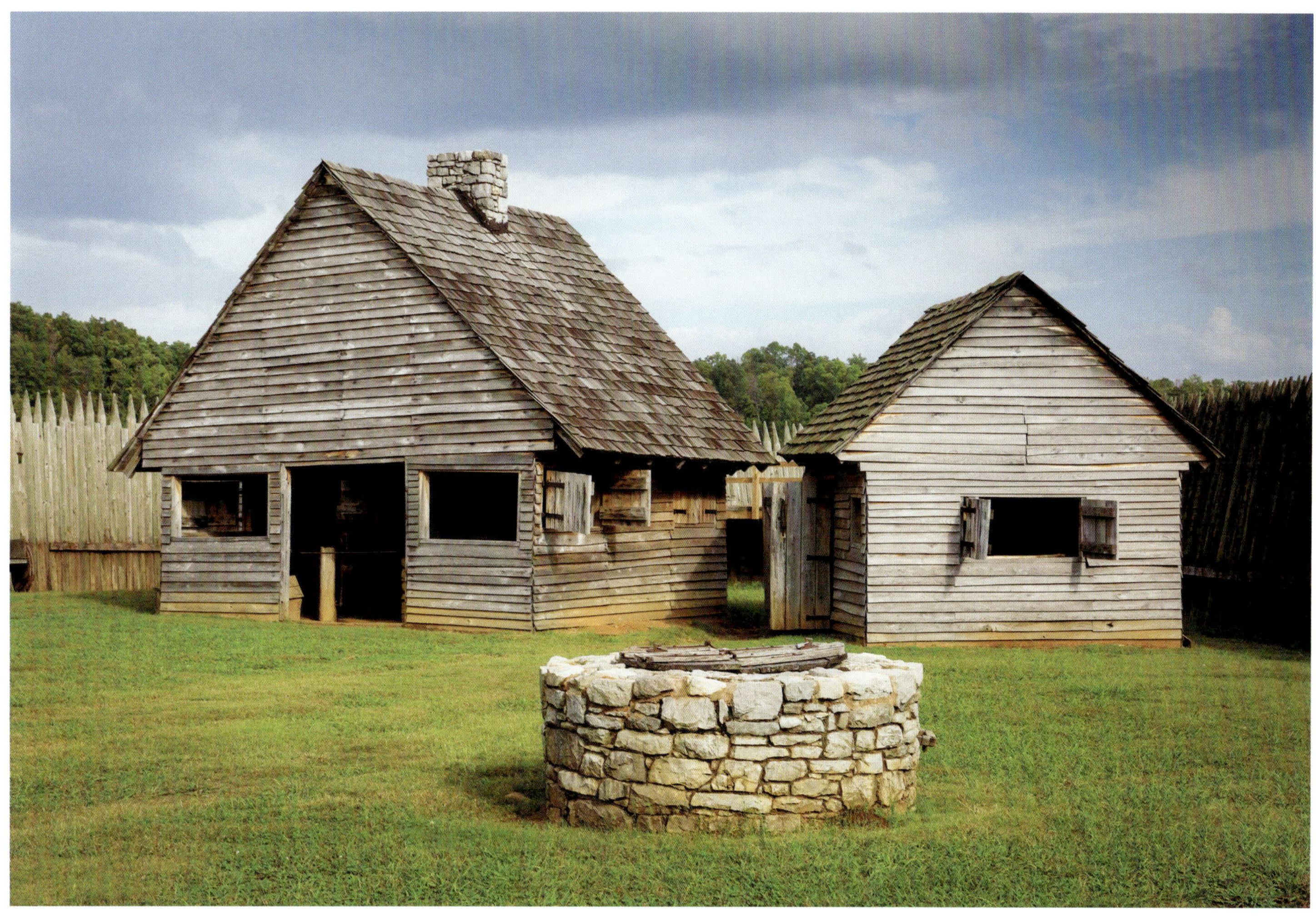

FORT LOUDOUN STATE PARK. Re-creation of the original British fort that occupied the lands of Tennessee below present-day Knoxville. Fort Patrick Henry, where Donelson prepared for his departure, was most likely built in a similar fashion.

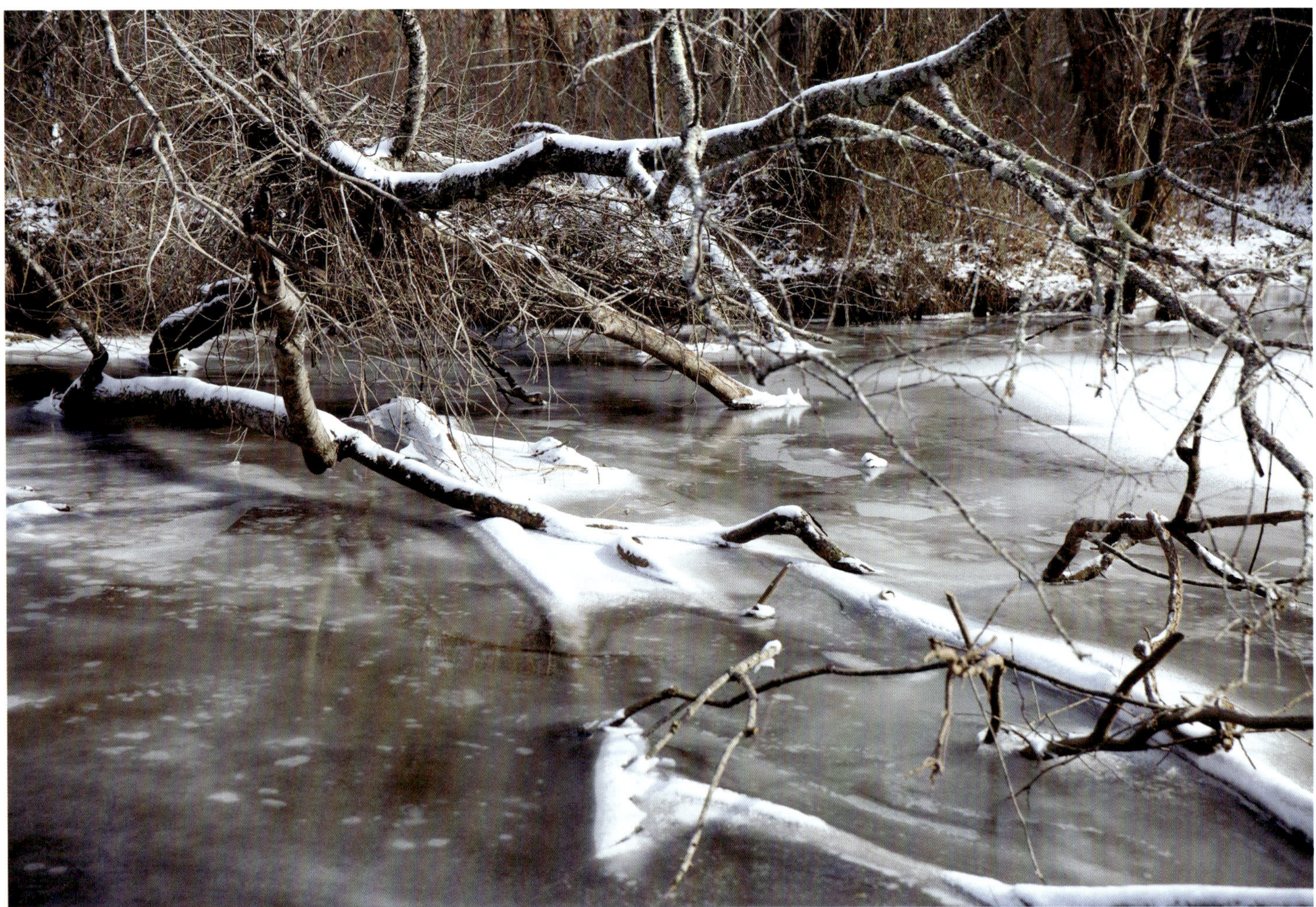

The “hard winter” wreaked mayhem on Donelson’s planned departure in December, delaying him for almost two unbearable months. This and all the following snowfall images were made with Will Perdue while filming the documentary *Voyage of Adventure*.

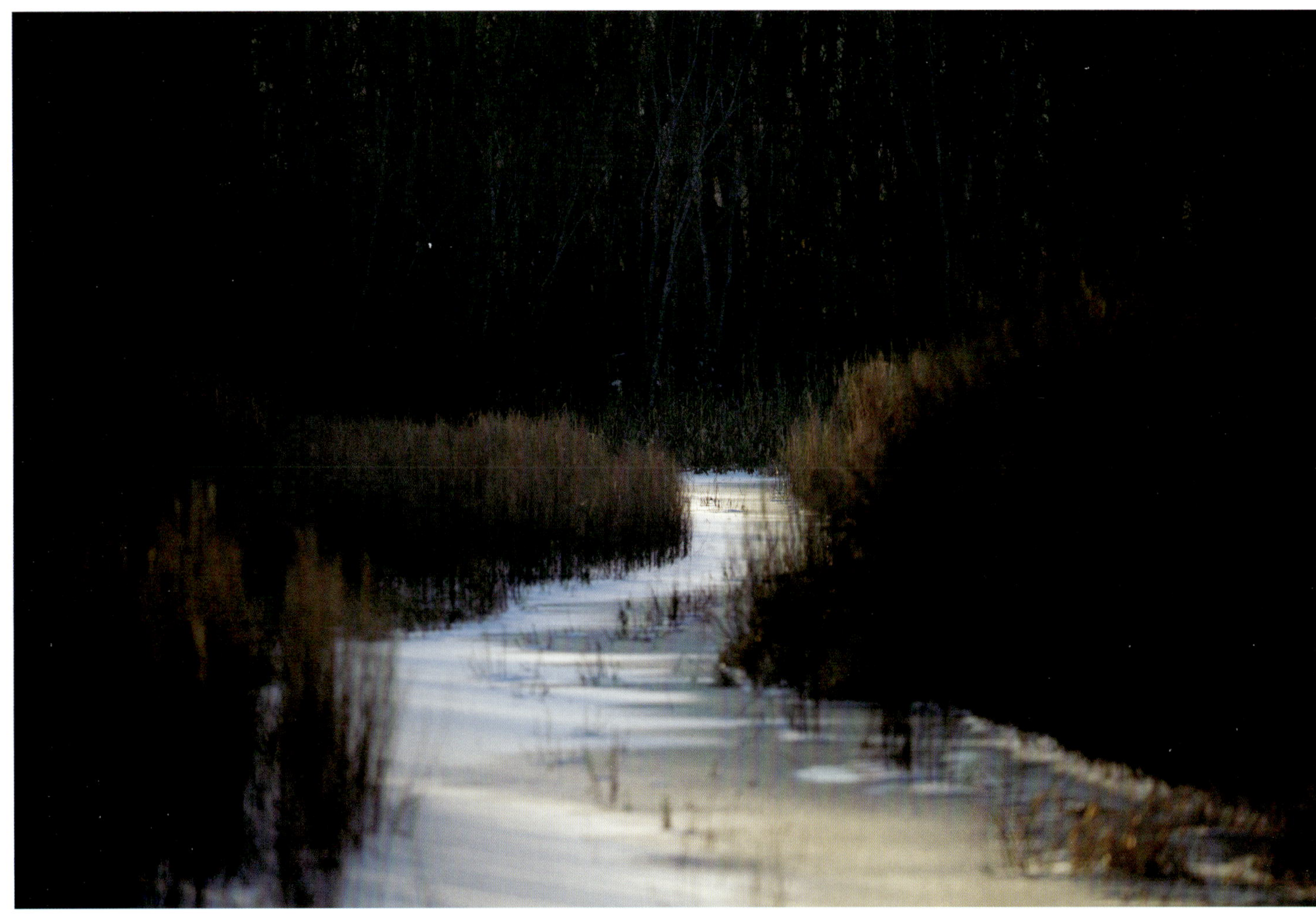

Their path was virtually unknown. Charts didn't exist. Food was scarce and the weather unusually cold. Danger and hardship lurked in every direction.

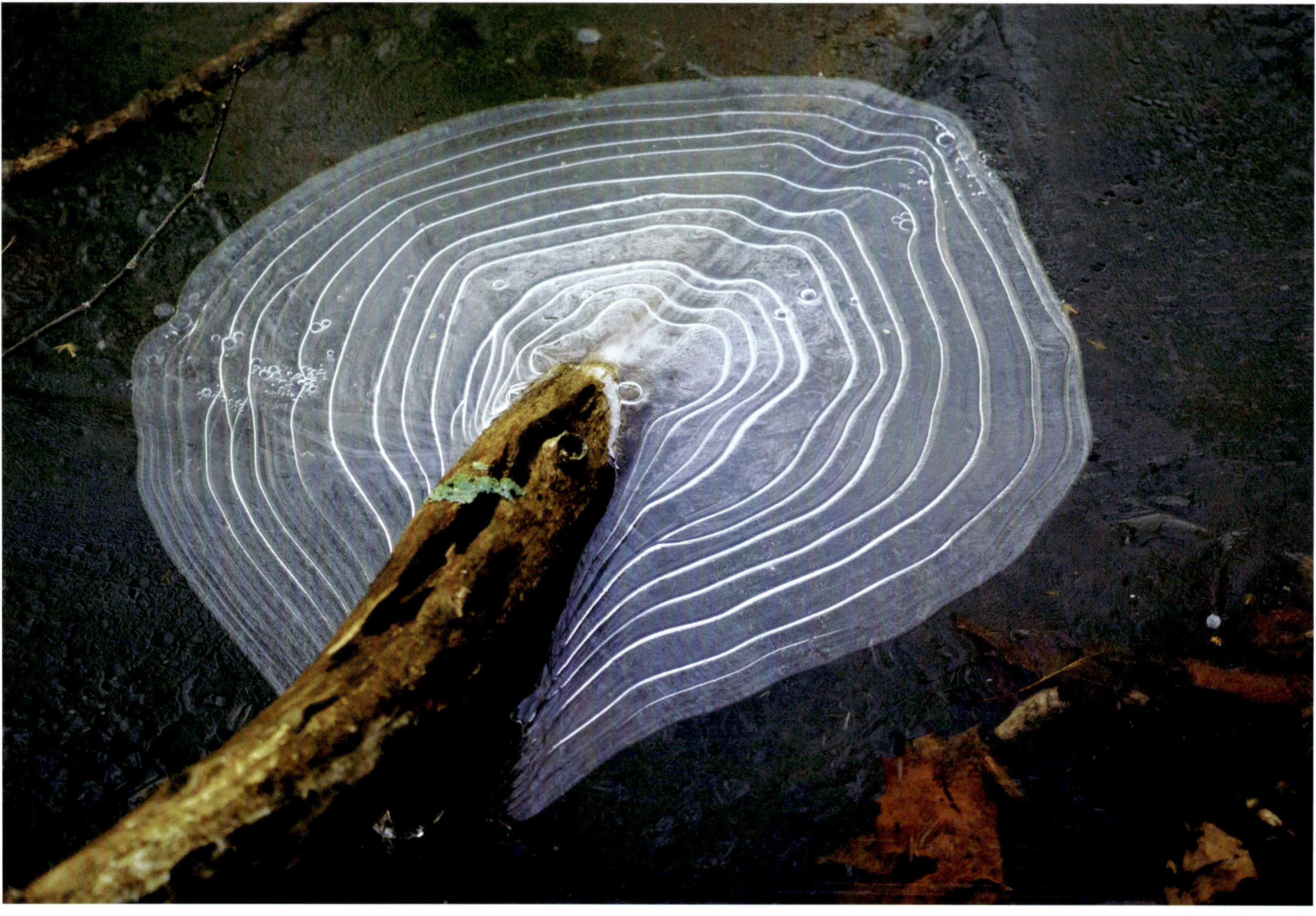

The frozen water in the feeder streams and ground cover lowered the water level on the Holston making it impossible to float the heavy flatboats. They were physically stuck until the spring thaw.

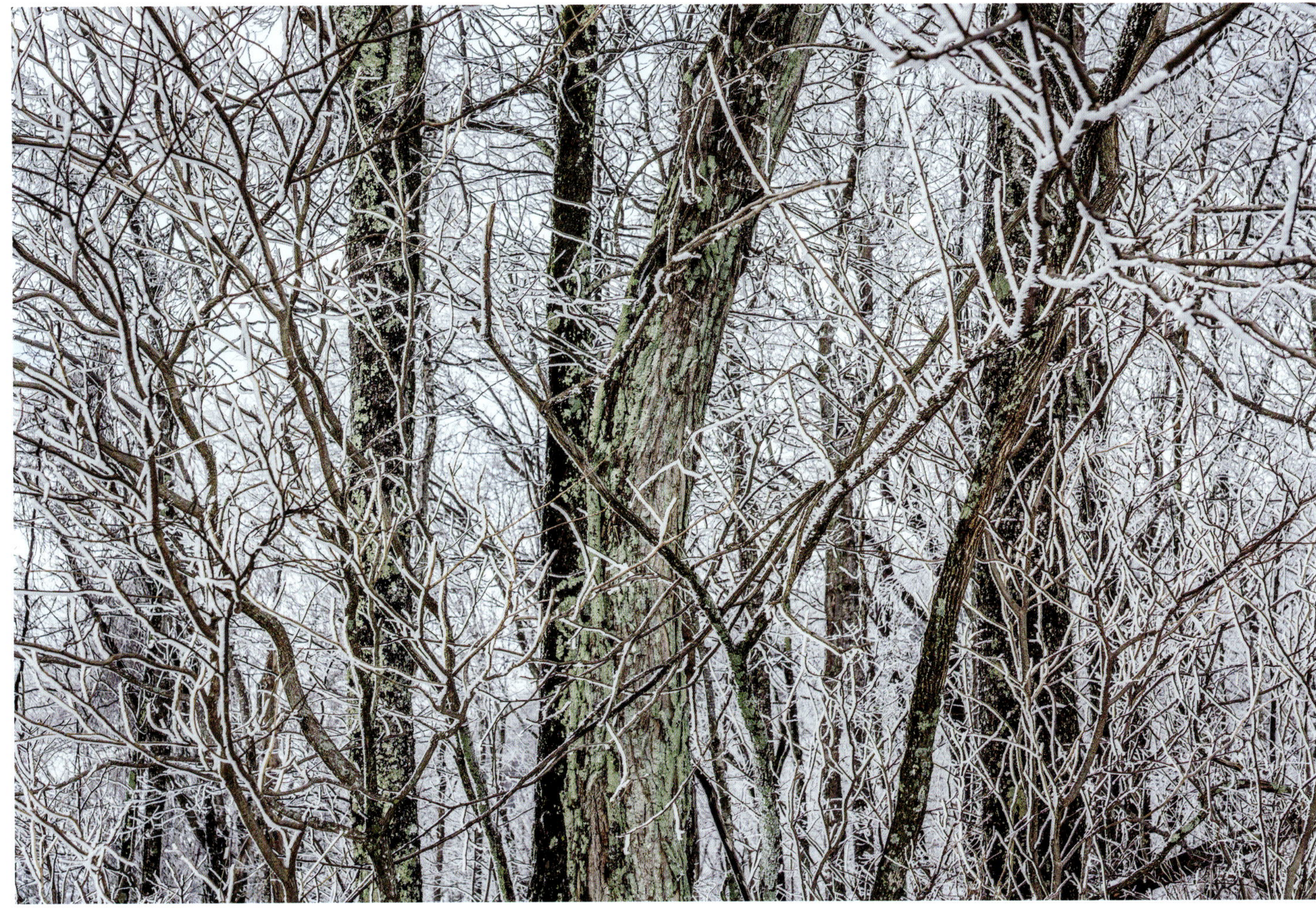

The forests were impenetrable as well. It is said animals were found frozen dead in their tracks.

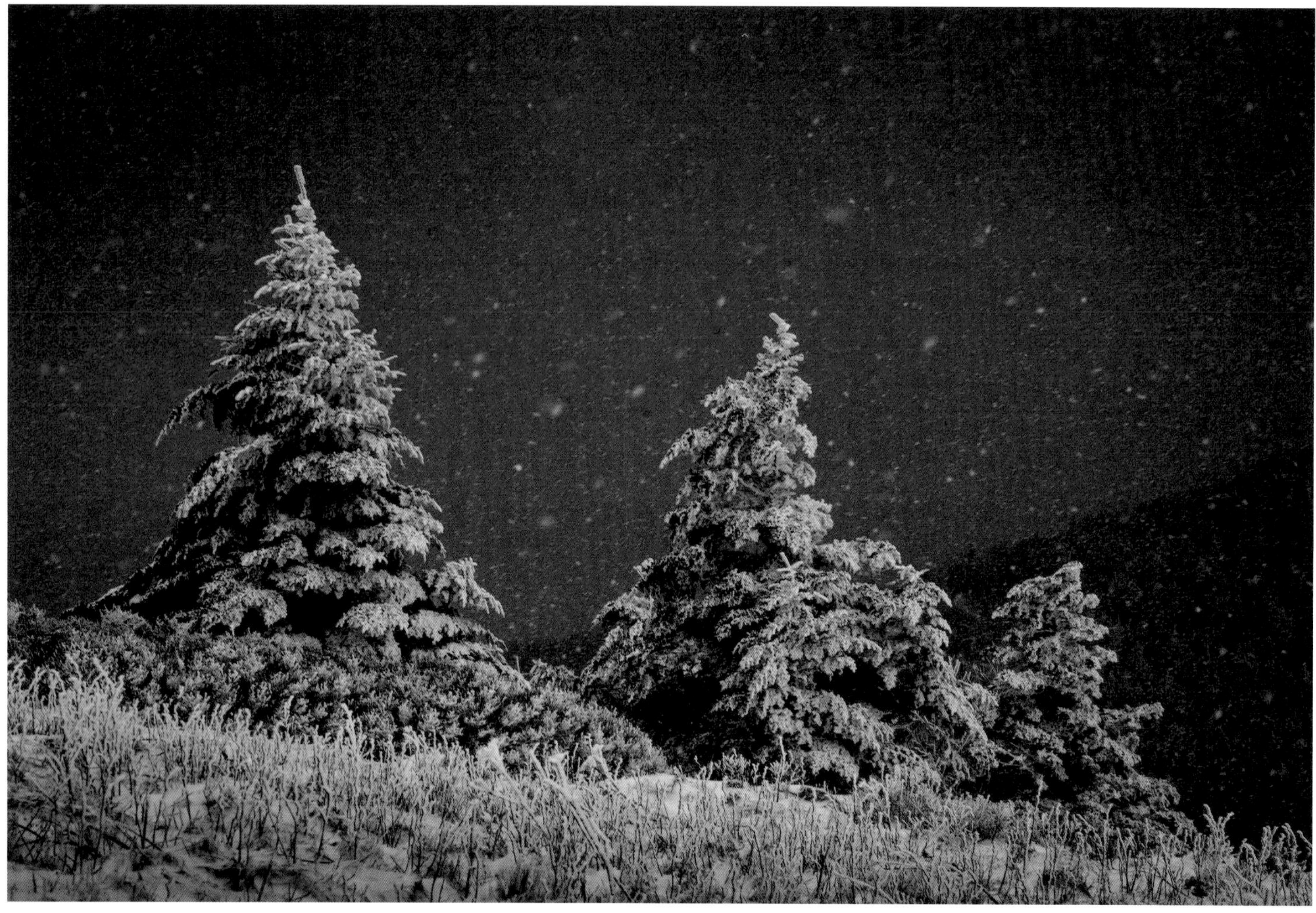

TOP OF ROAN MOUNTAIN AT DUSK. The cold and isolation the early travelers must have felt, hundreds of miles from anywhere with few resources to keep them alive, is nearly unimaginable.

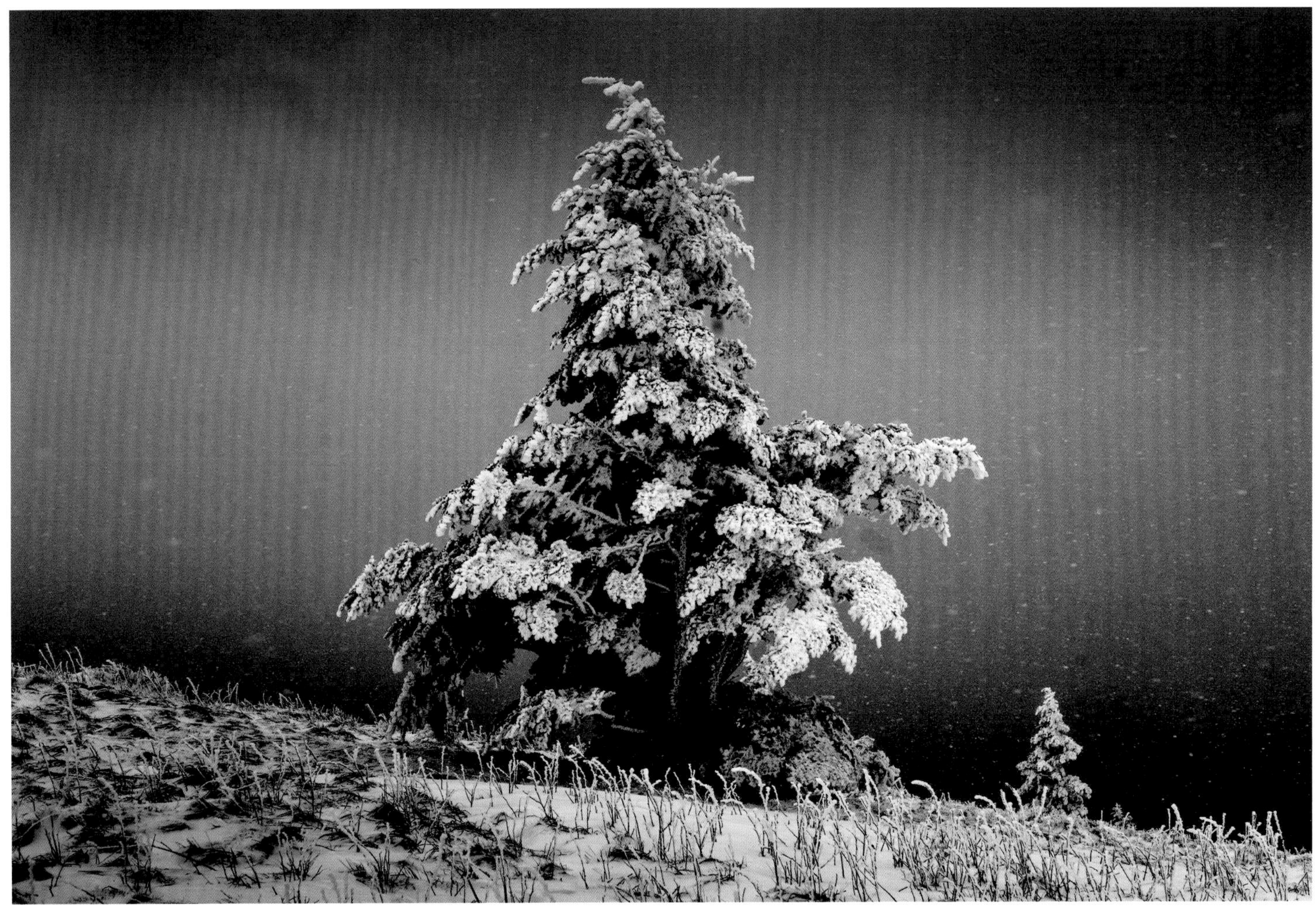

Starkness and desolation with little relief from the elements compounded their feelings of isolation.

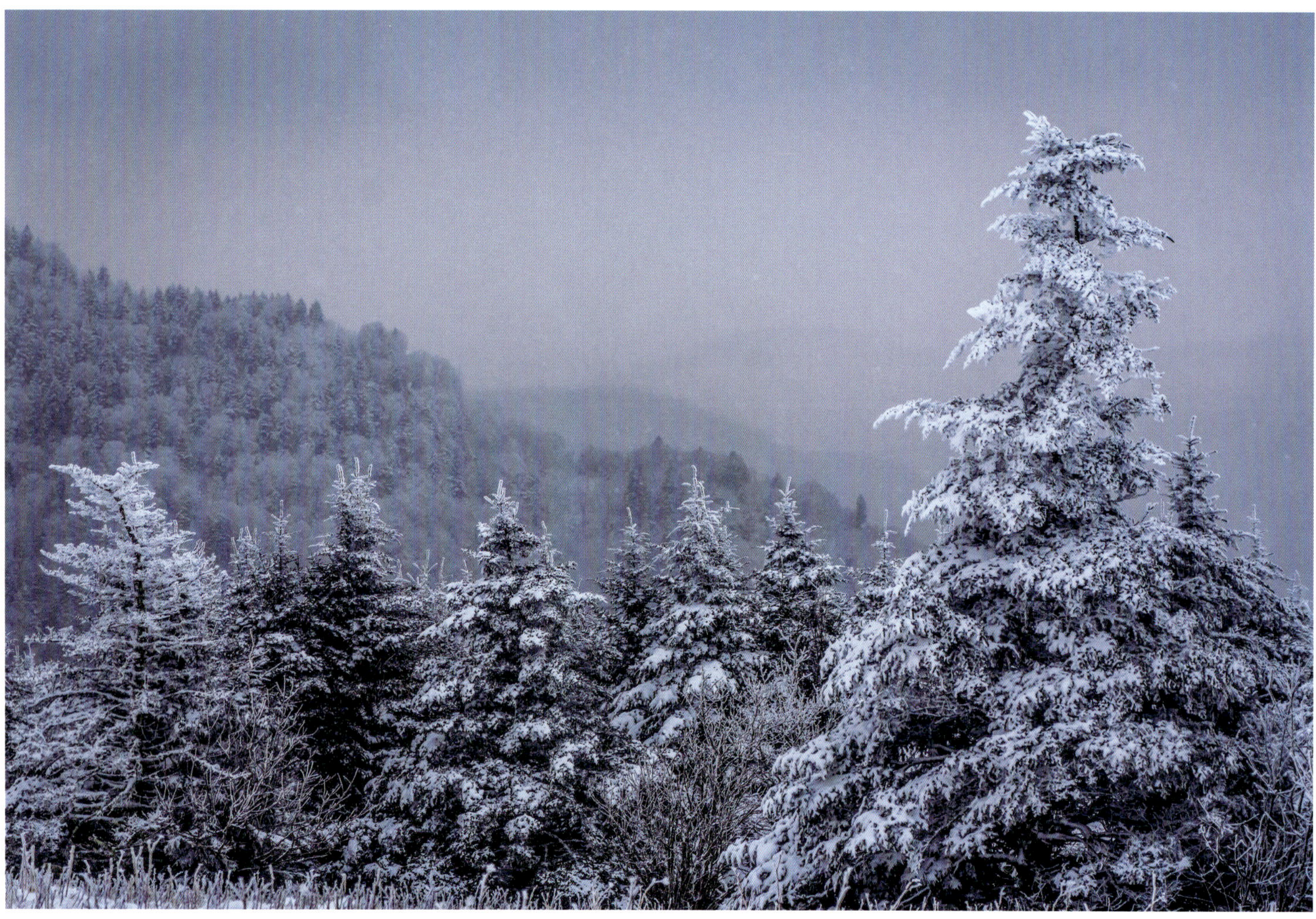

An ethereal view into an infinite landscape where no one is ever completely safe.

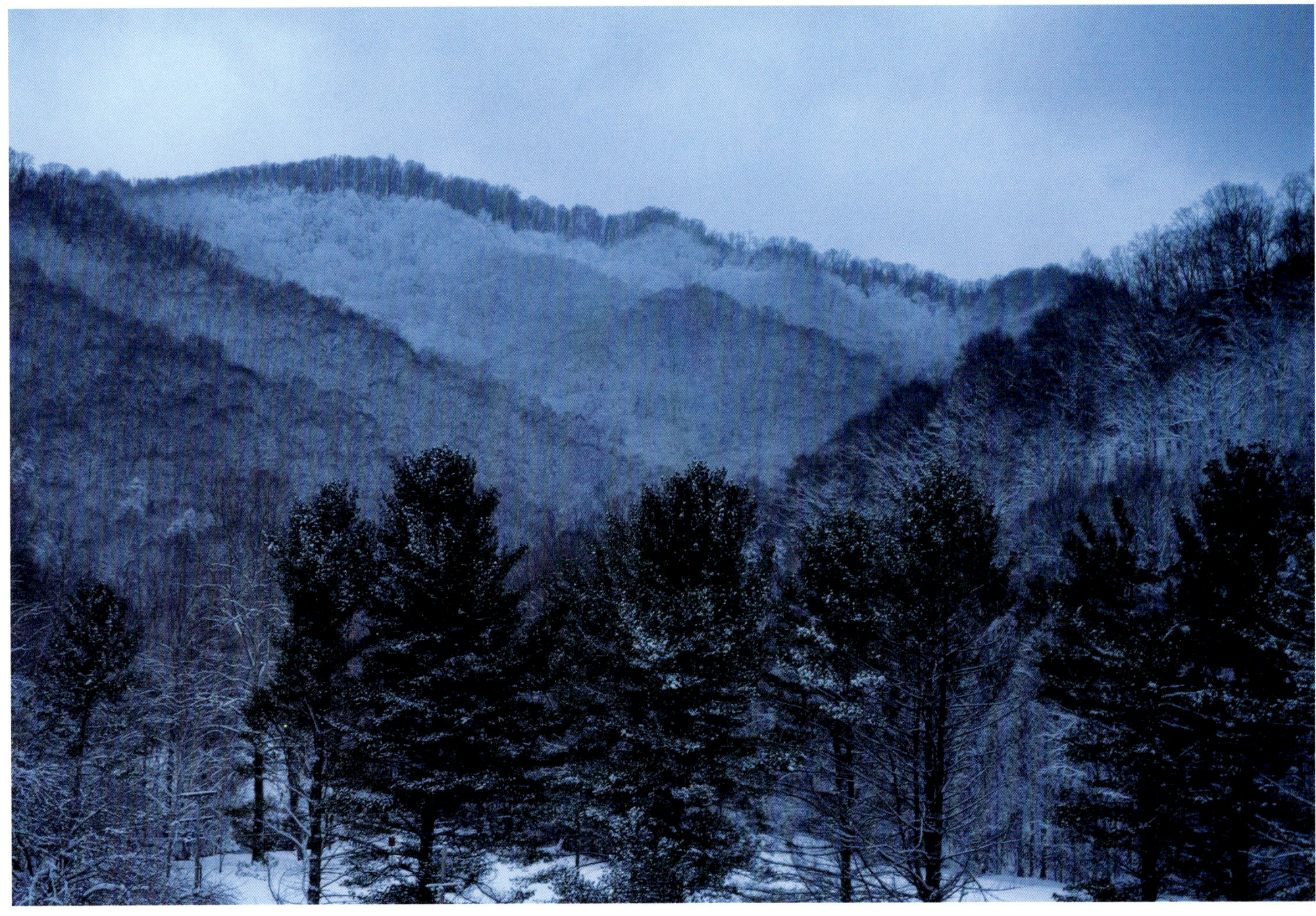

The impenetrable barrier. The rivers were a necessity for connecting the settlers to the new promised land.

Black Faces along the Cumberland River Basin

LEAROTHA WILLIAMS JR.

Professor of African American, Civil War and Reconstruction, and public history at Tennessee State University and coordinator of the North Nashville Heritage Project

When white Americans began their conquest of the area that encompasses the present-day Cumberland River Valley, men, women, and children of African descent accompanied them. With few exceptions, this group made the daunting journeys from North Carolina and Virginia in chains. As they gazed across the Cumberland at the site that would become Fort Nashborough, it must have been impossible for them to see this new territory as a land of opportunity as did their enslavers. Indeed, the new territory was to be an additional horror they, as enslaved Africans Americans, must endure and learn to negotiate.

The Cumberland area was different from the homes they had left in North Carolina and Virginia. Those areas—although their commitment to enslavement varied greatly during the 1790s—were mature slave societies. Virginia's tobacco culture had been well established after John Rolfe, the savior of the Jamestown colony, devised a profitable way to cure tobacco.[1] Those originating from North Carolina, an area dominated by small farms that with South Carolina composed the Carolina colony, may have found the geography strikingly similar to the places they had just departed, though lacking the well-maintained farms on which they labored daily. Indeed, their experience in this new territory would be reminiscent of what their ancestors had endured in Virginia and North Carolina almost two generations earlier.

The Cumberland Basin they saw upon their arrival would have been a place that was dominated by a variety of hardwoods, including oaks and hickory, and a few scattered shortleaf pines on the ridges surrounding the bluffs. As they received orders to disembark from the vessels that had brought them to their new homes, they would have observed towering maple trees, cedars, and tulip poplars growing from the rich soil along with river cane at the many cane breaks that dotted the Cumberland. While these trees provided an undeniable beauty to the new territory, they also became symbols of the extremely harsh conditions the enslaved people would endure along the Cumberland. The trees would have to be cut and the ground cleared before the land could produce the farms James Robertson and John Donelson envisioned, and the pines that grew in abundance away from the river would be needed to fuel the furnaces later owned by Montgomery Bell and others in Middle Tennessee. In many ways, the enslaved people's transition to the area and the labor required of them would make their existence mirror the lives of the Africans who had first arrived in America during its colonial period.

Though their identities have largely disappeared from history and our collective memories, students of the period can catch glimpses of these individuals. Records from the settlement provide the names of Dave, Fib, Febbie, Cumbo, George, and Patsy. But as is the case with most enslaved blacks from this period, the record provides little or no information about their day-to-day experiences, and few enslaved or free black individuals rise from the historical record unless they are connected in some way to a historical figure. Early accounts of the period tell of a black man named Robert who accompanied James Robertson on his initial voyage to what became Fort Nashborough and how he lost his life during a battle with Native Americans. Other blacks of note include Robert "Black Bob" Renfro who opened a tavern on the Public Square in the 1790s, and later a free black man named Jeffrey Lockelier who served faithfully under Andrew Jackson and at the courthouse until his death in 1830.[2]

One of the most interesting figures to emerge from this period was Jack Civil, who became one of the legendary figures of life on the Nashville frontier during the territorial period. His status after his arrival in Tennessee remains a mystery.

Some historians have claimed that Civil was one of the enslaved men brought to the region by John Donelson during his arrival in Tennessee, while others have identified him as a free man of mixed ancestry. Jack Civil gained notoriety in Nashville's history as a member of a group led by John Donelson that travelled to Clover Bottom to collect shares of cotton and corn. On the morning of their return, a group of Cherokee who had been hiding along the banks of the Stones River ambushed the party as they made their way back to Nashville. Many of the men who made the trip to Clover Bottom died during the attack. Civil, however, surrendered to the Cherokee after receiving a wound during the battle, an act that may have spared his life.

Shortly after the battle, his captors transported him to Chickamauga settlements near Lookout Mountain on the Tennessee River, and it was here that he joined them in their ongoing conflict against white settlers in the Middle Tennessee area. Many white settlers began circulating rumors that Civil had become an important figure among the Cherokee, participating in raids led from his settlement, a place off the Tennessee River they called "Nicka-Jack's" place.

After the destruction of the settlement by white settlers, Jack Civil would return to Nashville and inform Donelson and others that he had never killed or shot at a white person, but most of the community's leaders did not believe him. Civil had sufficient motive to be angry with the community's leaders as James Robertson had not submitted his name to the General Assembly as one of the settlers deserving of a land grant. When he eventually was able to secure a preemption claim, the legal documents supporting his right to the land were destroyed during inclement weather.

AS THE SETTLEMENT grew, it became a temporary stop for African Americans who came to the area as many were purchased by settlers desiring to create farms, establish furnaces, and engage in other activities. The day-to-day lives of these enslaved individuals, who constituted the majority of all African Americans who came to the Volunteer State, remain a mystery to most Tennesseans. Although the profits generated by their uncompensated labor still benefit the state today, the identities of the majority of these people who occupied the area around the Cumberland Basin remains elusive. As noted by historian Anita S. Goodstein, their status as enslaved people did not insulate them from the dangers of the frontier. They could also lose their lives and be kidnapped by indigenous groups as the contest for land rights grew more virulent in the newly settled area.[3]

Nevertheless, African Americans do appear in the historical record at times in the form of commodities, as goods that could be bought, sold, used to settle debt, and traded or won. In 1802, Jonathan Ramsey had two large tracts of land in Robertson County, Tennessee, he wished to sell, noting that he would accept payment in the form of "cash or negroes."[4] Four years later, four enslaved persons named Lydia, Robbin, Milly, and Polley were prizes that could be won in a Springfield, Tennessee, lottery along with a horse, a silver watch, and a table with a half dozen chairs.[5]

Even days during the year that were usually set aside as periods of joy and merriment could be transformed into days characterized by profound melancholy and despair. This was the case for four men enslaved by a Robertson County minor named Henry Hart, men who were scheduled to be auctioned off on New Year's Eve to provide funds for the child's upkeep.[6]

For much of the territorial and early statehood periods, the enslaved who make it into the historical record were known only by the names of their enslavers, a fact that only recognizes them as passive observers or victims of the events that occurred around them. Thus we know nothing about the black man who lost his life or the black woman who was taken prisoner while on a Cumberland salt boat near Clarksville other than their owners' last name was Shelby.[7] Nonetheless, enslaved Africans made up a significant portion of the residents of the Middle Tennessee counties that had been organized by the turn of the nineteenth century. In 1800, 25 percent of the residents of Davidson, Montgomery, Robertson, Smith, Sumner, and Williamson Counties arrived in this area in chains. Among the more than eight thousand enslaved blacks who came to this area during Tennessee's territorial and early statehood period, around forty percent remained in Davidson County.[8]

While historians have done an excellent job at chronicling the history of the communities and counties that developed in the Cumberland River Basin, information about the day-to-day lives, experiences, and culture of the enslaved people that provided the labor necessary to build and maintain the farms, plantations, and furnaces remains obscure. Though the voices of people were silenced during this period, scrutiny of extant sources reveal that the world created for them by Robertson, Donelson, McGavock, and others was one that was characterized by hard labor extracted through the use of fear of violence upon their person, friends, or family. An advertisement that farmer and future president of the United States Andrew Jackson placed in the *Tennessee Gazette* provides a glimpse into the fear and violence necessary to maintain the institution on the Cumberland frontier. In the ad, Jackson seeks an unnamed mulatto whom he thought had acquired papers stating that he was free and absconded from the Hermitage. Jackson offered a fifty-dollar reward for the return and promised "ten dollars extra, for every hundred lashes any person will give him, to the amount of three hundred."[9] Eight years later, an enslaved man identified as "Ned," who Jackson hired out to the Nashville Inn, freed himself by escaping from the Inn with several changes of clothes and shoes, long boots, and a pair of saddlebags. Jackson mused that he may have been "taken off by a villain" and entertained the thought the Ned may have "run off" on his own. The number of escapes noted in the papers starting with the establishment of the fort and other Cumberland settlements reveals that although enslaved, the desire for freedom persisted among African Americans brought to the area during its early period.[10]

Several events played significant roles in the development of the Cumberland settlements and the growing presence of African Americans in the area between 1790 and 1805. Eli Whitney's patent of the cotton gin in 1794—a device he boasted could help one man and a horse clean as much cotton as fifty men could over the course of a day—and the United States' purchase of the Louisiana Territory would have a dramatic effect on the Cumberland settlements. As Nashville matured from a frontier town to a fledgling Southern city, its importance as a slave port increased; it ultimately became the second most important city in the state for planters desiring to enslave black men and women, making it an important space in the history of African Americans in the South. Indeed, the Cumberland became a portal for African Americans, one that could lead to destinations where they would spend the majority of their days picking cotton in the Deep South; it could also be a vital avenue on their journey to freedom once federal forces reached Nashville during the Civil War.

One of the challenges facing enslaved blacks brought to this area was the difficulty of creating the family ties and communities needed to survive and negotiate the slave experience in the region and in an environment that had reduced them to commodities their enslavers could extract a profit from. During slavery, the status of a child followed that of its mother; consequently, if the mother was enslaved, all the children she had faced the curse of enslavement. Individuals seeking to buy black women, such as Timothy Demonbreun who advertised for an enslaved girl or woman who was "trusty and well acquainted with kitchen duty," looked to earn income from their labor and later from their offspring. The twelve-year-old girl and the "one likely wench and child" and offered by Nashville's Jeremiah Brown could be viewed by potential purchasers as investments that would continue to earn income for generations.[11]

Although attempts to create family bonds were severely challenged by law and custom, enslaved blacks along the Cumberland formed and nurtured strong family ties when possible. During the autumn of 1817, an enslaved woman named Mary hurriedly left the home of her enslaver, Jason Thompson, wearing only "an old blue bombazet frock." Mary did not have a scarf on her head or shoes on her feet when she left, and she was notably pregnant at the time she escaped. Thompson believed that she would try to make her way toward Lexington, Kentucky, or perhaps travel as far away as Charlotte, Virginia. The account of her running away without proper clothing suggests a sense of desperation and a desire not to bring an enslaved child into the world.[12] Likewise, an enslaved man named Lewis absconded from the Tennessee Iron Works during the night of April 7, 1822. Many believed that his wife, who lived on a farm near the bend of the Cumberland, assisted him with his escape by hiding clothing he would need on his journey. Although his destination was unknown by Anthony Van Leer and Co., the business that had hired him out, it was noted that he had been "frequently seen" near the area where his wife lived.[13]

As the farms around the Cumberland flourished, growing corn, tobacco, and cotton, freedom became an unobtainable dream for the enslaved men and women who worked the fertile soil as well as for those who deforested the land to feed the many furnaces that dotted the landscape adjacent to the rivers. Within two generations after the ancestors of enslaved people arrived with the first settlers, the Tennessee State Assembly prohibited manumission in Tennessee except on the express condition that the freed African American should be immediately removed from the state and imposed strict fines for free blacks who visited Tennessee and remained beyond thirty days.[14] This made the choice provided to emancipated slaves as undesirable as the one faced by those who fled the enslavers: the choice between freedom and permanent separation from friends and families. In short, they faced what amounted to the psychological death of those whom they loved and cared for.

In many instances, breaking tools or participating in work slowdowns served as ways to engage in simple day-to-day resistance of the work regime.

The world in which they lived was highly regimented, with their enslavers controlling or seeking to control every aspect of their existence. For those that grew tobacco—a crop which was one of the most labor intensive in the state—their care for the crop had to be meticulous in order for their enslavers to earn a profit. To grow tobacco, the enslaved sowed the seeds in a sheltered place and took great care to protect them from frosts. During the late spring, they then took the time to plant the small plants in the fields. Much of the tedious labor of growing tobacco involved keeping the ground free of weeds, removing insects, and taking meticulous care of the leaves. When the leaves were ready, they were cut, dried, and fermented. They were then dried again, bundled, placed in casks, and shipped.[15] The tobacco cultivated in this area was often shipped to the Clarksville tobacco market, the profits from which would later make men like George A. Washington of Robertson County's Wessyngton Plantation one of the wealthiest men in the state.[16]

When considering the lives of the enslaved who arrived and created lives along the Cumberland River Basin, historians often describe the quaint farms, plantations, and furnaces where they worked but overlook the ways in which they resisted enslavement. In many instances, breaking tools or participating in work slowdowns served as ways to engage in simple day-to-day resistance of the work regime. *The American Farmer* admonished planters to keep their tools serviceable and in good order, noting that they should know where "they ought to be, and are; and the knowledge of these facts makes his hands careful, and attend to their duty—whereas, a negligent master most generally has servants and slaves, whose great delight is to kill time."[17]

Scores of African Americans resisted by deserting the spaces where they were enslaved, many within the first decade of the settlement of the Cumberland River Basin. Advertisements for enslaved persons who left farms and plantations seeking freedom dominated early Middle Tennessee newspapers. In many ways, the Cumberland River—the waterway which brought many of them to the area during the late eighteenth and early nineteenth centuries—had the potential to serve as the means by which they could obtain freedom. A courageous enslaved man or woman could under the right circumstances stowaway on a barge or steamer heading up the Cumberland on a voyage that would get the close to the Ohio River and freedom.

Most, however, resisted by creating a culture that enabled physical and mental survival. It was a culture that enabled them to endure the trauma their enslavers imposed upon them in an effort to make a profit. More importantly, they created a culture that still animates life in the Volunteer State today, and any story that celebrates life along the Cumberland River Basin that does not include and at times center their experience in the narrative provides an incomplete account of life, culture, and history in Tennessee.

NOTES

1. For more information on Virginia's tobacco culture see G. Melvin Herndon, *Tobacco in Colonial Virginia: "The Sovereign Remedy"* (Williamsburg: Virginia 350th Anniversary Celebration Corporation, 1957); Phillip D. Morgan, *Slave Counterpoint: Black Culture in the Eighteenth-Century Chesapeake and Lowcountry* (Chapel Hill: University of North Carolina Press, 1998); and Allan Kullikof, *Tobacco and Slaves: The Development of Southern Cultures in the Chesapeake, 1680–1800* (Chapel Hill: University of North Carolina Press, 1986).
2. *Tennessee Gazette*, July 7, 1802.
3. Anita S. Goodwin, "Black History on the Nashville Frontier, 1780–1810," *Tennessee Historical Quarterly* 38, no. 4 (Winter 1979): 401.
4. *Tennessee Gazette*, March 3, 1802.
5. *Democratic Clarion*, April 11, 1802.
6. *Tennessee Gazette*, December 24, 1800.
7. *History of Tennessee from the Earliest Time to the Present: Together with an Historical and a Biographical Sketch of Montgomery, Robertson, Humphreys, Stewart, Dickson, Cheatham, and Houston Counties* (Nashville: Goodspeed Publishing Co, 1886), 757.
8. Social Explorer Dataset (SE), Census1800, digitally transcribed by Inter-university Consortium for Political and Social Research, edited, verified by Michael Haines, compiled, edited, and verified by Social Explorer.
9. *Tennessee Gazette*, October 3, 1804.
10. *Nashville Banner and Nashville Whig*, September 19, 1815.
11. For more information on the value placed upon enslaved people, see Daina Ramey Berry's *The Price for Their Pound of Flesh: The Value of the Enslaved, from Womb to Grave, in the Building of a Nation* (Boston: Beacon Press, 2017).
12. *Nashville Banner and Nashville Whig*, September 22, 1817.
13. *Tennessee Watchman*, May 24, 1822
14. Acts of Tennessee, 1831, Chap. 102, Sec.2.
15. Francis S. Wiggins, *The American Farmer's Instructor, or, Practical Agriculturalist* (Philadelphia: Orrin Rogers, 1840), 203.
16. For more on tobacco production on the Wessyngton plantation see John Baker's *The Washingtons of Wessyngton Plantation: Stories of My Family's Journey to Freedom* (New York: Atria Books, 2009).
17. *The American Farmer*, 4th series, vol. 5 (1849).

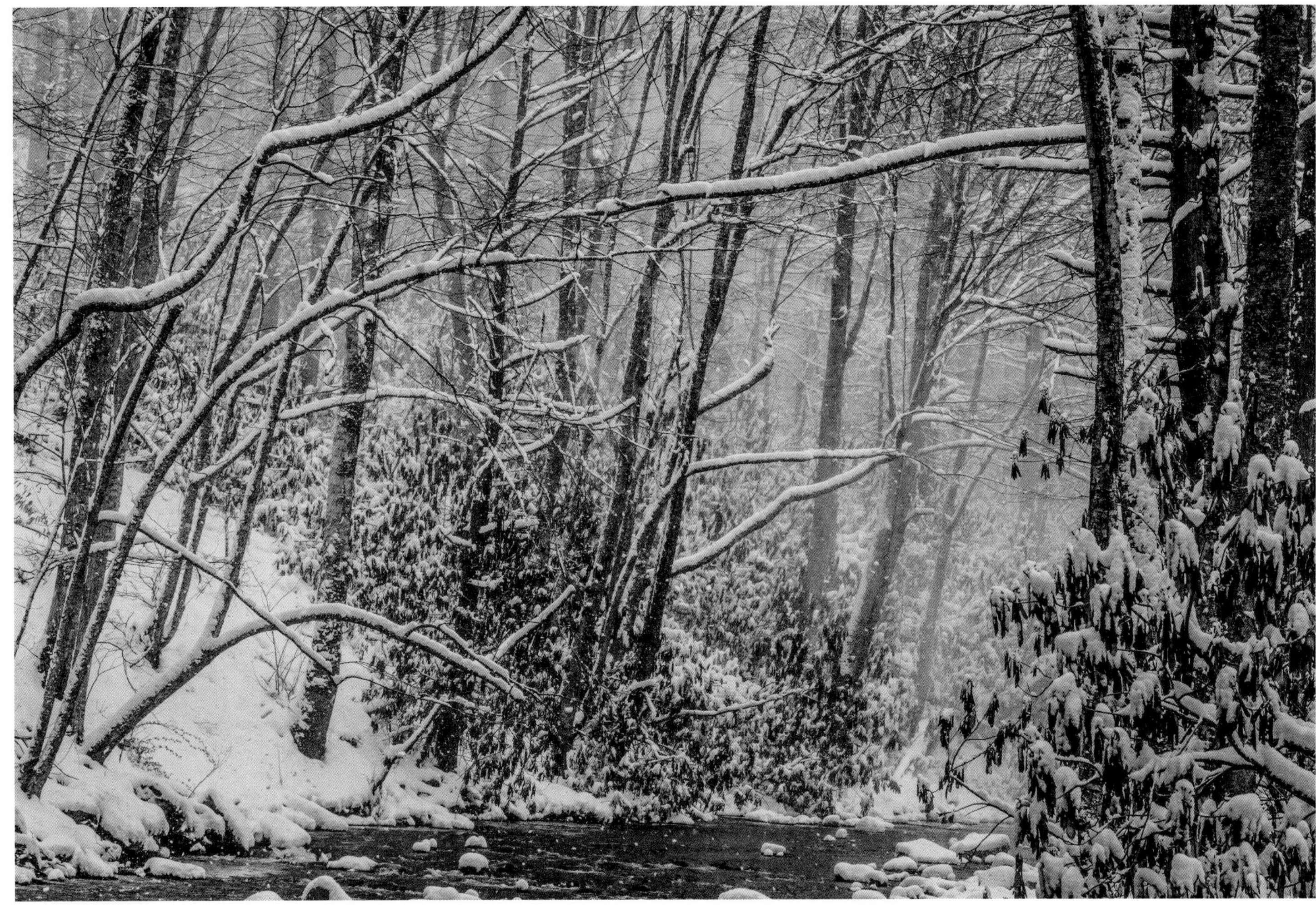

Icy woods, similar to what Donelson's party of men, women, and children would have seen as they waited, shivering, for the weather to clear.

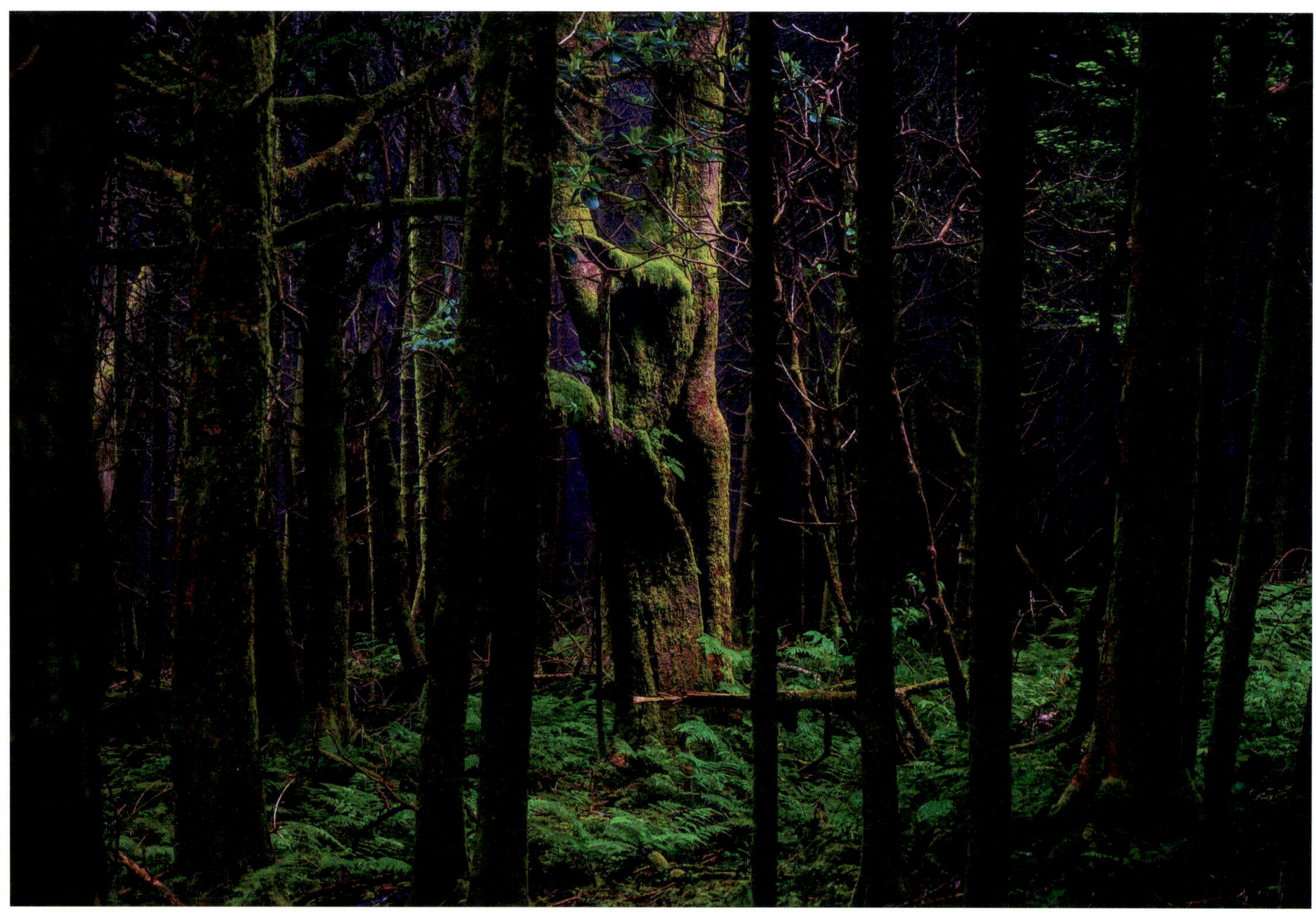

APPALACHIAN RAINFOREST.

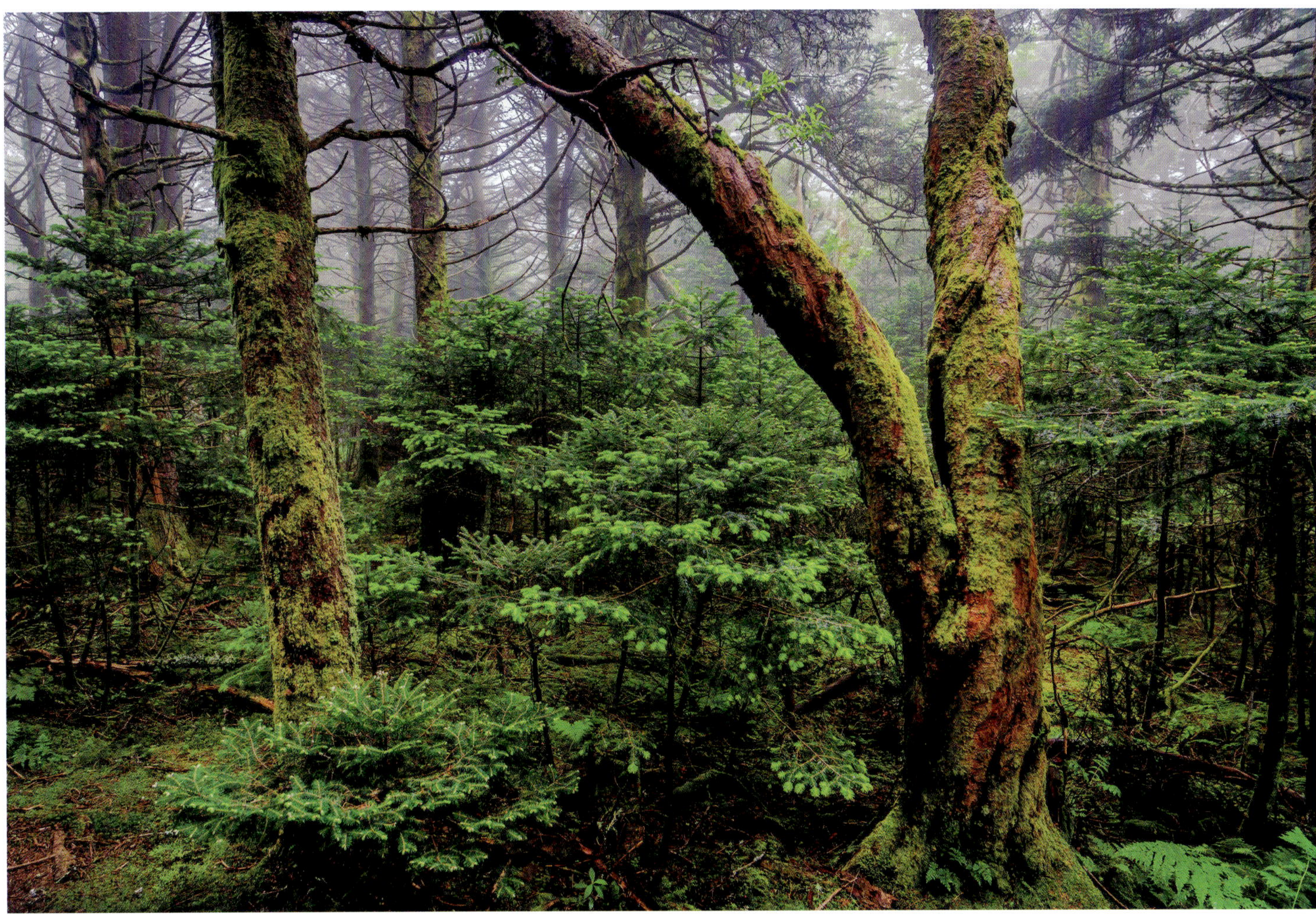

The woods not only precluded the movement of goods and implements necessary for the clearing and tilling of the land, they were also considered too dangerous for travel by women and children whom, it was believed, would be safer on the boats, far away from shore. That assumption proved untrue.

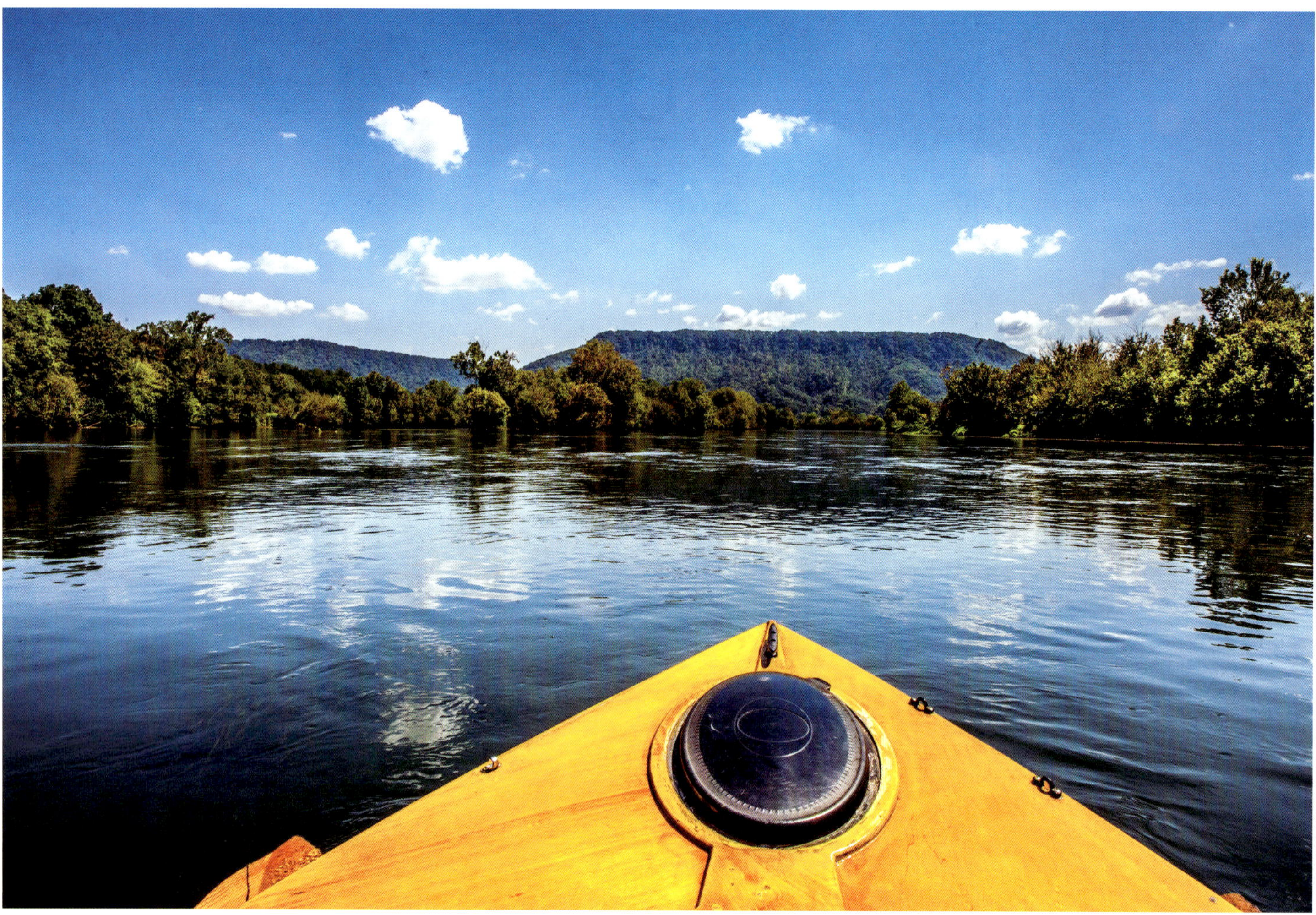

HOLSTON RIVER, BELOW KINGSPORT, TENNESSEE, SEPTEMBER 5. View of the obstructing mountains behind me as I made my way down river away from town. Whereas the Donelson party was impeded by the low waters caused by the harsh winter, I was fuming because the closing of the river at Holston munitions plant forced me to put in miles below Donelson's start and made me question who controls the rivers.

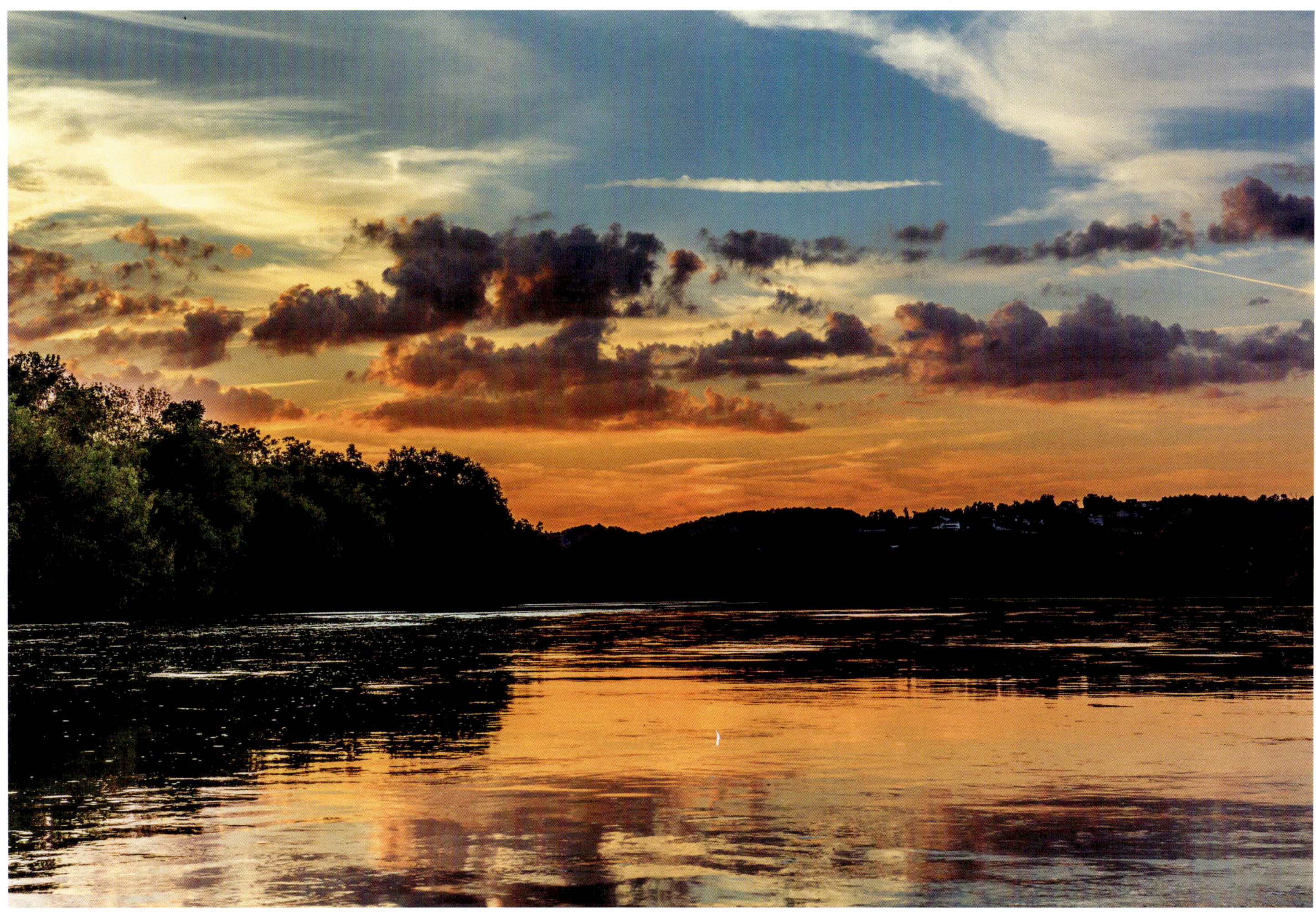

HOLSTON RIVER, BELOW KINGSPORT, TENNESSEE, SEPTEMBER 5. Sunset view of my first night on the river. Donelson may have viewed a similar sky, but for him the trees were barren and the cold almost unbearable. For the next two months, like the Donelson party, I would be on my own.

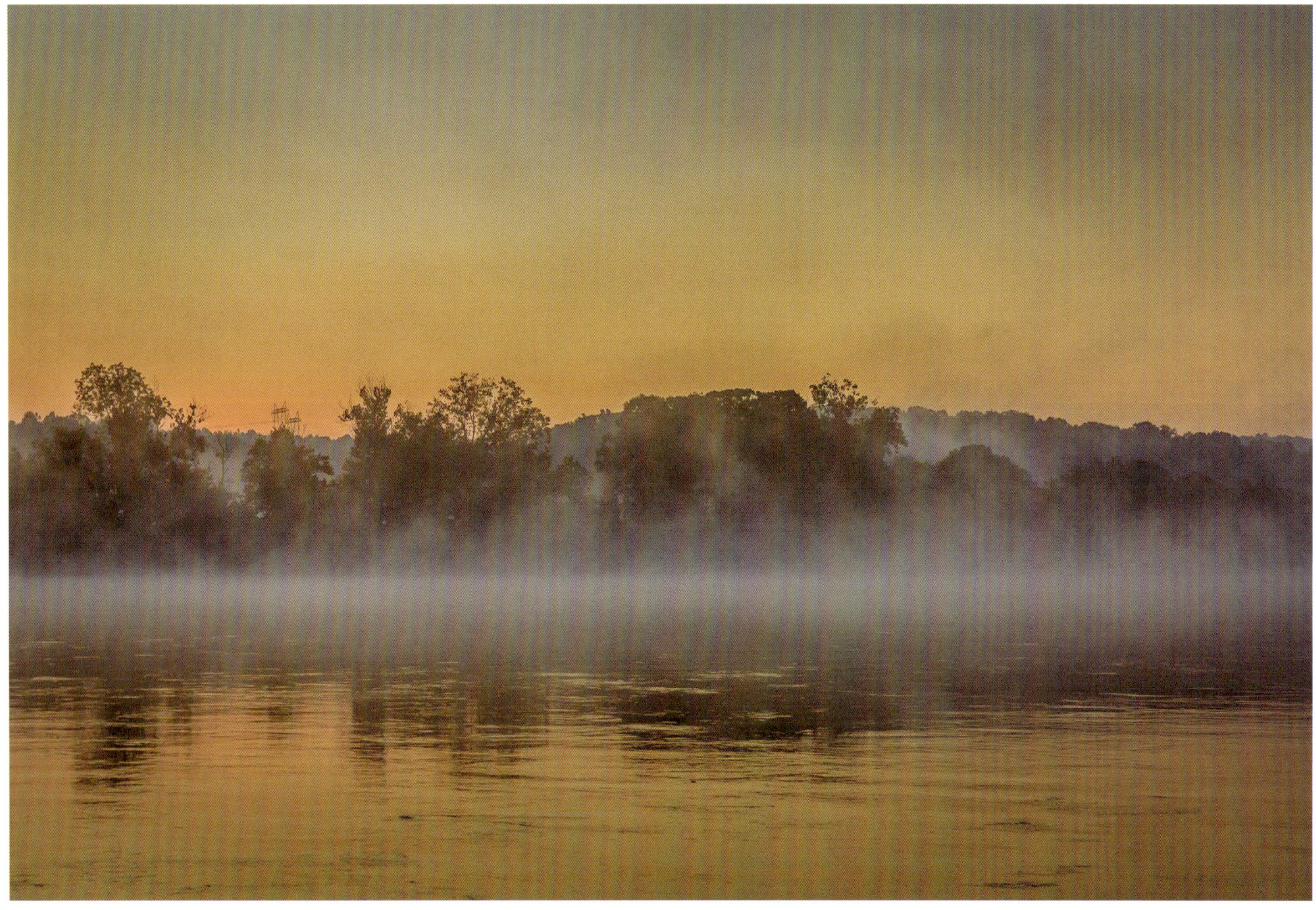

HOLSTON RIVER, BELOW KINGSPORT, TENNESSEE, SEPTEMBER 6. A spectacular fog-infused sunrise awaited me after fewer than twenty-four hours on the water. The surrounding beauty and the endorphins awakened by a strenuous row filled me with joy.

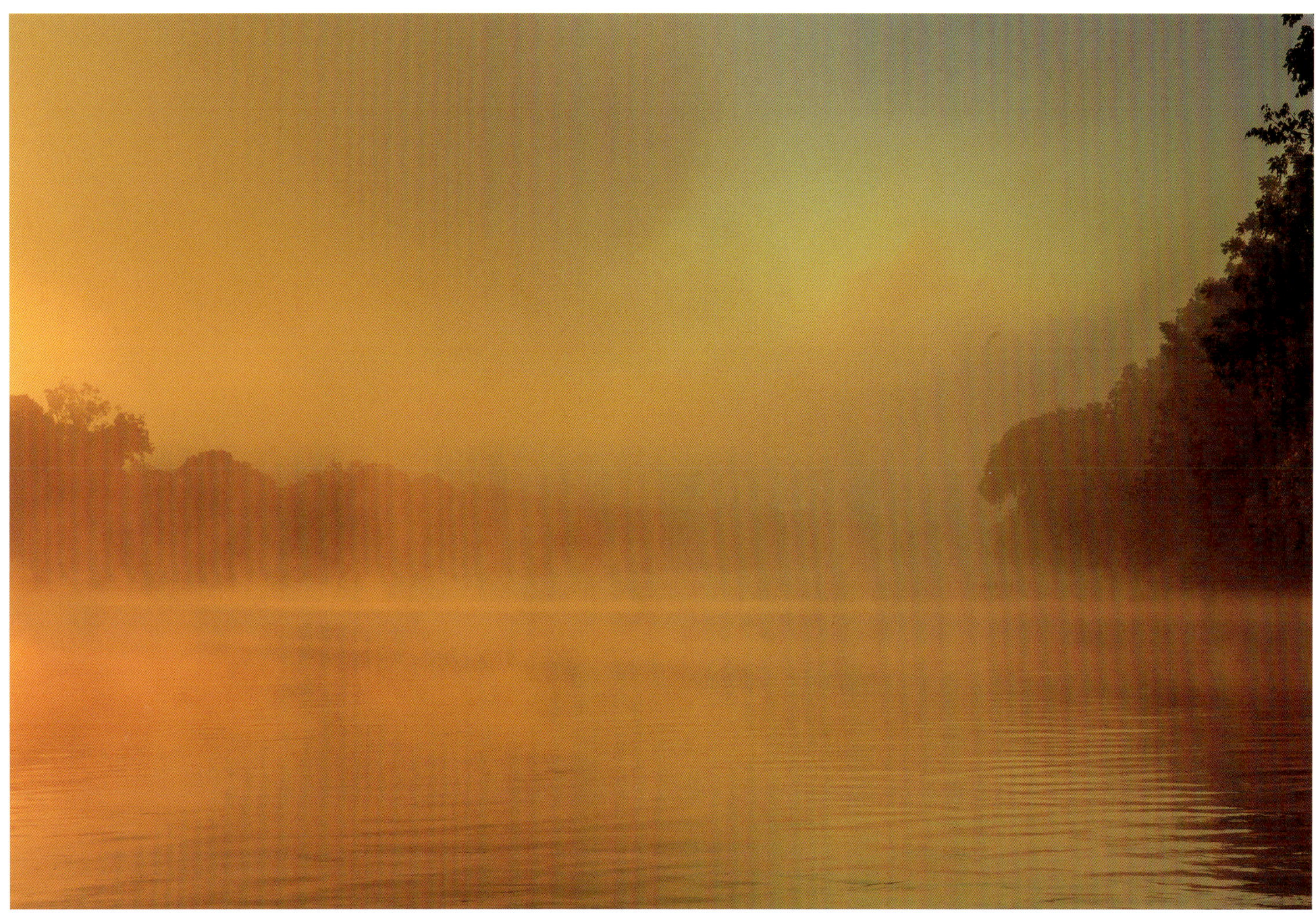

HOLSTON RIVER, BELOW KINGSPORT, TENNESSEE, SEPTEMBER 6. The pooling waters caused by the river's impoundment by the John Sevier Fossil Plant dam not too far downstream slowed my progress, causing my days on the Holston to be much longer than Donelson's.

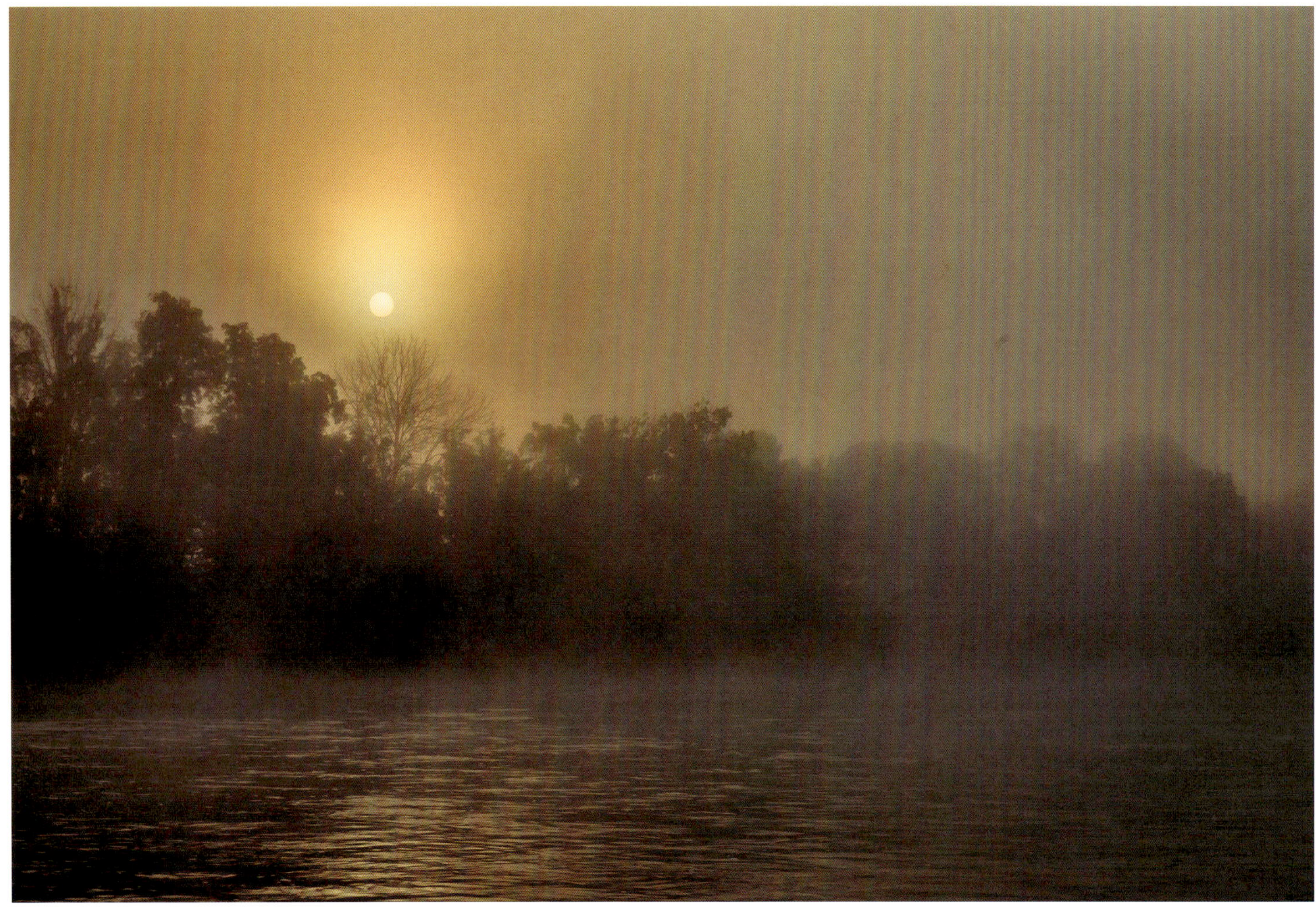

HOLSTON RIVER, BELOW KINGSPORT, TENNESSEE, SEPTEMBER 6. Morning sun rising over the trees softened by the Gaussian mist that wafts over the night-chilled water.

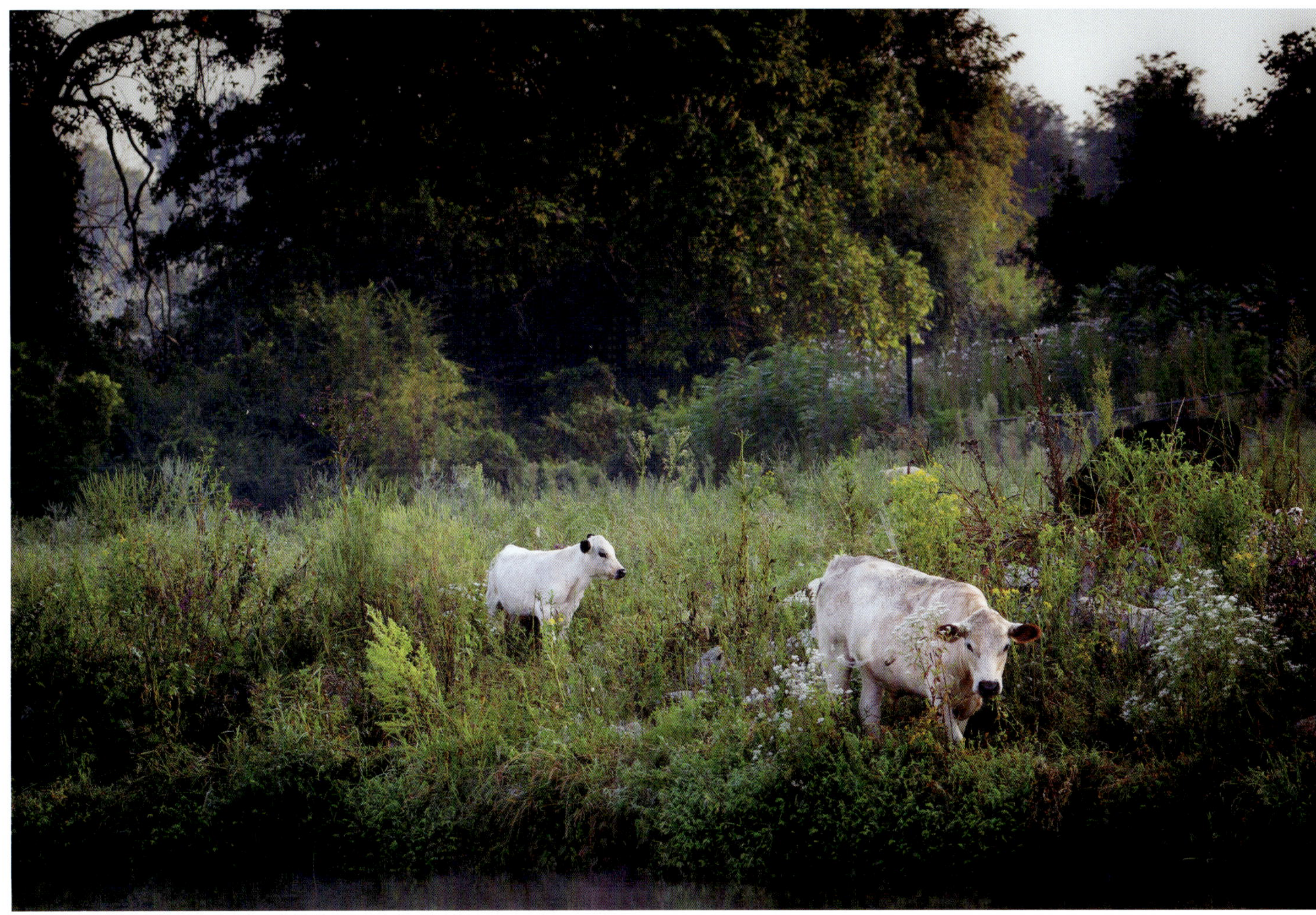

HOLSTON RIVER, BELOW KINGSPORT, TENNESSEE, SEPTEMBER 6. Livestock would come down to the river to check me out. For days at a time the wandering bovines were my only contact with modern civilization. Unfortunately their presence has added to the pollution that inundates our waters, putting marine life at risk and contaminating the drinking water of the communities that reside downstream.

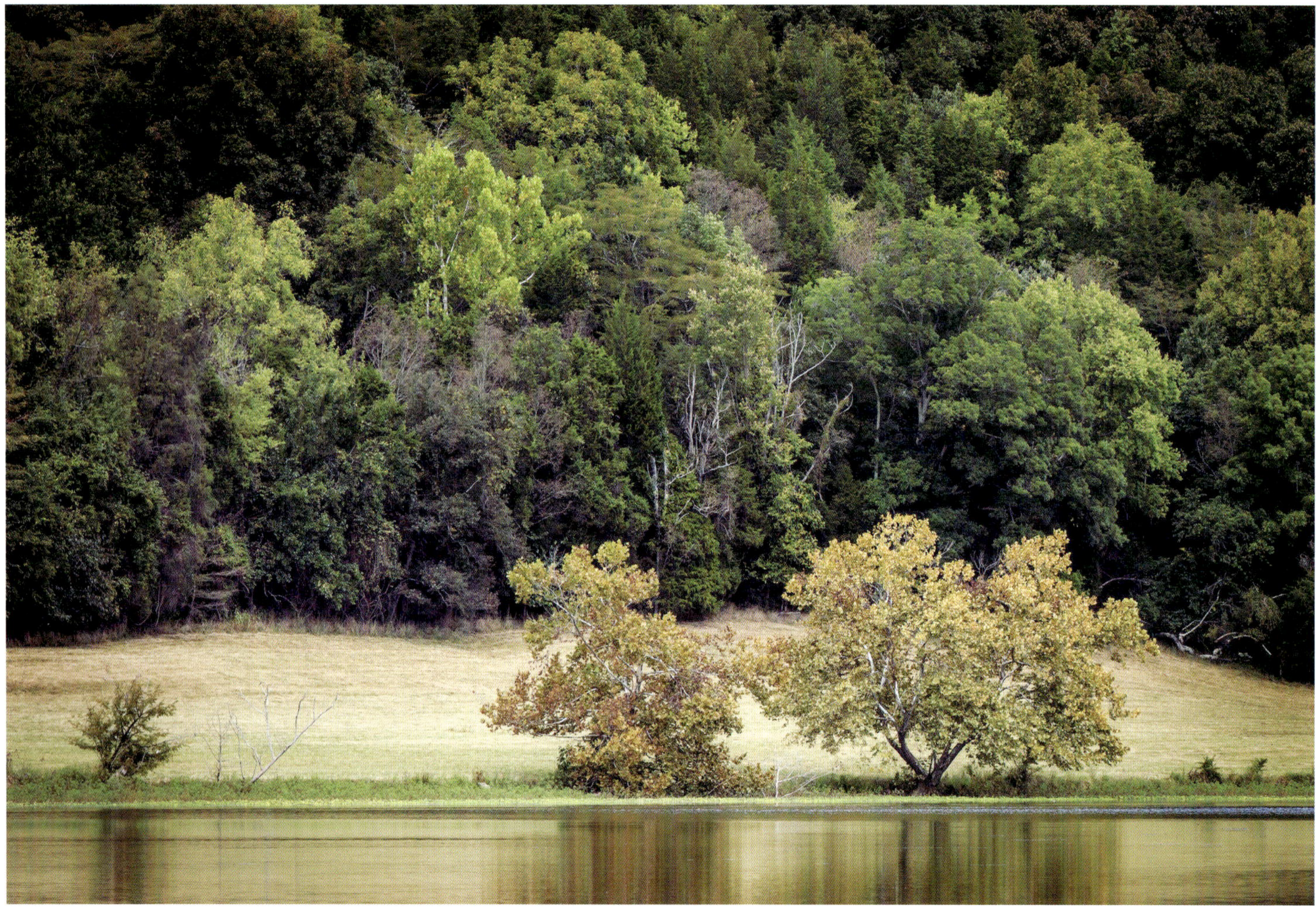

HOLSTON RIVER, BELOW KINGSPORT, TENNESSEE, SEPTEMBER 6. The spreading river flowed quietly across the pastoral landscape. The soft gurgling of the river and the sweet chirping of the birds combined to create a most unusual symphony.

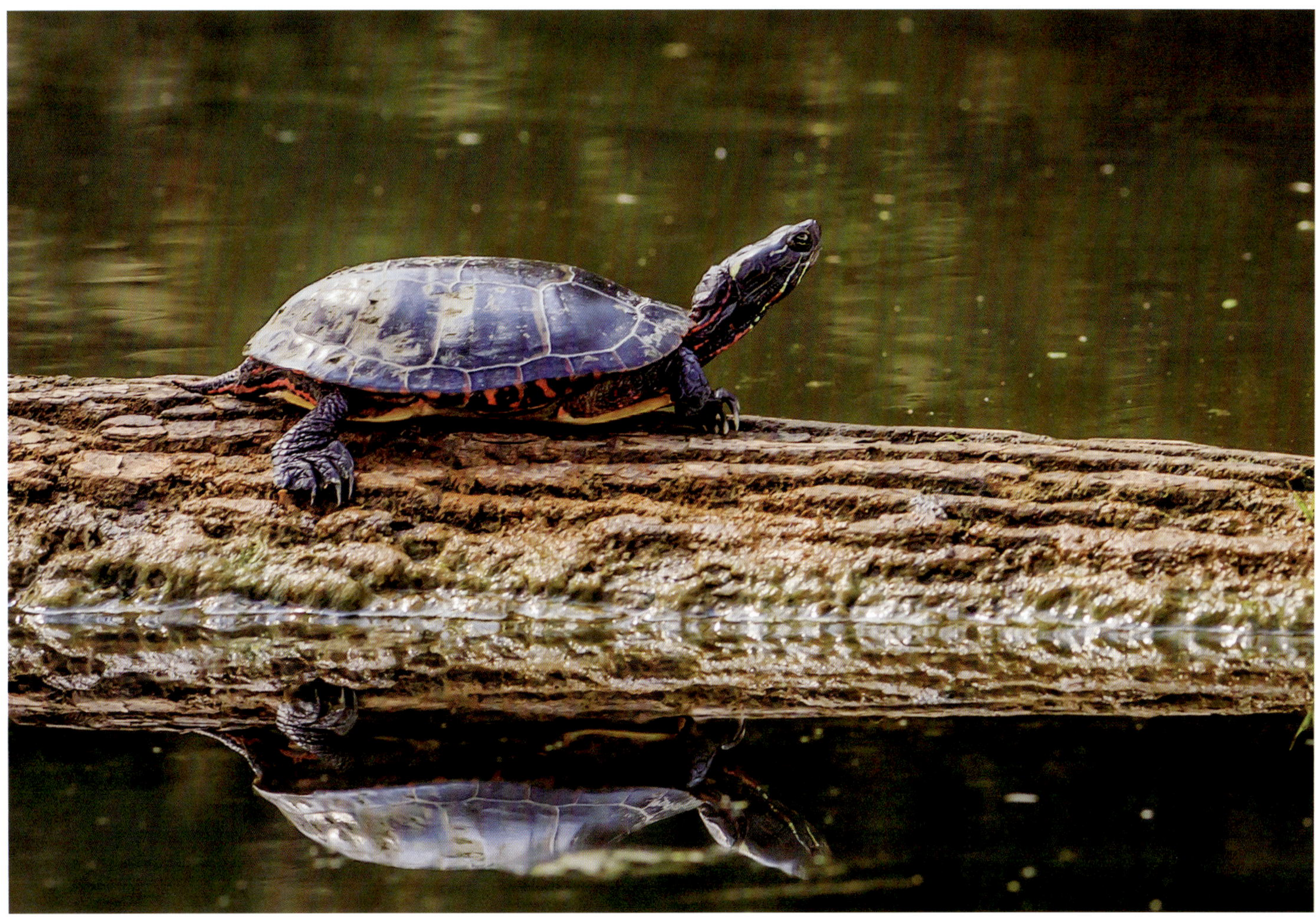

HOLSTON RIVER, BEECH CREEK, ROGERSVILLE COMMUNITY, TENNESSEE, SEPTEMBER 6. The turtles proved to be surprisingly agile, waking from their warming sunbaths and leaping into the security of the water as soon as my presence became alarming. For such a rural part of Tennessee, I saw few other wild creatures along the riverine.

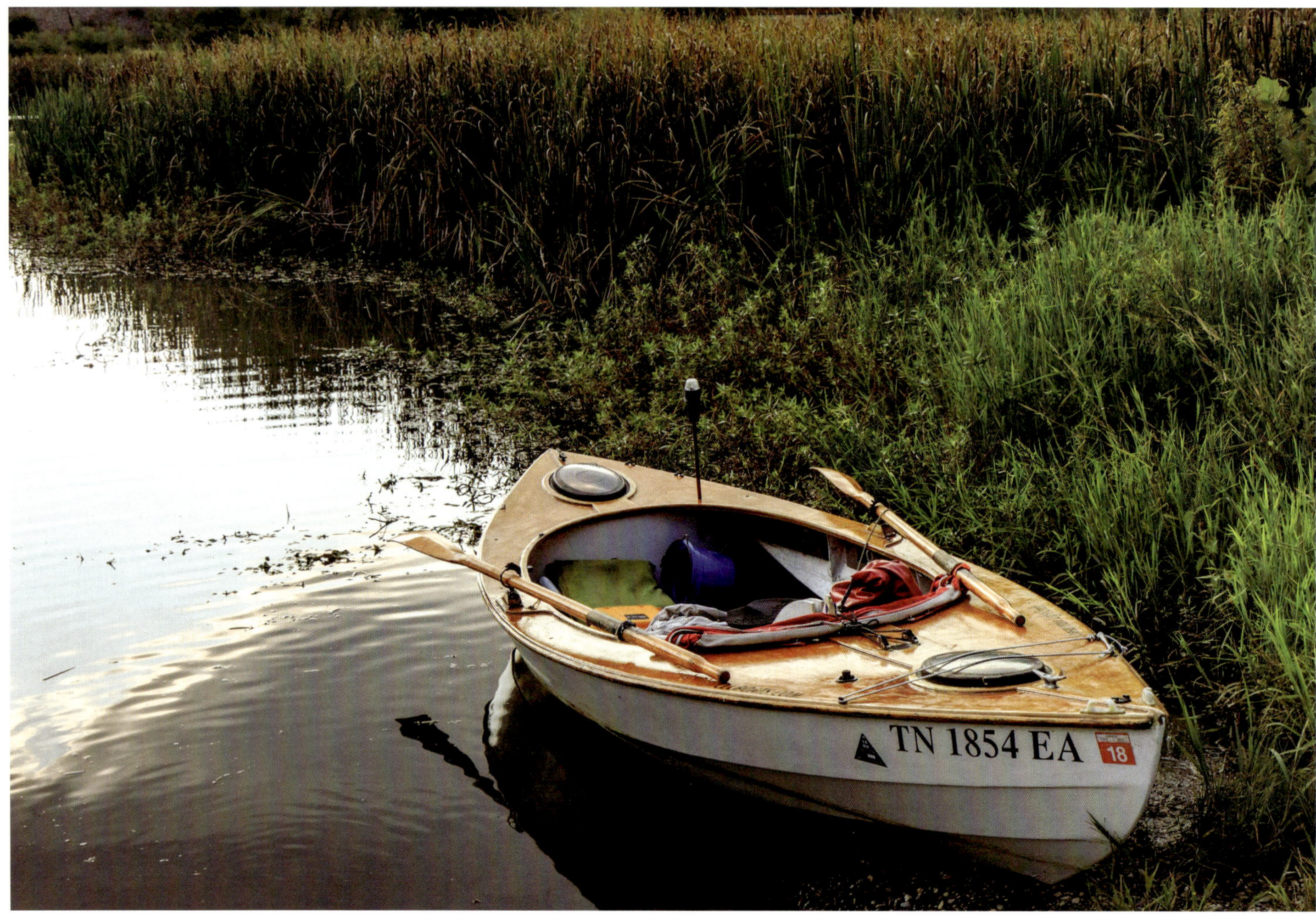

HOLSTON RIVER, BEECH CREEK BOAT RAMP, TUNNEL HILL ROAD, ROGERSVILLE, TENNESSEE, SEPTEMBER 6. My progress was thwarted by the dam at the John Sevier Fossil Plant that encased the river directly below me.

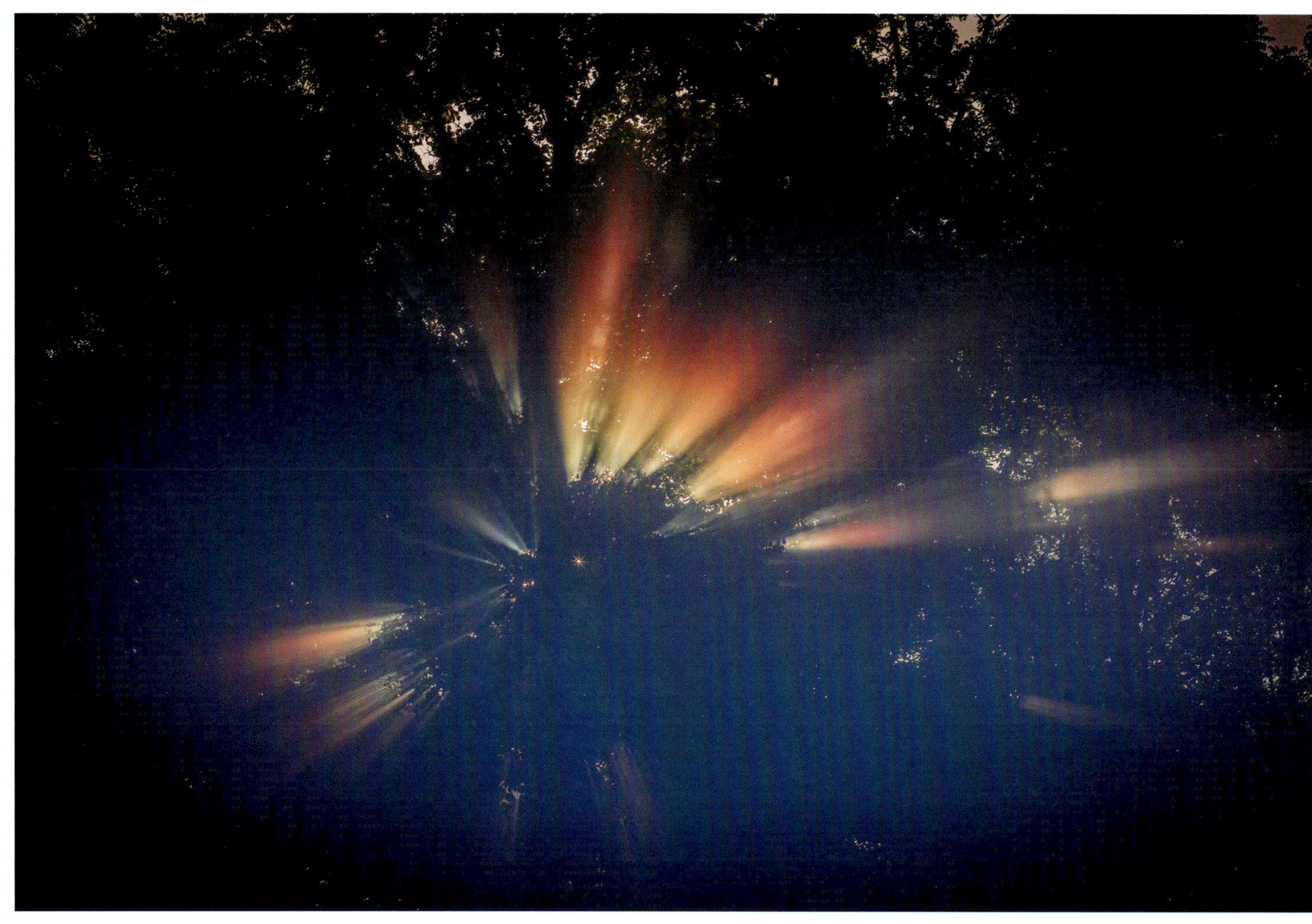

HOLSTON RIVER, BELOW KINGSPORT, TENNESSEE, SEPTEMBER 6. Sunlight bursting through the trees. This image or one similar to it could have been taken most any day on any of the Tennessee rivers.

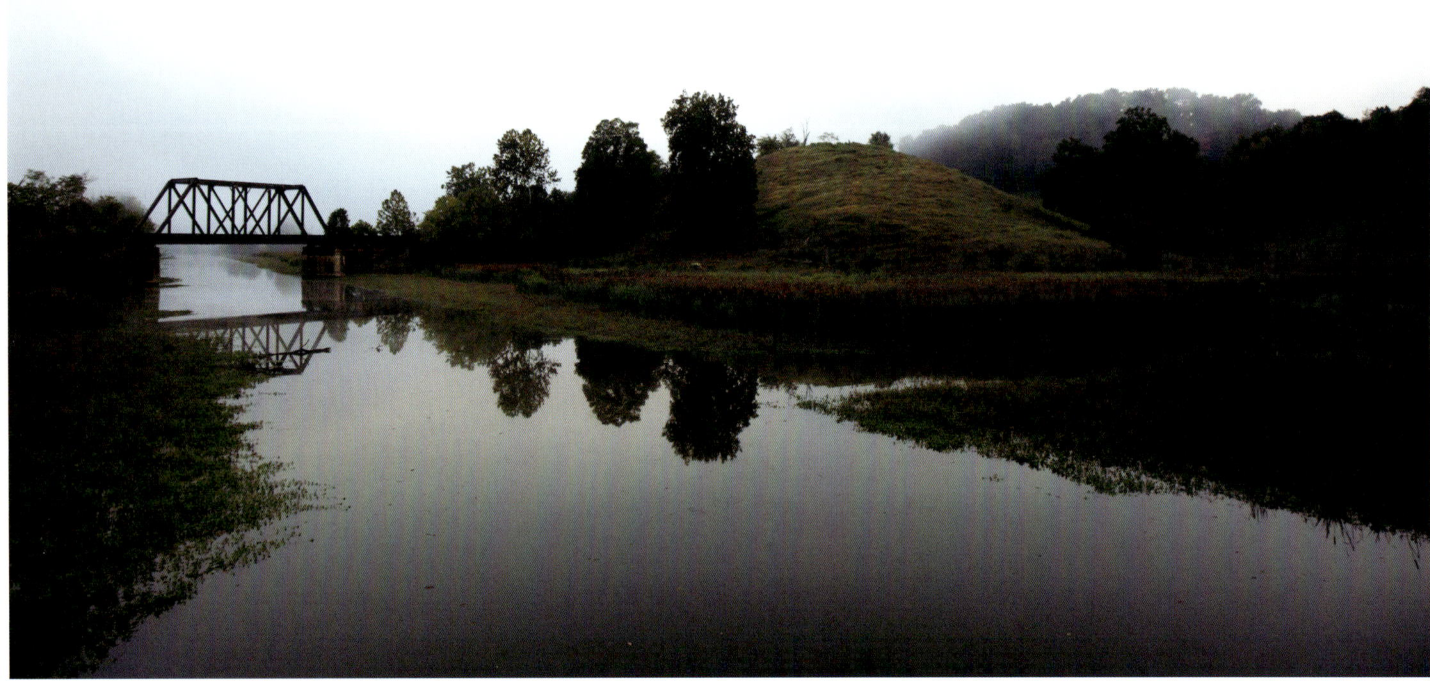

HOLSTON RIVER, RAILROAD BRIDGE OVER BEECH CREEK, ROGERSVILLE COMMUNITY, TENNESSEE, SEPTEMBER 6. As darkness began to fall all I could do was sit and wait to see if my ride would show up to trailer me to the other side of the dam. While I waited, fishermen loading their boats into the water warned me of the dangers caused by the meth epidemic. Nothing was safe. People would do most anything to get their next fix.

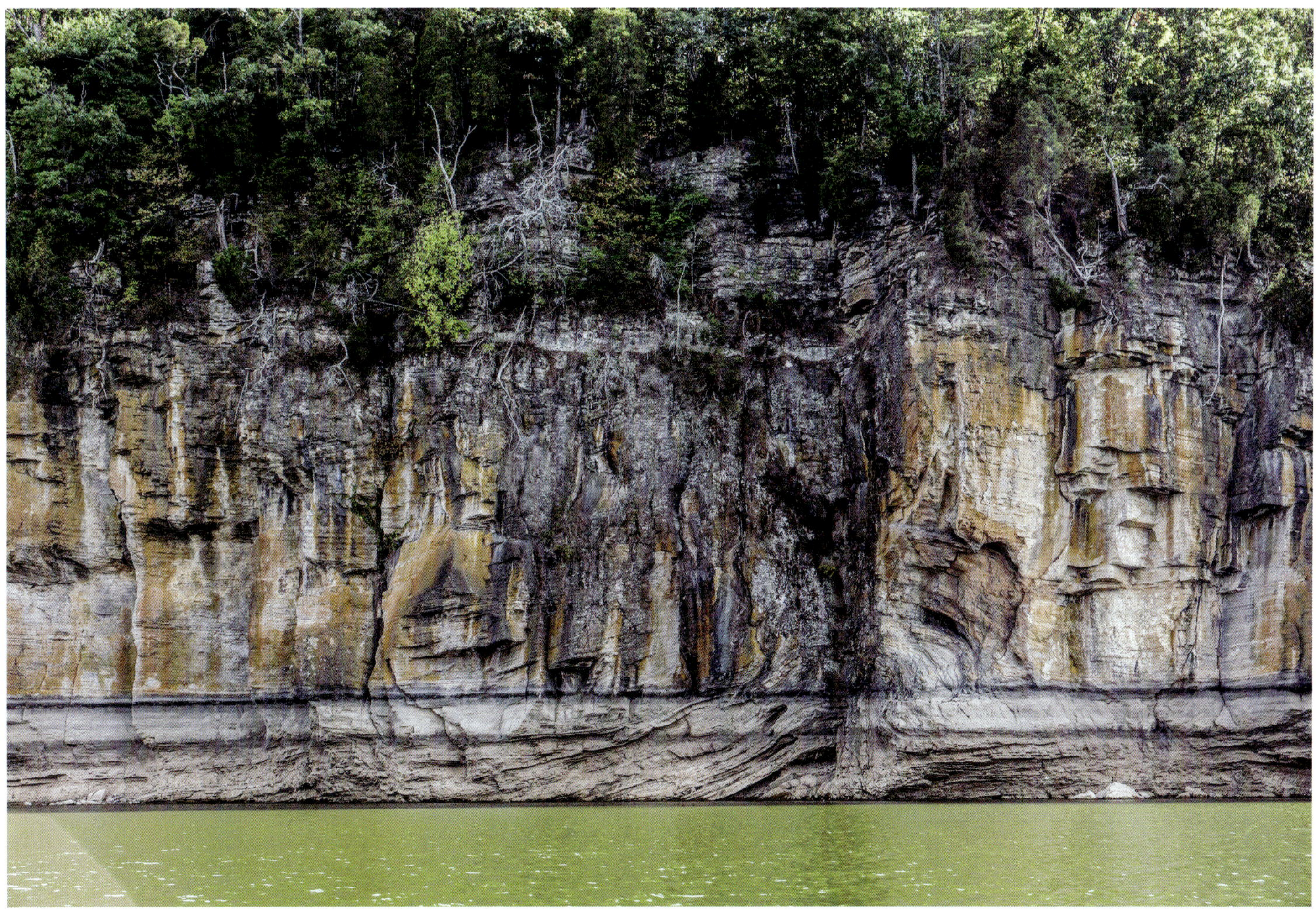

HOLSTON RIVER, HEADWATERS OF CHEROKEE LAKE, SEPTEMBER 7. Site where I launched after my friend Mark Fly, a professor at the University of Tennessee, trailered my boat around the John Sevier Fossil Plant dam. The cliffs were so distinctive I became absorbed picking out all the different faces and images in its facade.

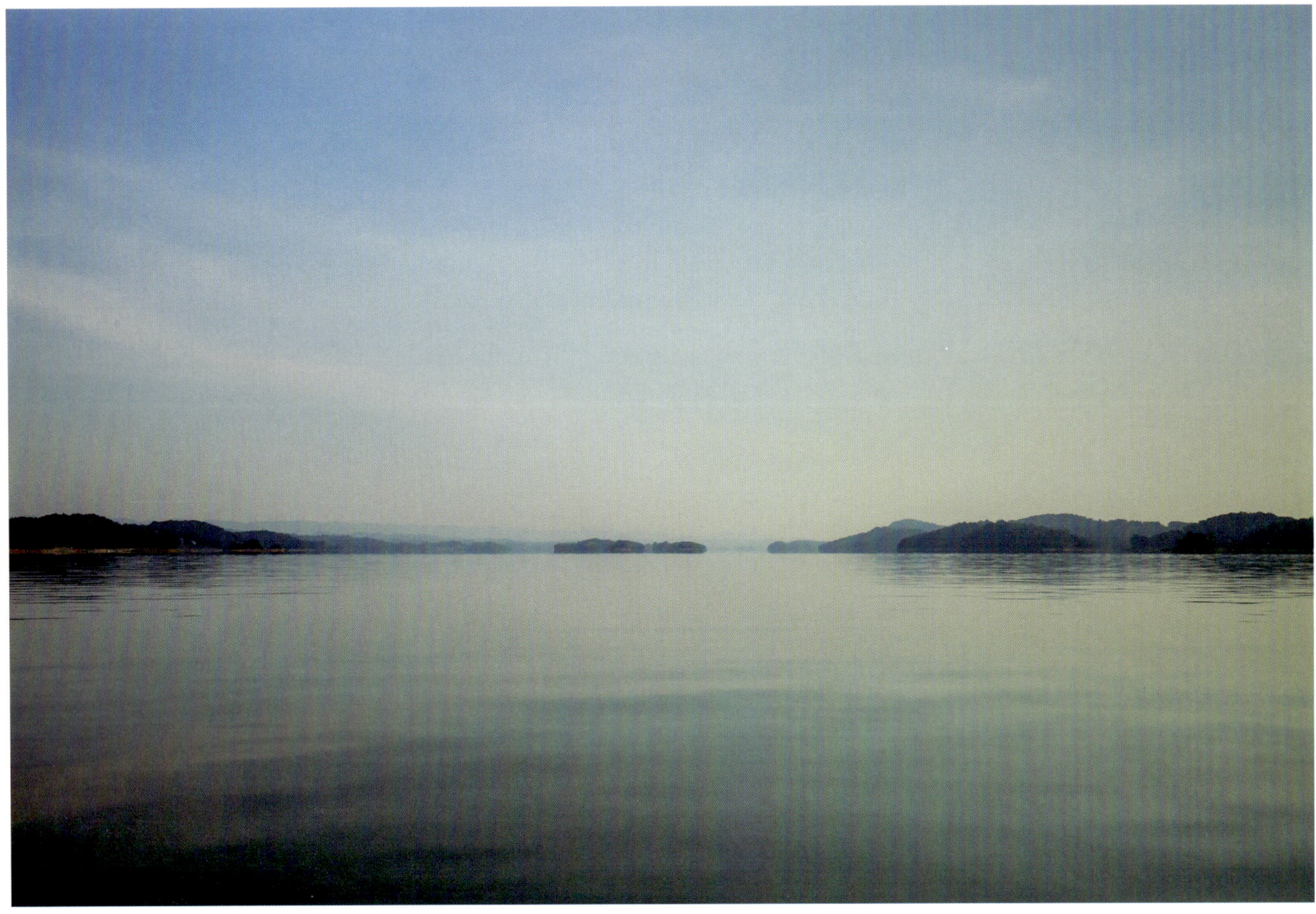

CHEROKEE LAKE/HOLSTON RIVER, SEPTEMBER 9. What were once hilltops now rise out of the man-made lake to form islands on the surface of the impounded water. A local fisherman by the name of James Adams generously helped me ferry my boat across the dam, allowing me to continue forward. Throughout my journeys I have been continually amazed by the kindness of strangers.

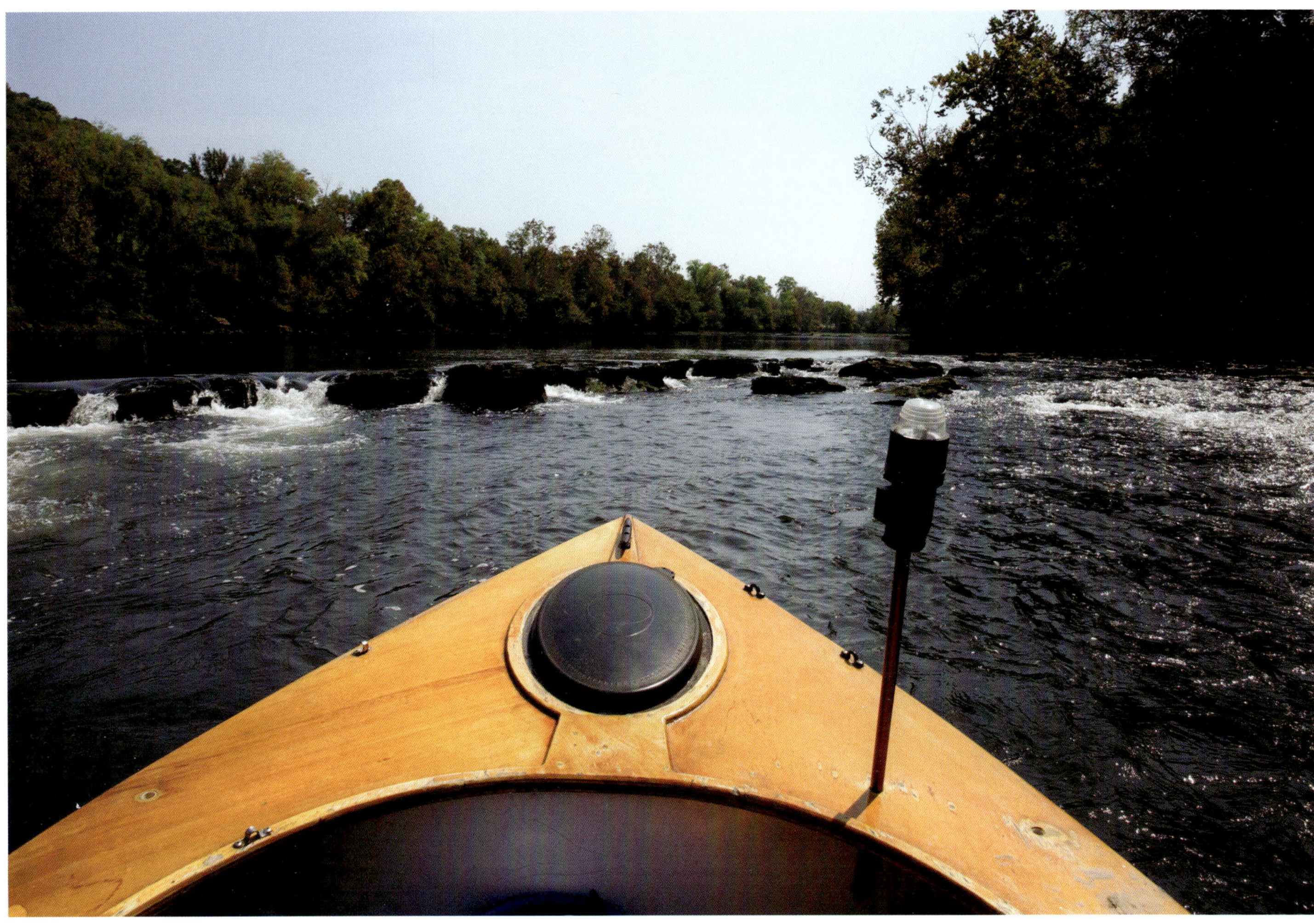

HOLSTON RIVER, BELOW THE CHEROKEE DAM, SEPTEMBER 9. The water level is low when the hydroelectric dam is not generating. The exposed rocks made passage in my wooden boat very tricky.

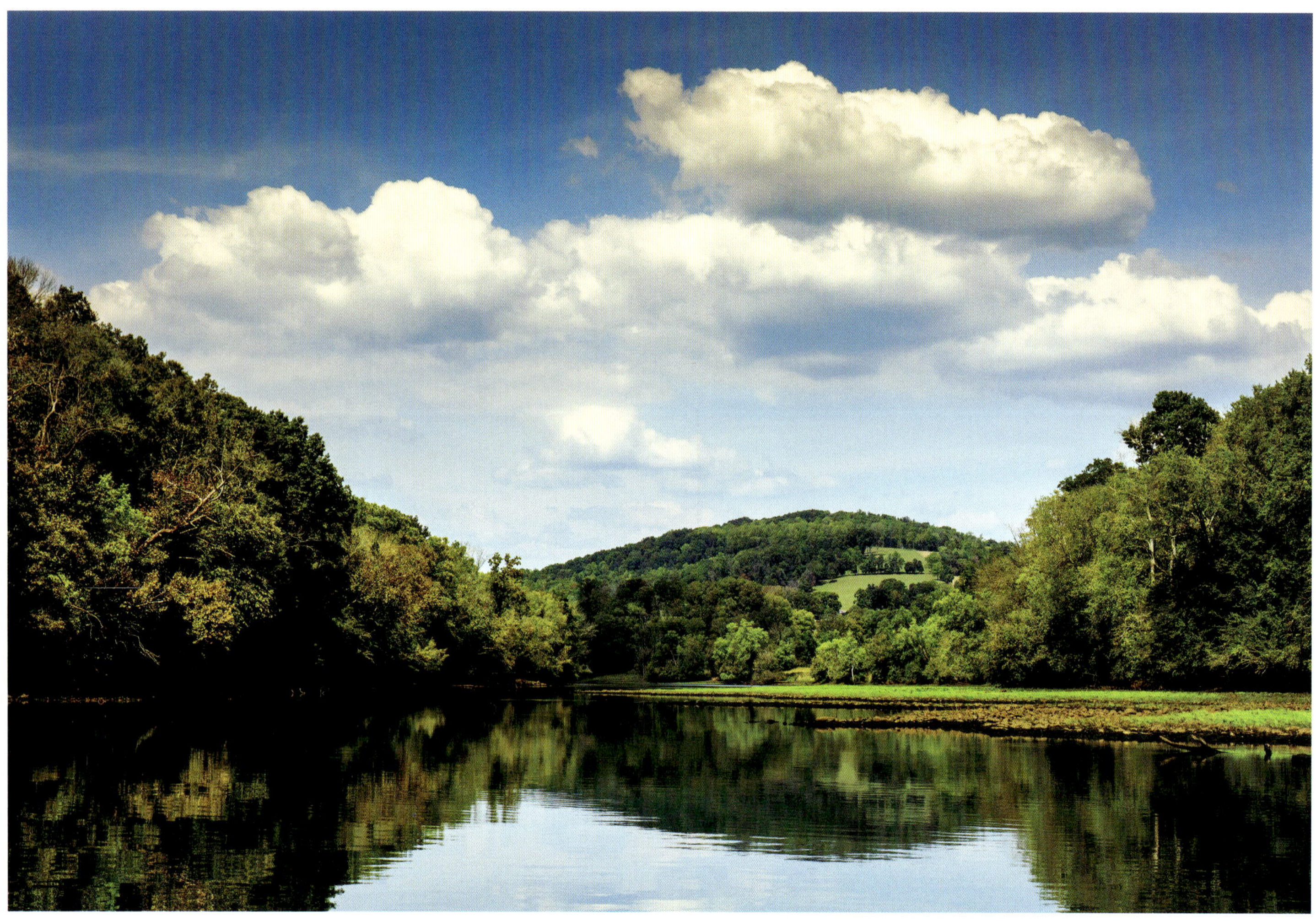

HOLSTON RIVER, BELOW THE CHEROKEE DAM, SEPTEMBER 9. The river calming in the pooling waters added to the sense of peace and surreality that enveloped the landscape.

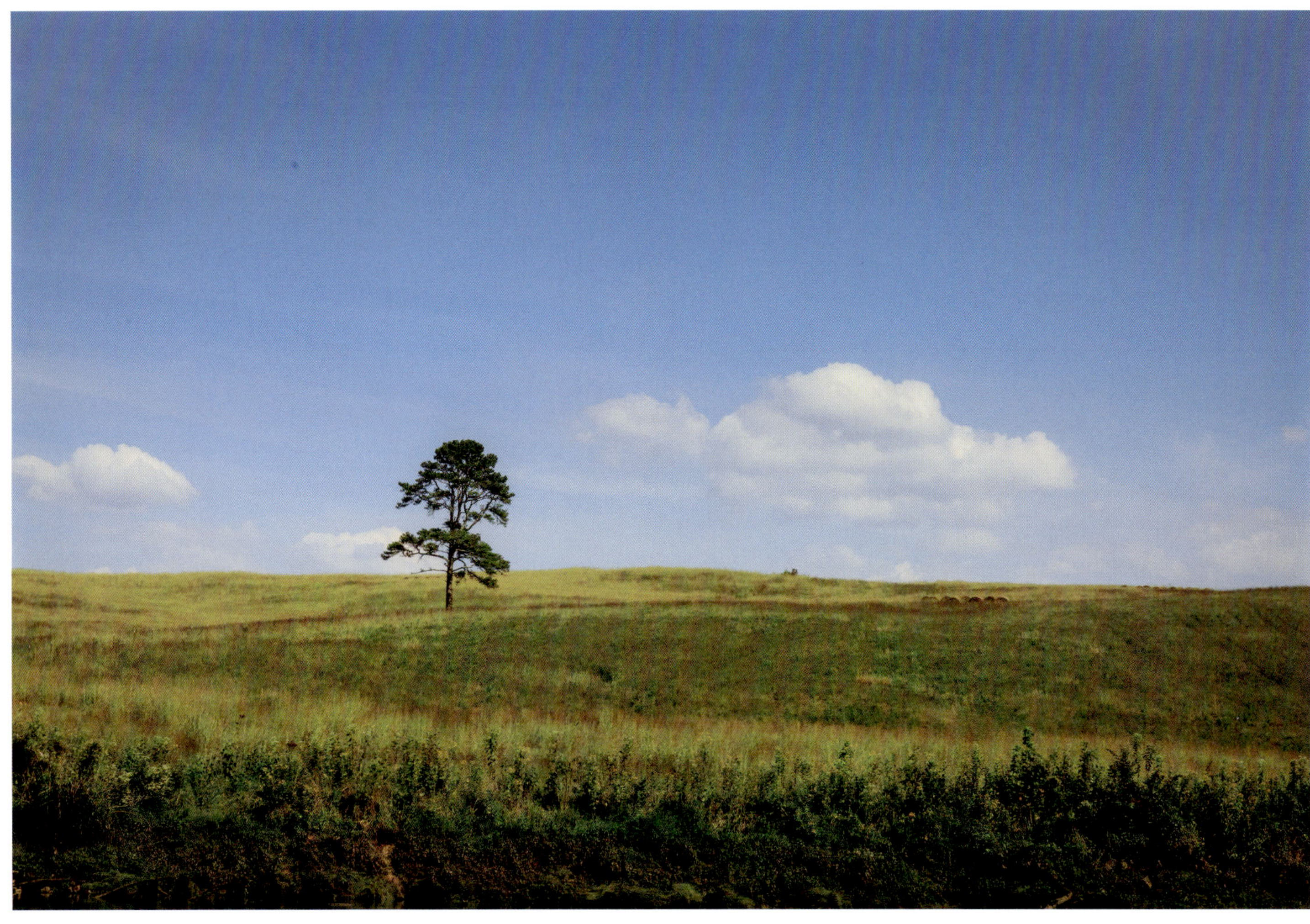

HOLSTON RIVER, SEPTEMBER 9. A solitary tree dominates the landscape along the fields that have been cleared for grazing.

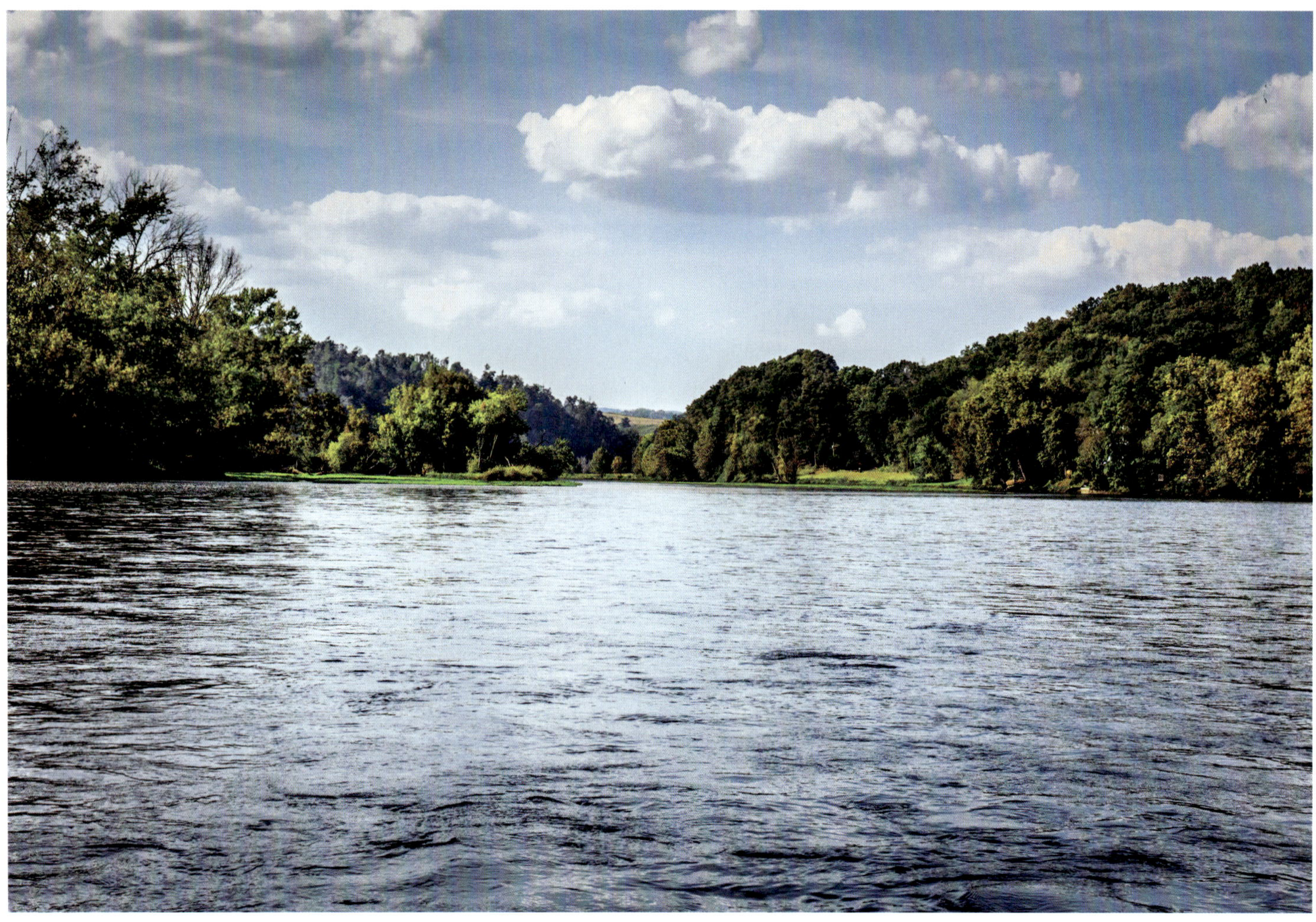

HOLSTON RIVER, SEPTEMBER 9. The otherwise clear water of the highlands river reflects the metallic sky, camouflaging the life that moves underneath.

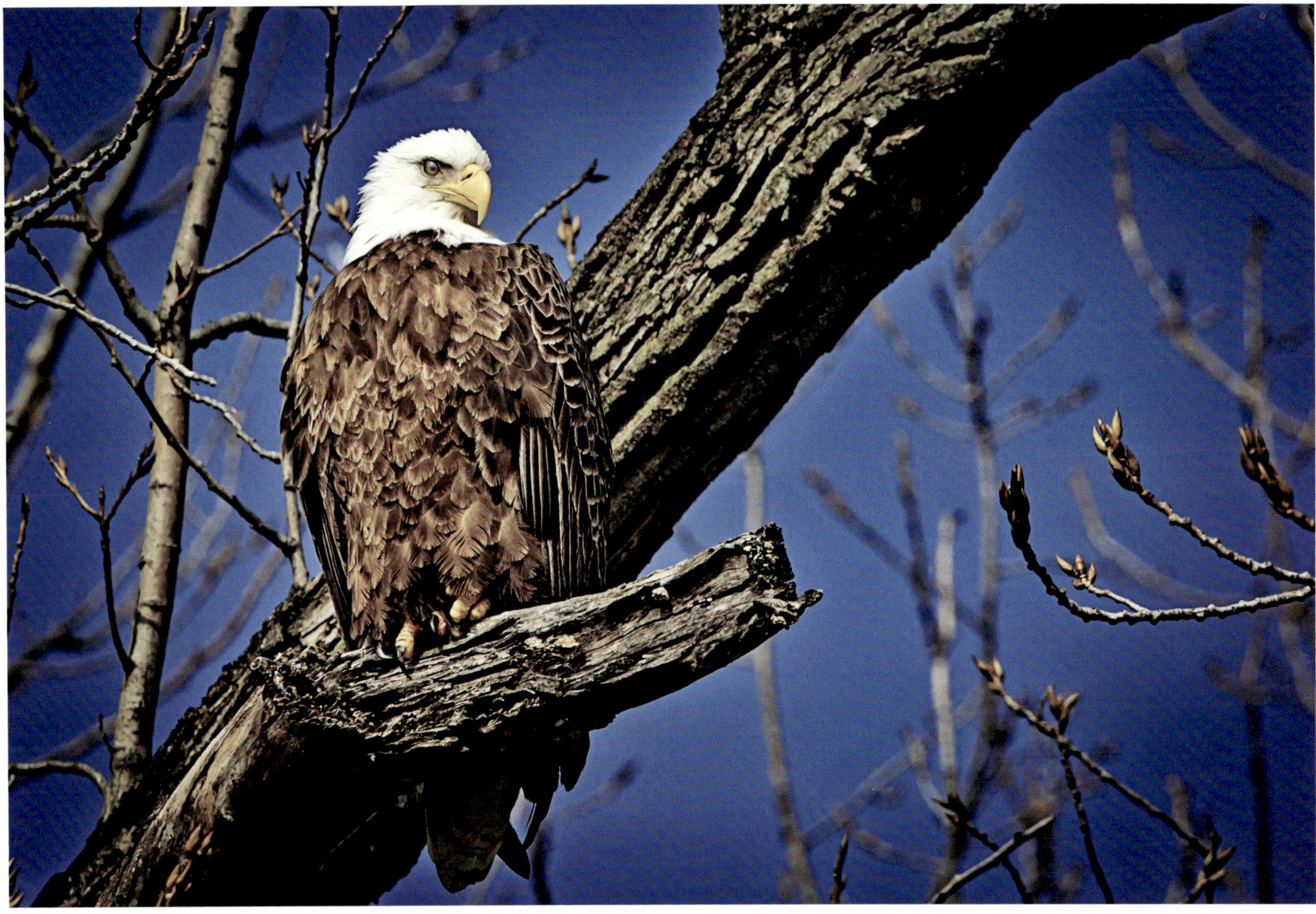

One of the joys of traveling in nature is seeing the healthy return of the bald eagle.

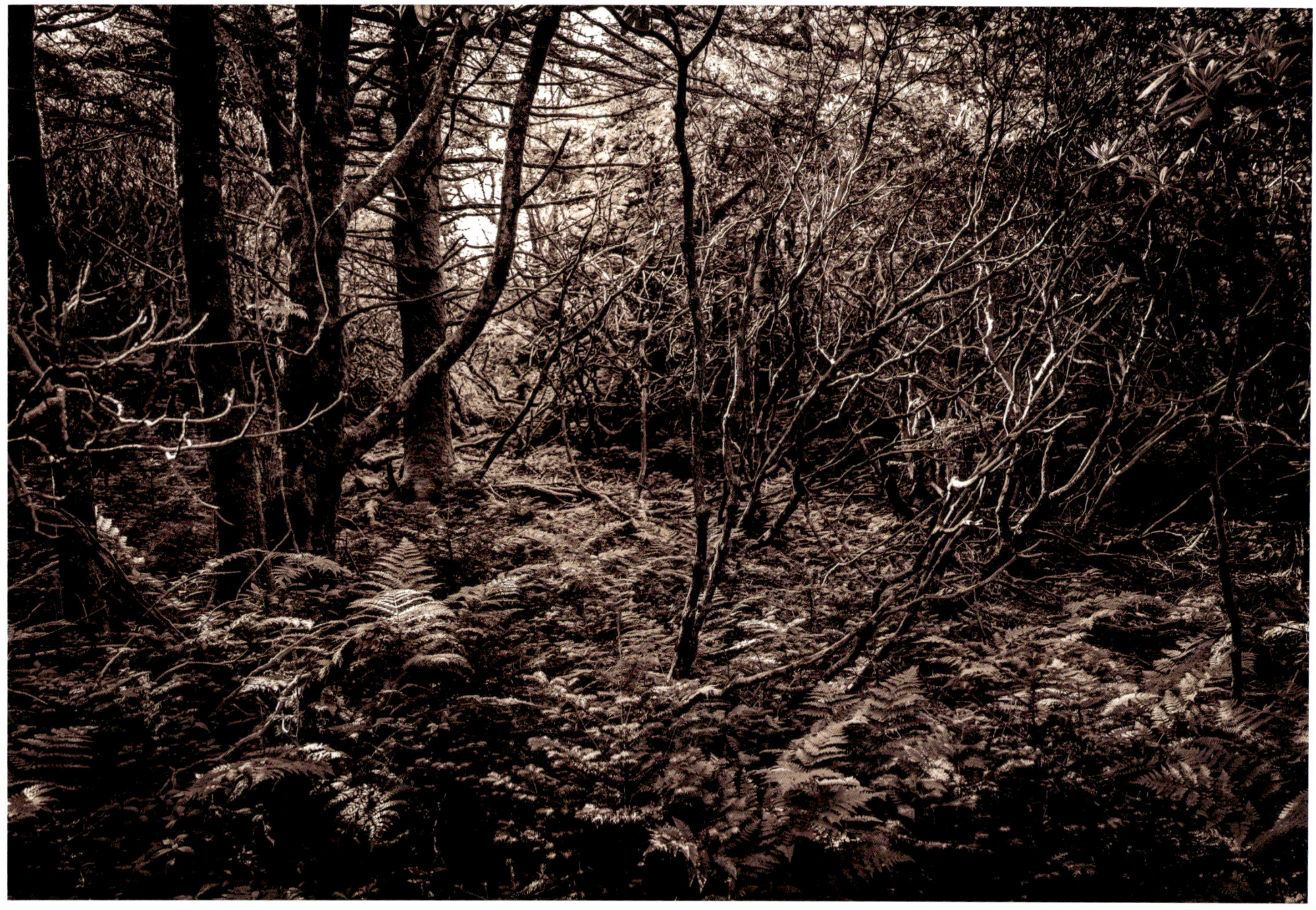

My typical surroundings when I pulled off along the bucolic countryside to camp at night.

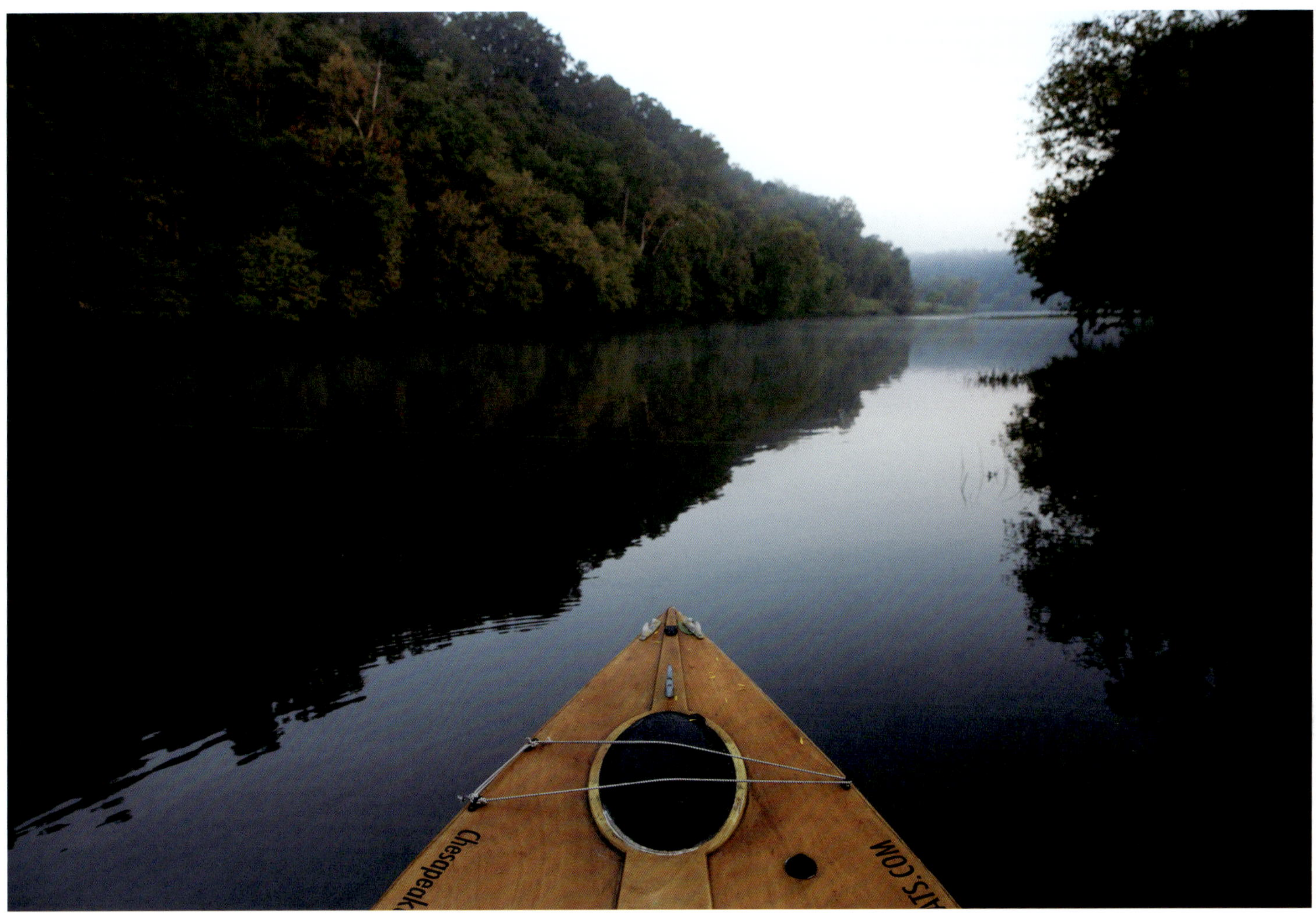

HOLSTON RIVER, SECOND DAY BELOW THE DAM, SEPTEMBER 10. The Holston flows through a primarily rural environment offering views similar to what the Donelson party may have seen almost 240 years prior. What will the river look like 240 years from now?

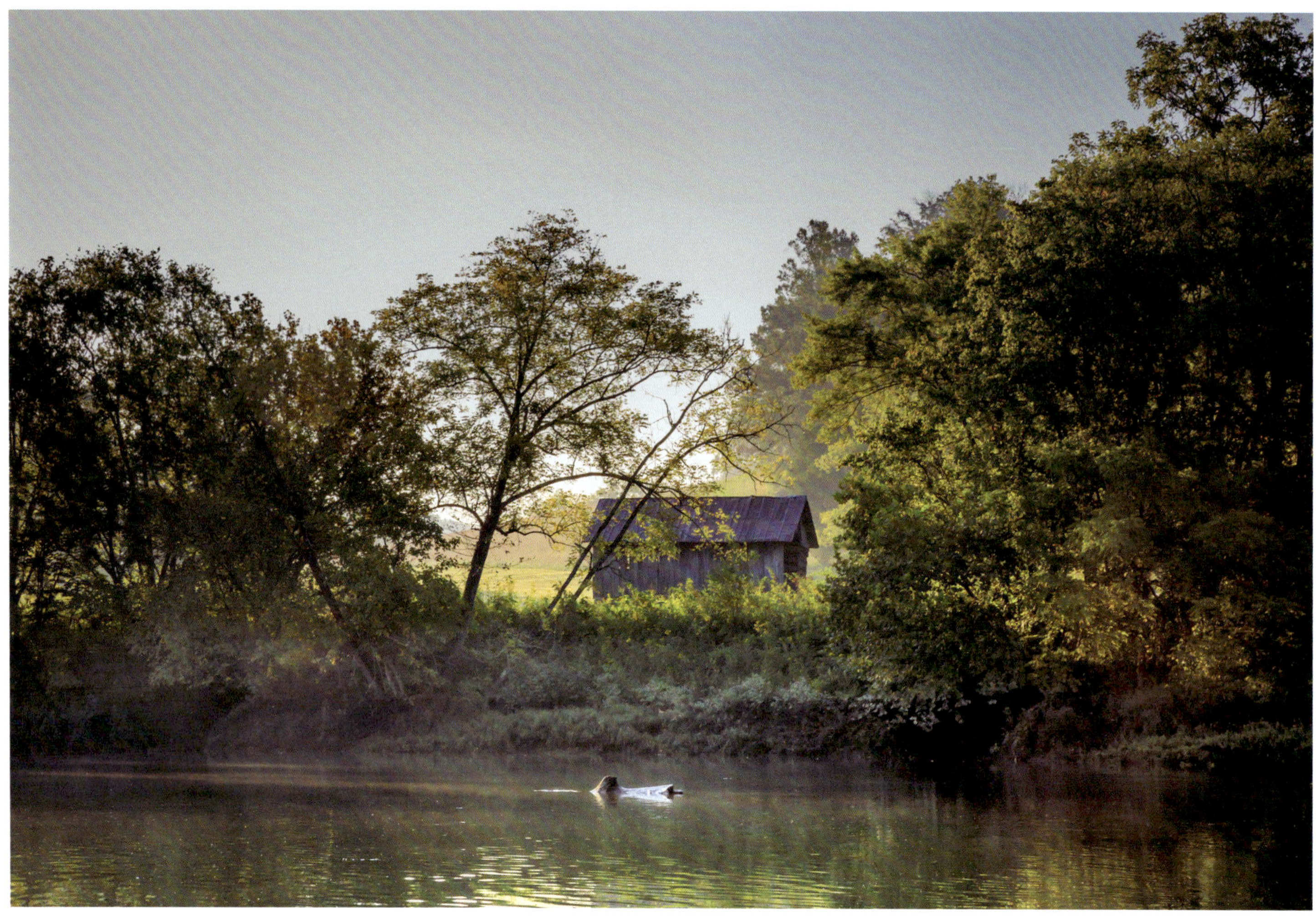

HOLSTON RIVER, EARLY EVENING, SEPTEMBER 10. Tranquil sunset river passage. All is calm. All is right with the world. The pastoral scene does not reflect all the blood, sweat, and tears that went into clearing and farming that field.

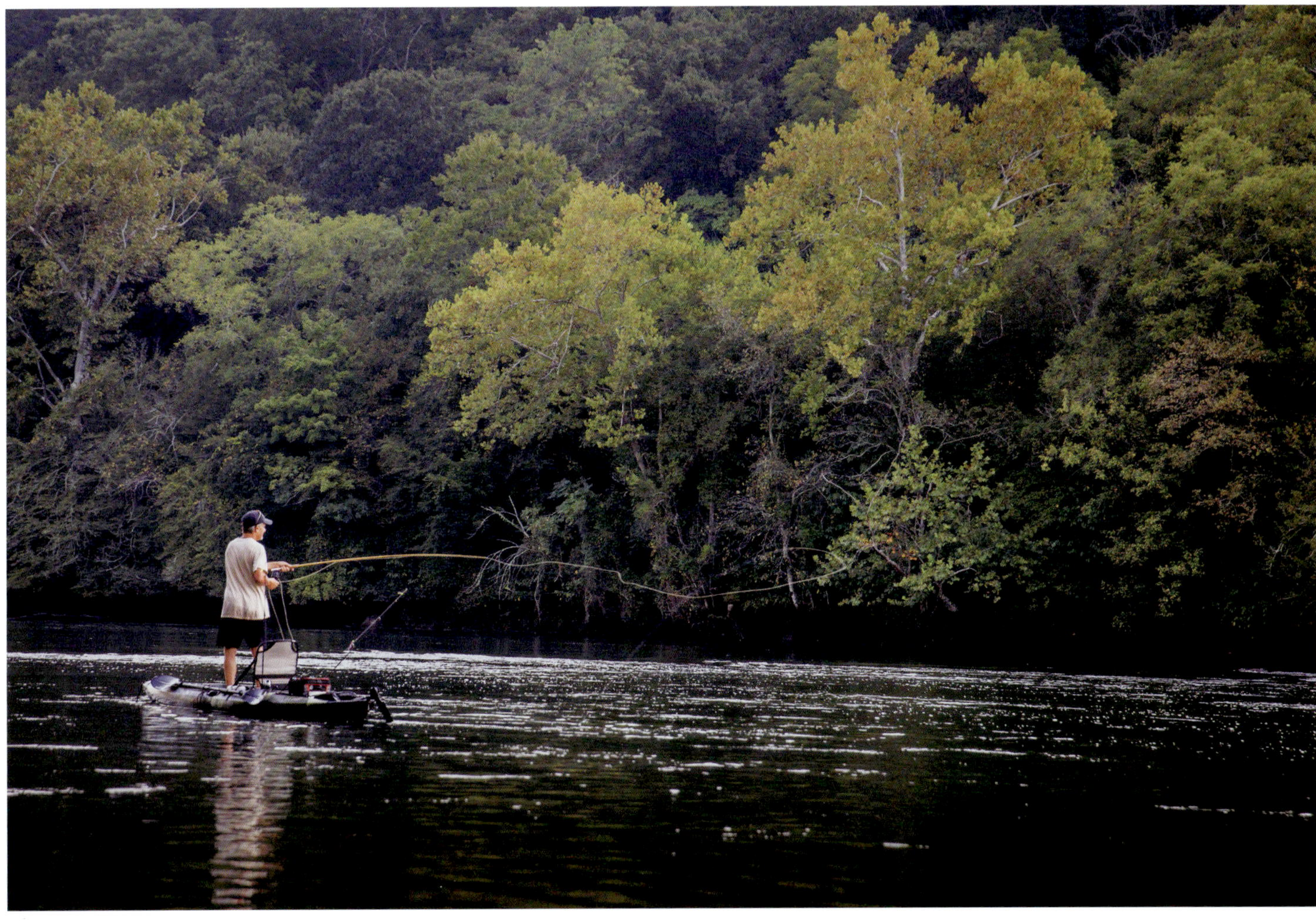

HOLSTON RIVER, KNOX COUNTY, TENNESSEE, SEPTEMBER 10. Fisherman standing on his kayak fishing next to an island. Aside from the necessary portages, I mostly had the river all to myself.

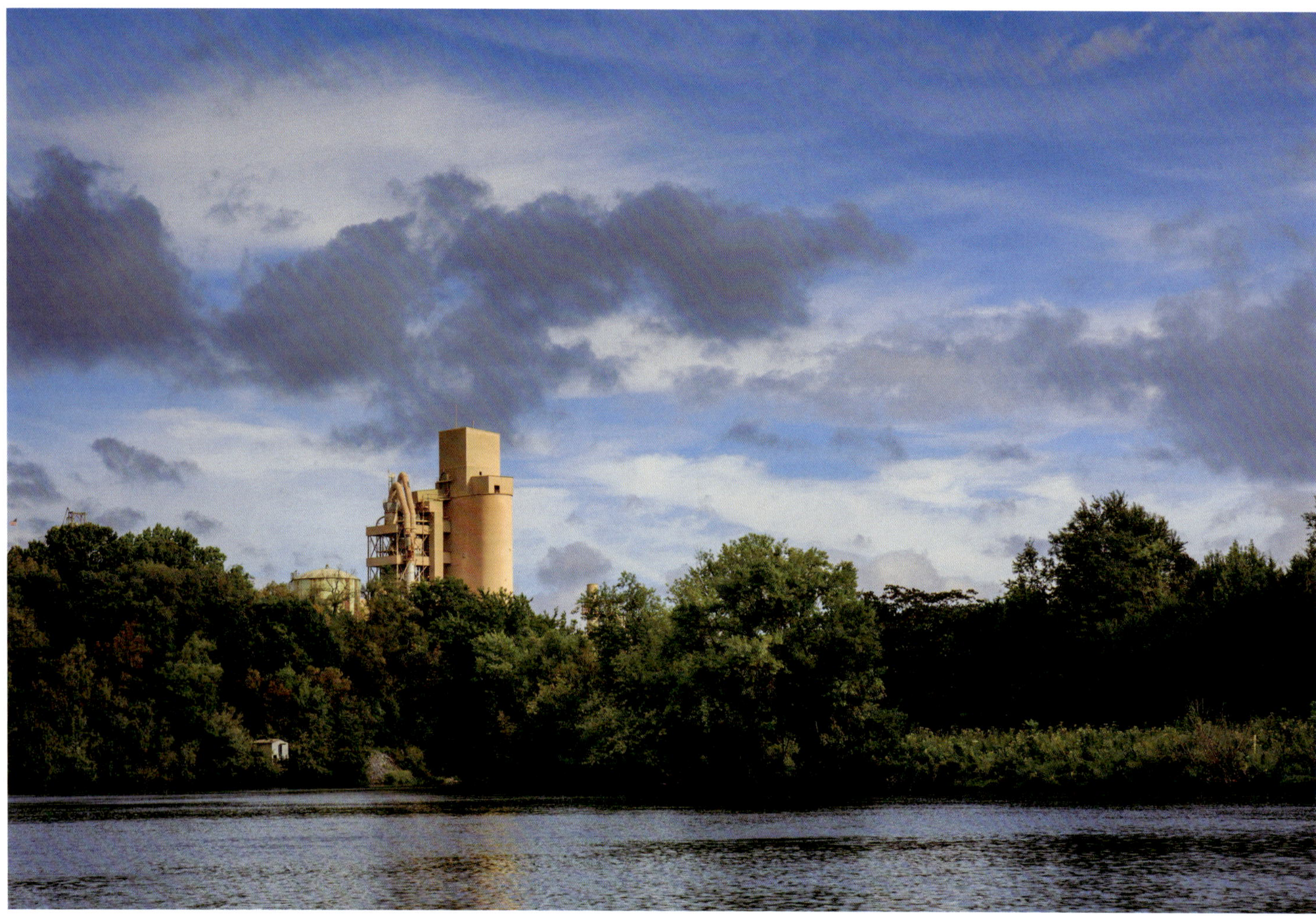

HOLSTON RIVER, KNOX COUNTY, TENNESSEE, SEPTEMBER 11. Grain mill at the confluence of the Holston and French Broad Rivers forming the headwaters of the Tennessee River. The colliding rivers caught one of the boats in the Donelson flotilla, sending it into the shoals of Dickinson Island where it promptly sank. No one was hurt, but many stores were lost.

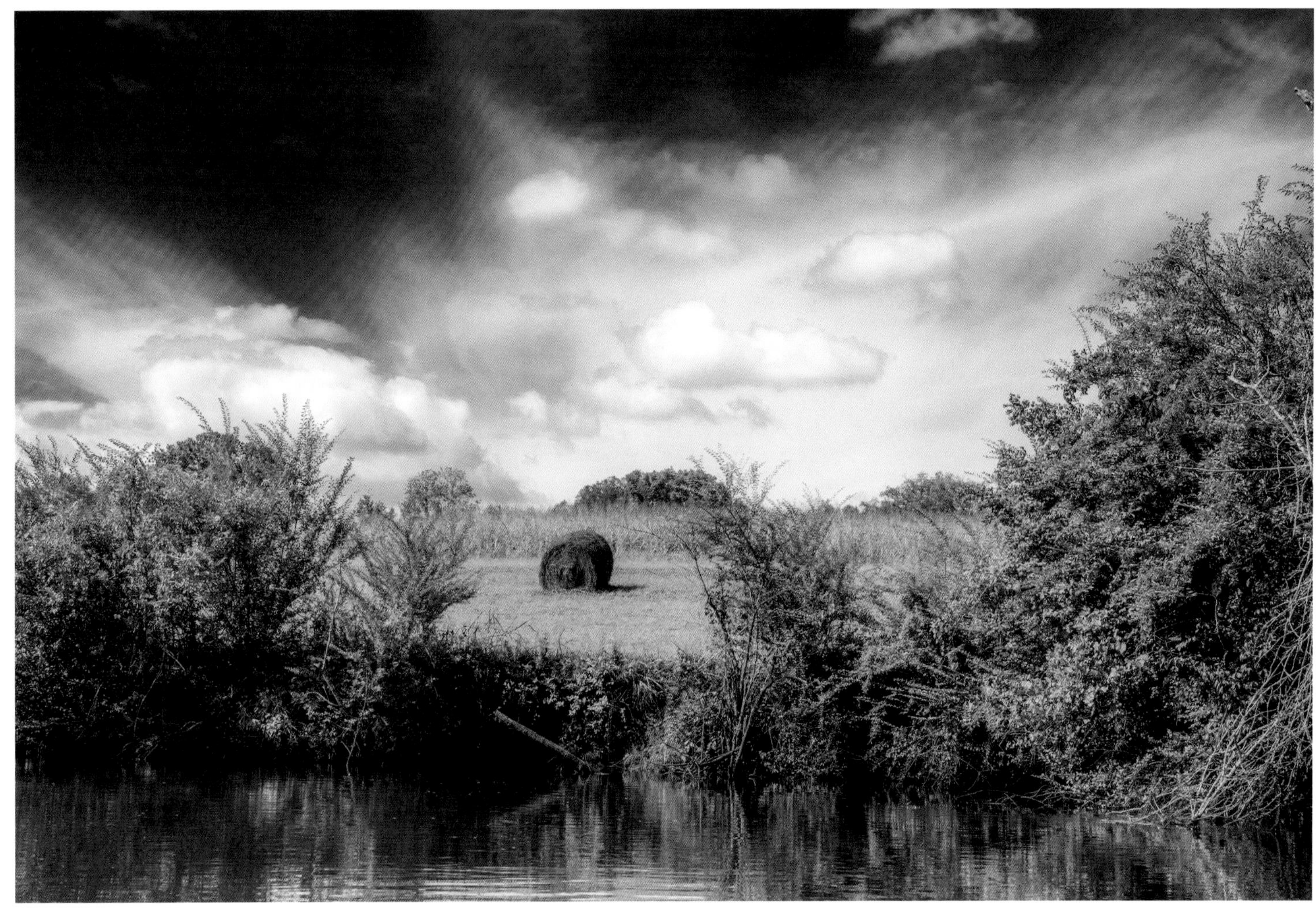

TENNESSEE RIVER, KNOX COUNTY, TENNESSEE, SEPTEMBER 11. Farmland on the northern shore of the river close to the Knoxville city limits. Donelson's boat carried thirty enslaved people. If not for them, Donelson's flatboat would not have been able to navigate the treacherous shoals of the Holston River.

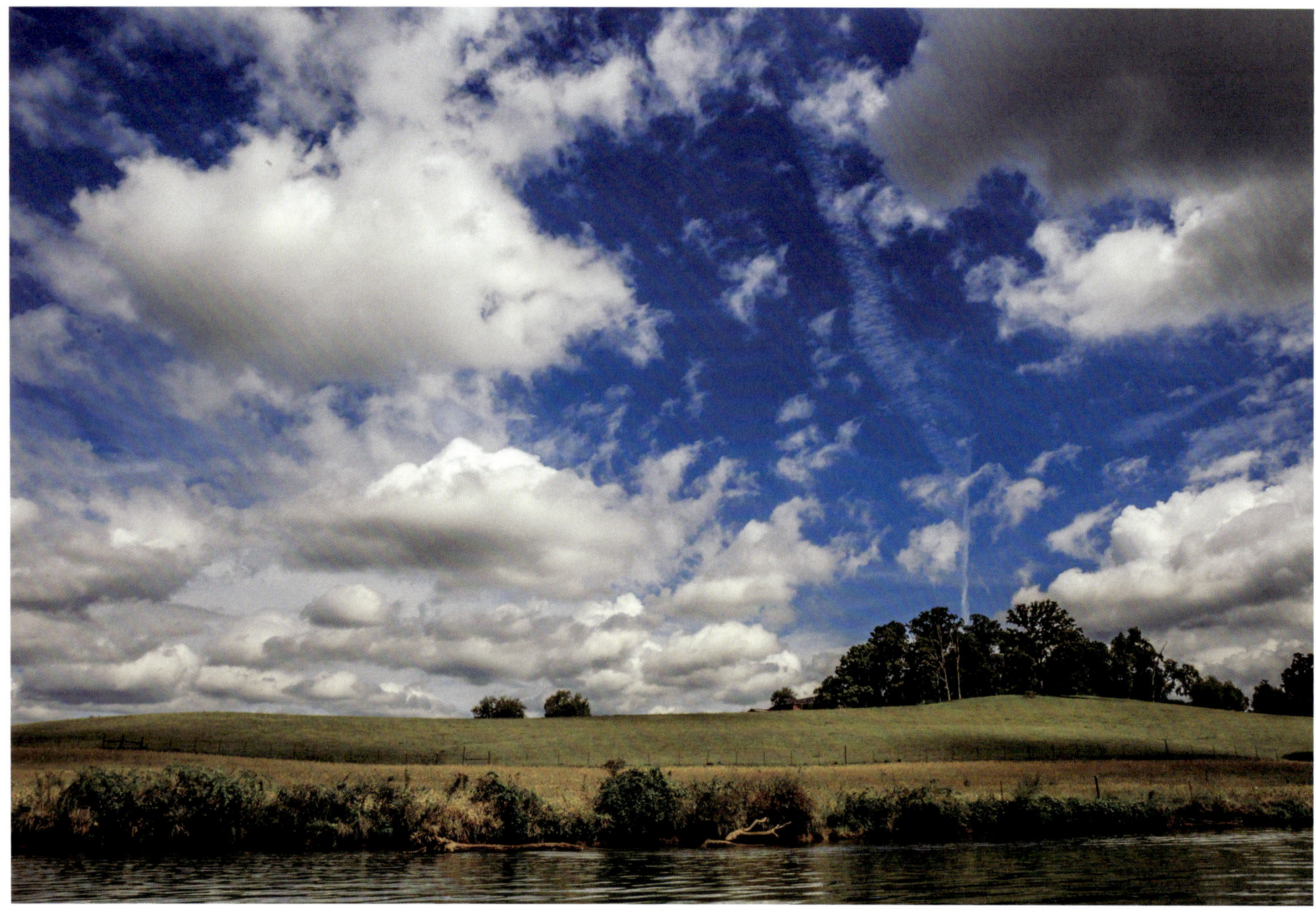

TENNESSEE RIVER, KNOX COUNTY, TENNESSEE, SEPTEMBER 11. Cloud-infused sky overshadows the river. “Thank God they cannot cut down the clouds! All kinds of figures are drawn on the blue ground with this fibrous white paint.” —Henry David Thoreau

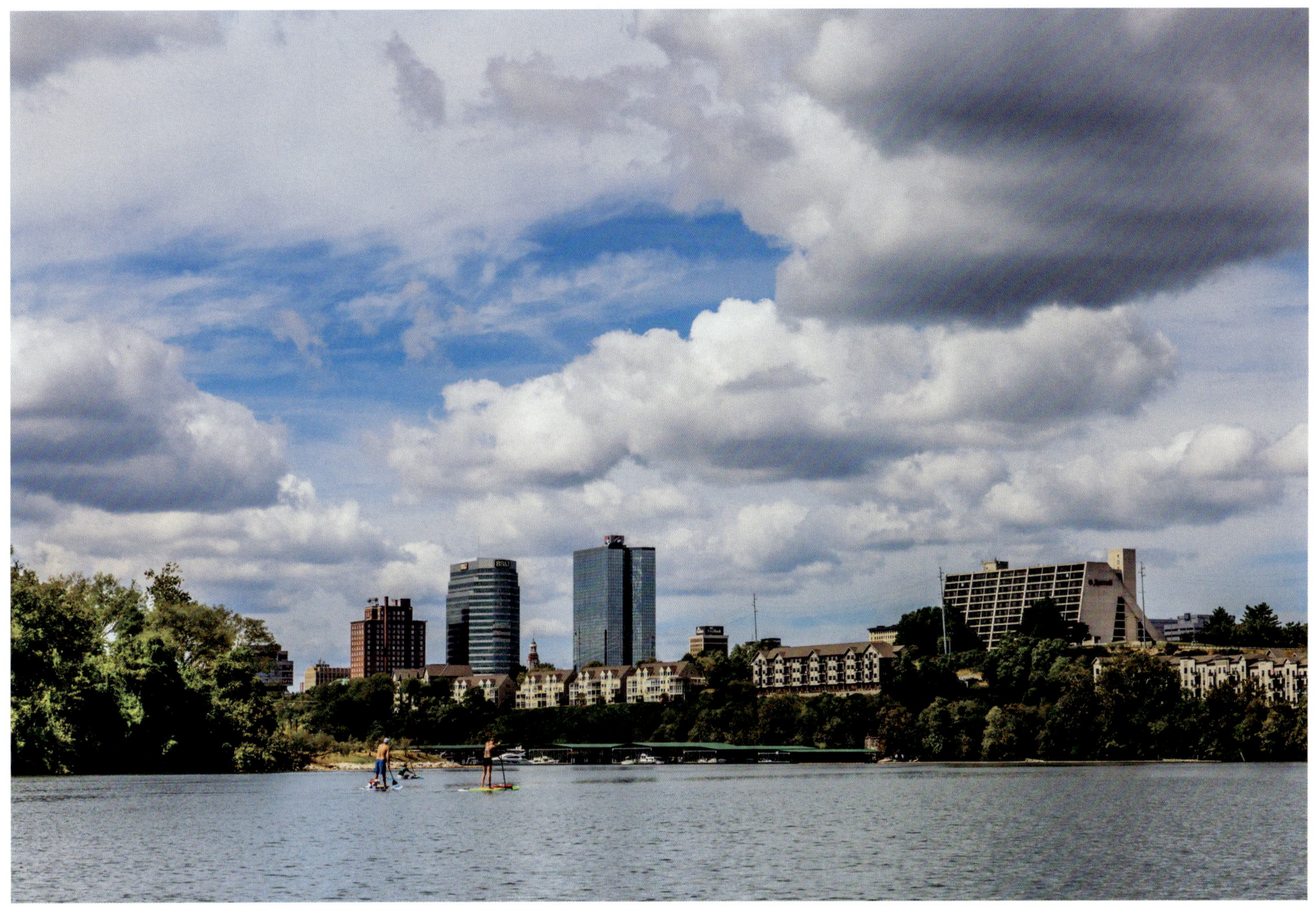

TENNESSEE RIVER, KNOXVILLE, TENNESSEE, SEPTEMBER 11. After almost a week of quiet solitude the river came alive with activity. Here the river was deep and swift, carrying the Donelson party upwards of fifty miles per day.

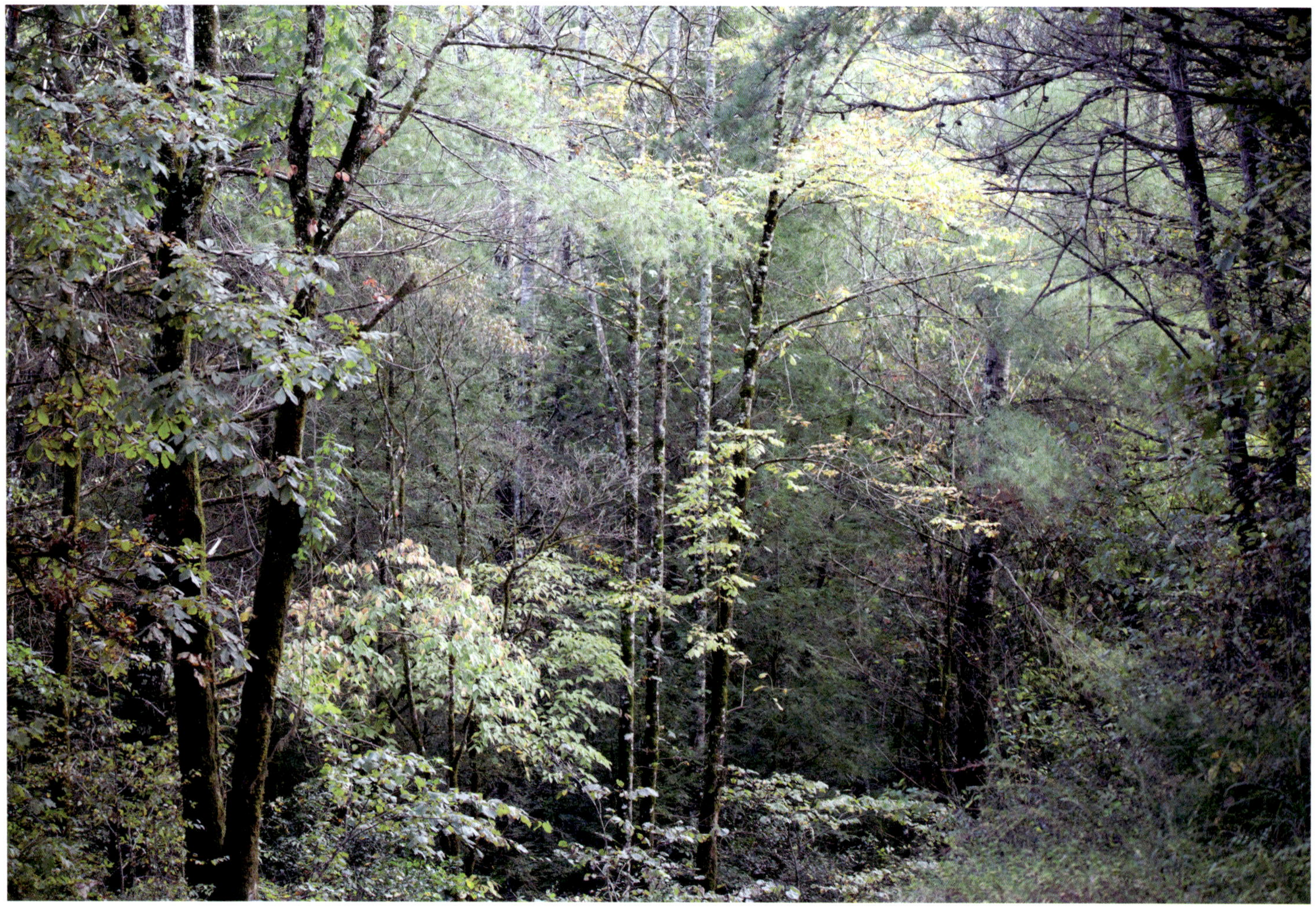

A typical early fall Tennessee landscape. Van Gogh wrote, “If one loves nature, beauty can be found anywhere.”

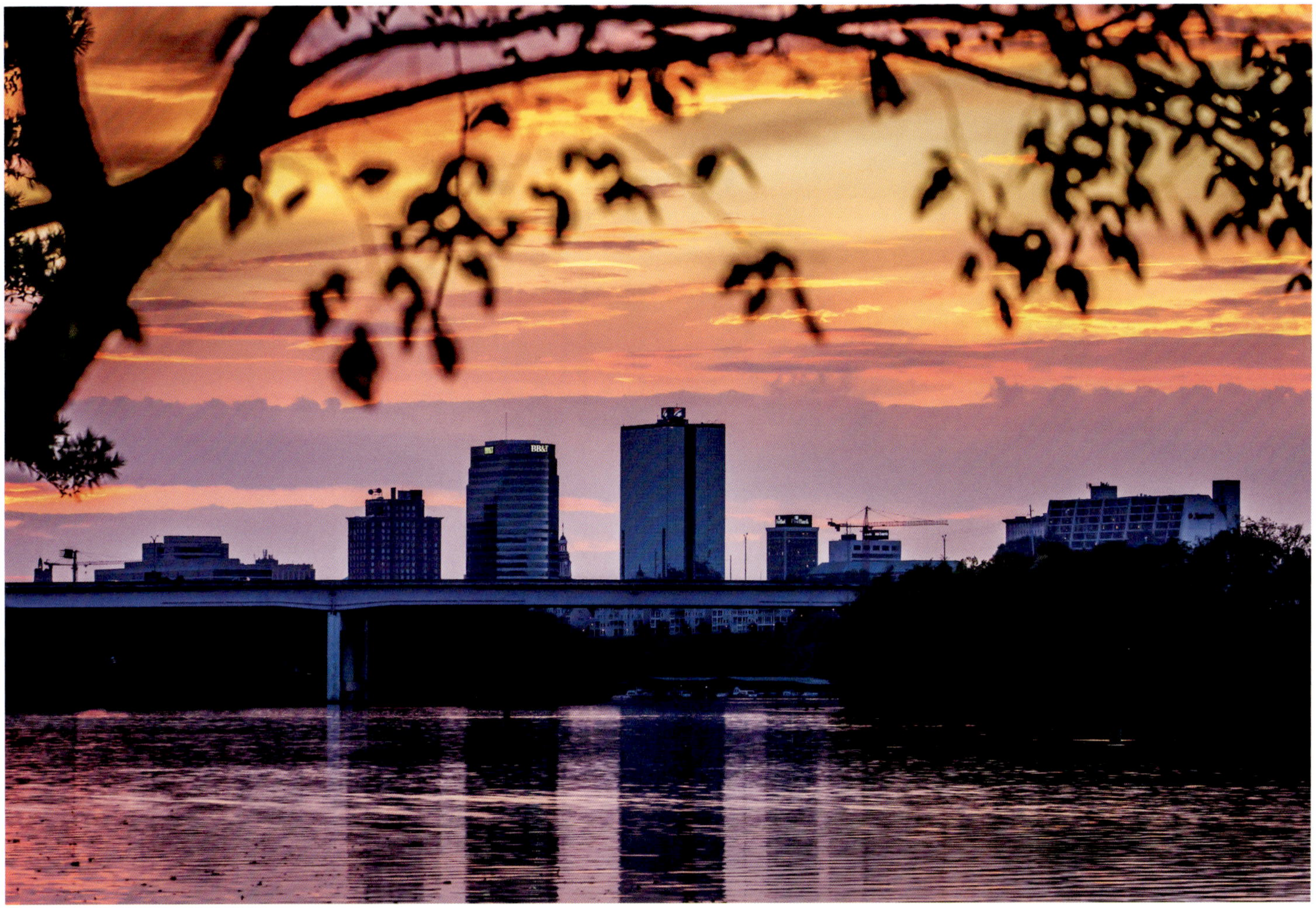

TENNESSEE RIVER, KNOXVILLE, TENNESSEE, SEPTEMBER 11. View of the Knoxville skyline. Stayed with Mark Fly while I replaced a torn sail and my cell phone that had been lost in the water.

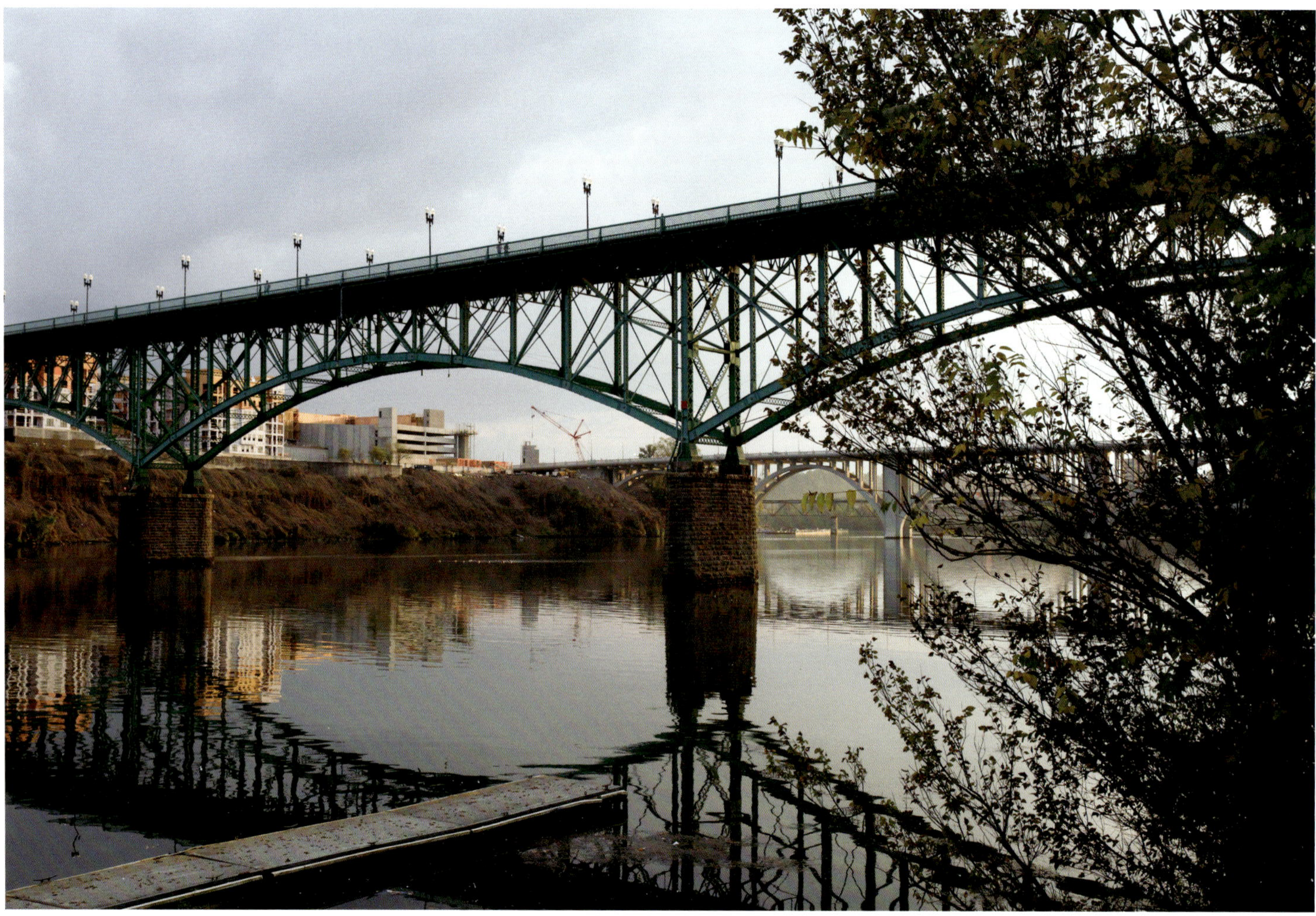

TENNESSEE RIVER, KNOXVILLE, TENNESSEE, SEPTEMBER 12. View of the downtown bridges and the eastern shore. What Donelson saw was just riverbank and possibly smoke from fires in a few trappers' encampments.

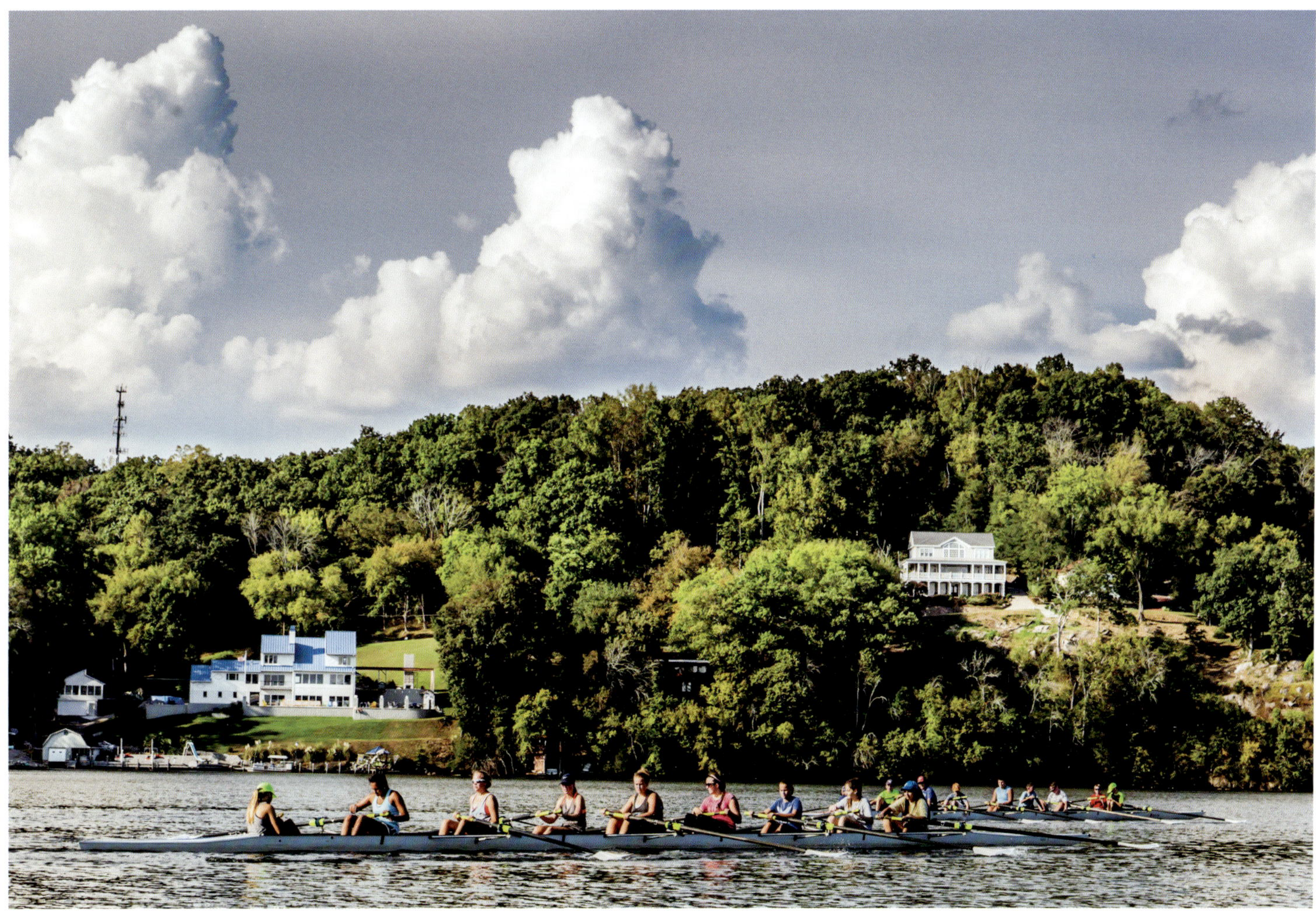

TENNESSEE RIVER, KNOXVILLE, TENNESSEE, SEPTEMBER 13. Women's rowing team practicing against a landscape of expensive homes. I wonder what the children of the flotilla—road weary, cold, and hungry—would have thought had they passed by such a scene?

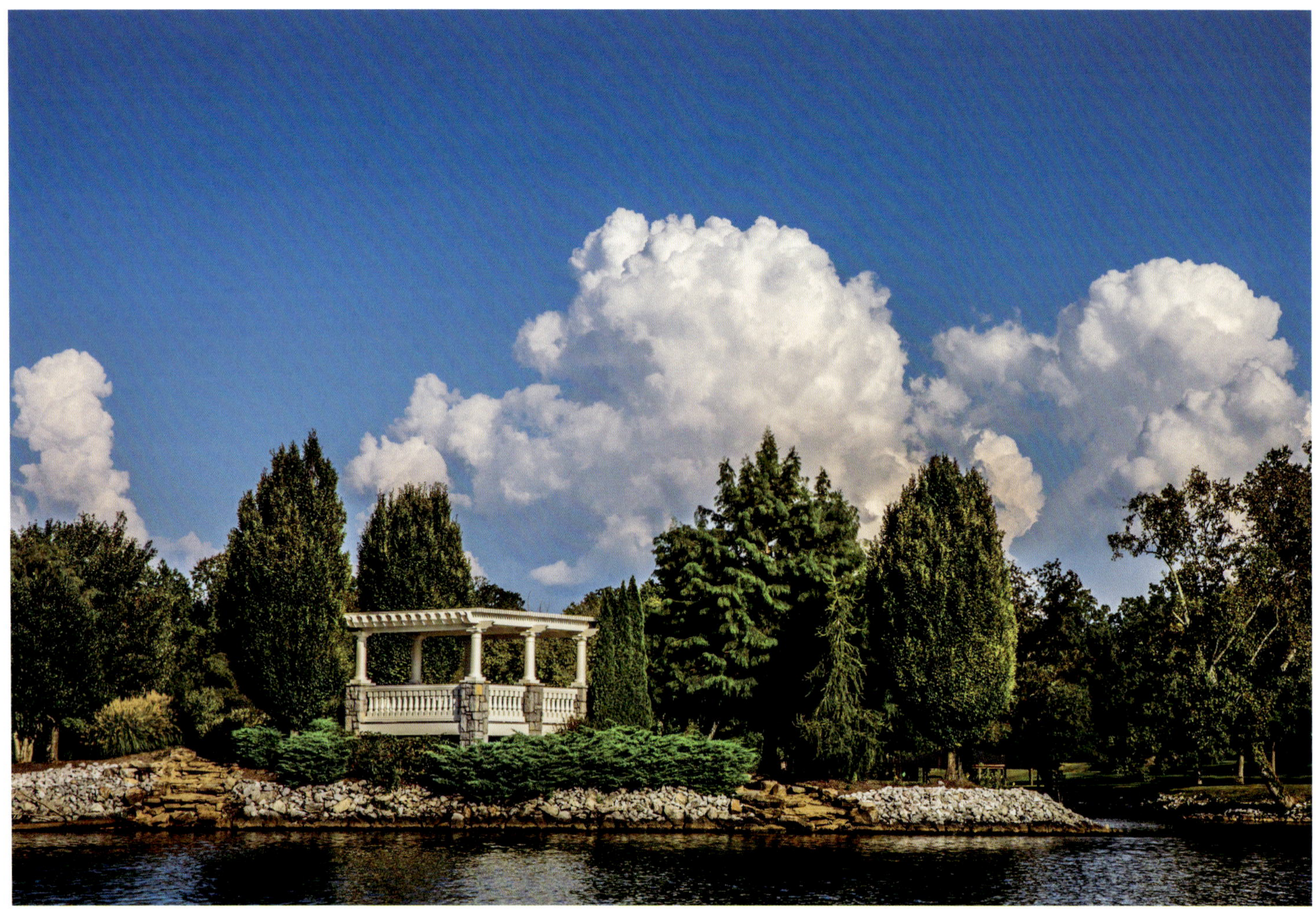

TENNESSEE RIVER, KNOXVILLE, TENNESSEE, SEPTEMBER 13. The riverside estates had constrained nature. With no other activity apparent, the world for a moment was ghostly in its silence.

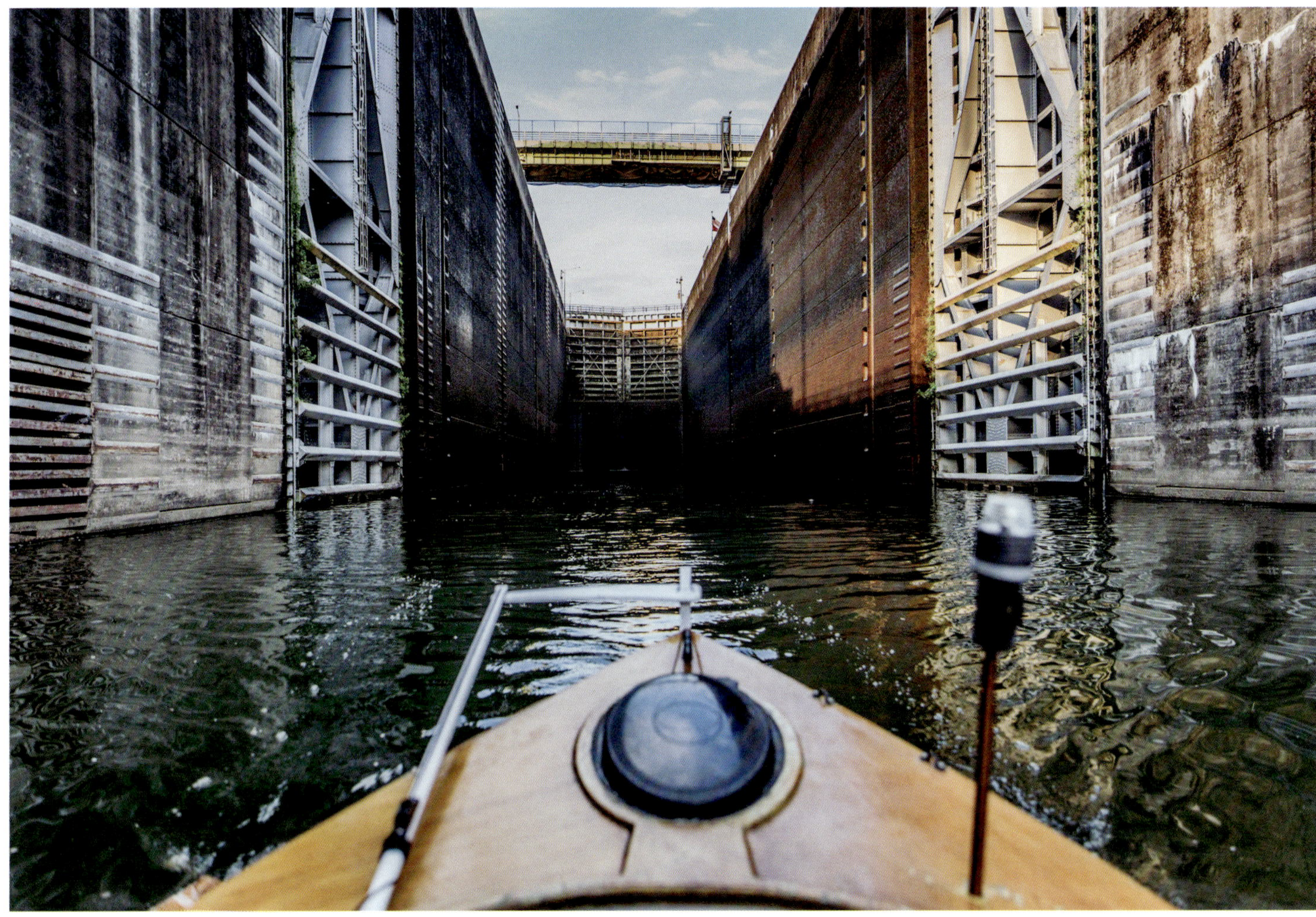

TENNESSEE RIVER, FORT LOUDOUN LOCK, SEPTEMBER 14. My first lock through of the journey. The lockmaster was especially gracious, saying he had never locked through a rowboat before. When I told him I had made it myself, he was duly impressed. After that I had ten more locks to transit before I reached Nashville.

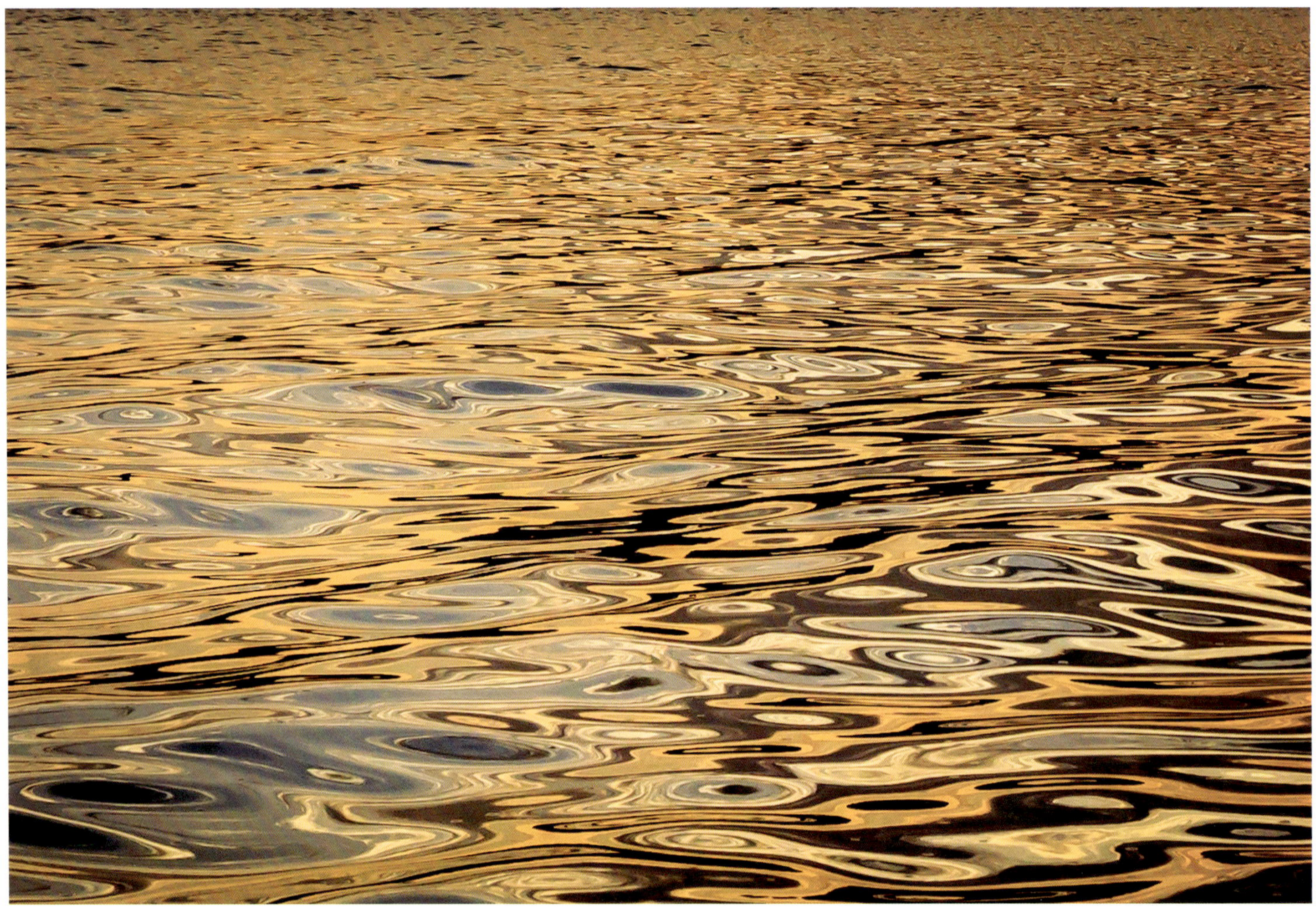

TENNESSEE RIVER, ROANE COUNTY, TENNESSEE, SEPTEMBER 16. Sunset reflecting on the water.

I WAS NEARLY asleep around 10 p.m. when I heard the drone of something mechanical approaching. It was too far away to determine if it was coming from land or water. Then from around the bend I was hit with blinding lights like nothing I had ever seen before. A strange craft lumbered across the water toward me. I could make it out as a pontoon boat, ringed with a brilliant string of tungsten halogen lights at the waterline. It was moving at an excruciatingly slow speed. As it grew closer I could hear voices resonate above the engine and generator noises. The boat, following the path of the shoreline, was heading directly toward me without regard. As the conversation became audible I realized that the couple talking were bow hunting and using their lights to attract and kill fish. Their path was determined and my position was not going to sway or embarrass them. In between the swooshes of arrows and thrashing of the stricken prey, they talked mainly about their day as if this were just part of their routine. I couldn't tell if they were doing this as sport or for commerce. I had no idea if it was legal or not. The rig was blinding and they went about their activity as if I didn't exist. They came close to my boat as they entered and exited the narrow cove I had anchored in. Not once did they dim the lights or make any other acknowledgment of my existence. I wanted say something but the circumstance was so unusual all I could do was sit in disbelief. Eventually they disappeared behind the next bend like an apparition, never to be seen again.

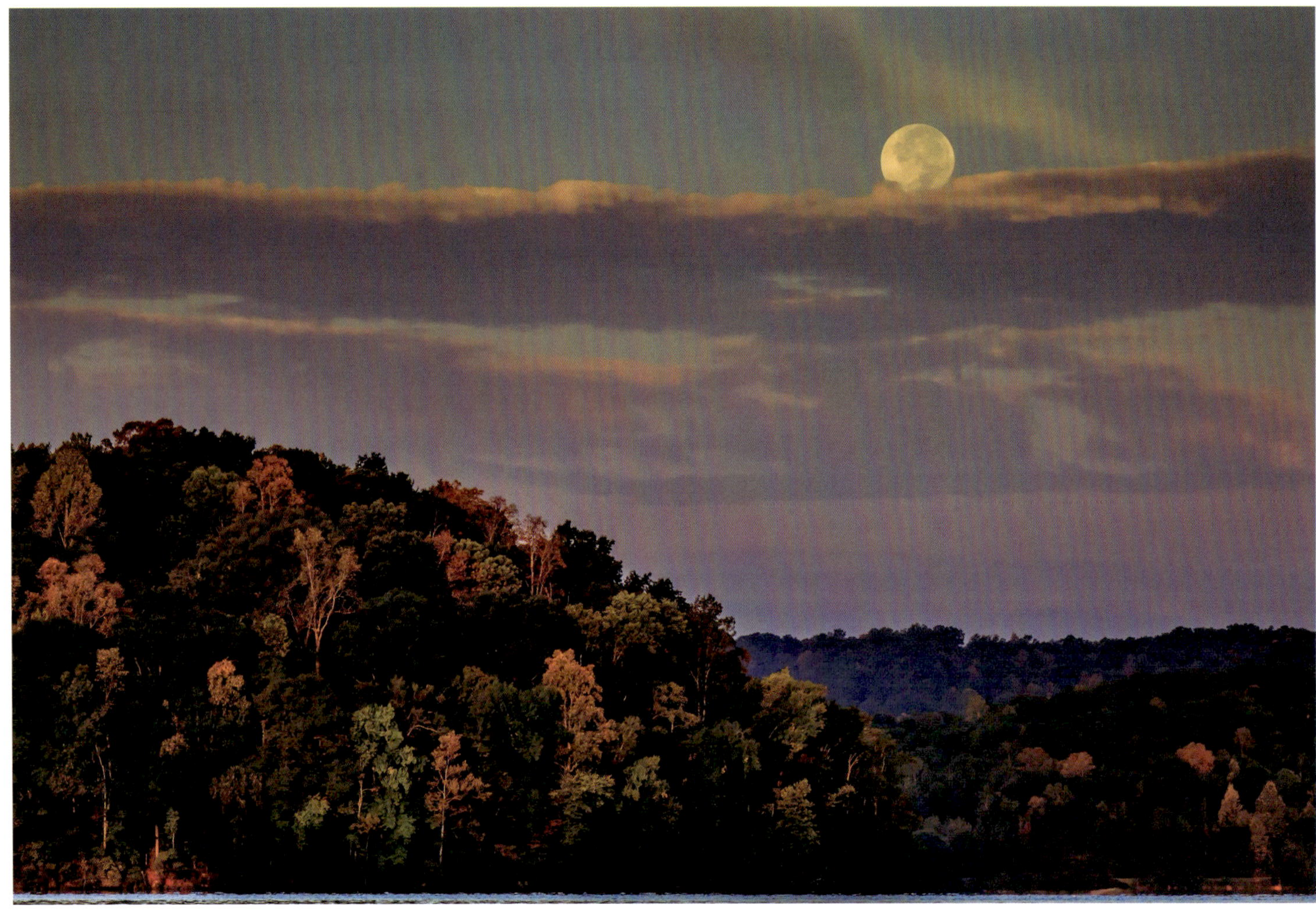

TENNESSEE RIVER, THIEF NECK ISLAND, ROANE COUNTY, TENNESSEE, SEPTEMBER 17. Moon set over the river. It's for moments like this that I came. "I do not wish to take a cabin passage, but rather go before the mast and on deck of the world, for there I could best see the moonlight amid the mountains. I do not wish to go below." —Henry David Thoreau.

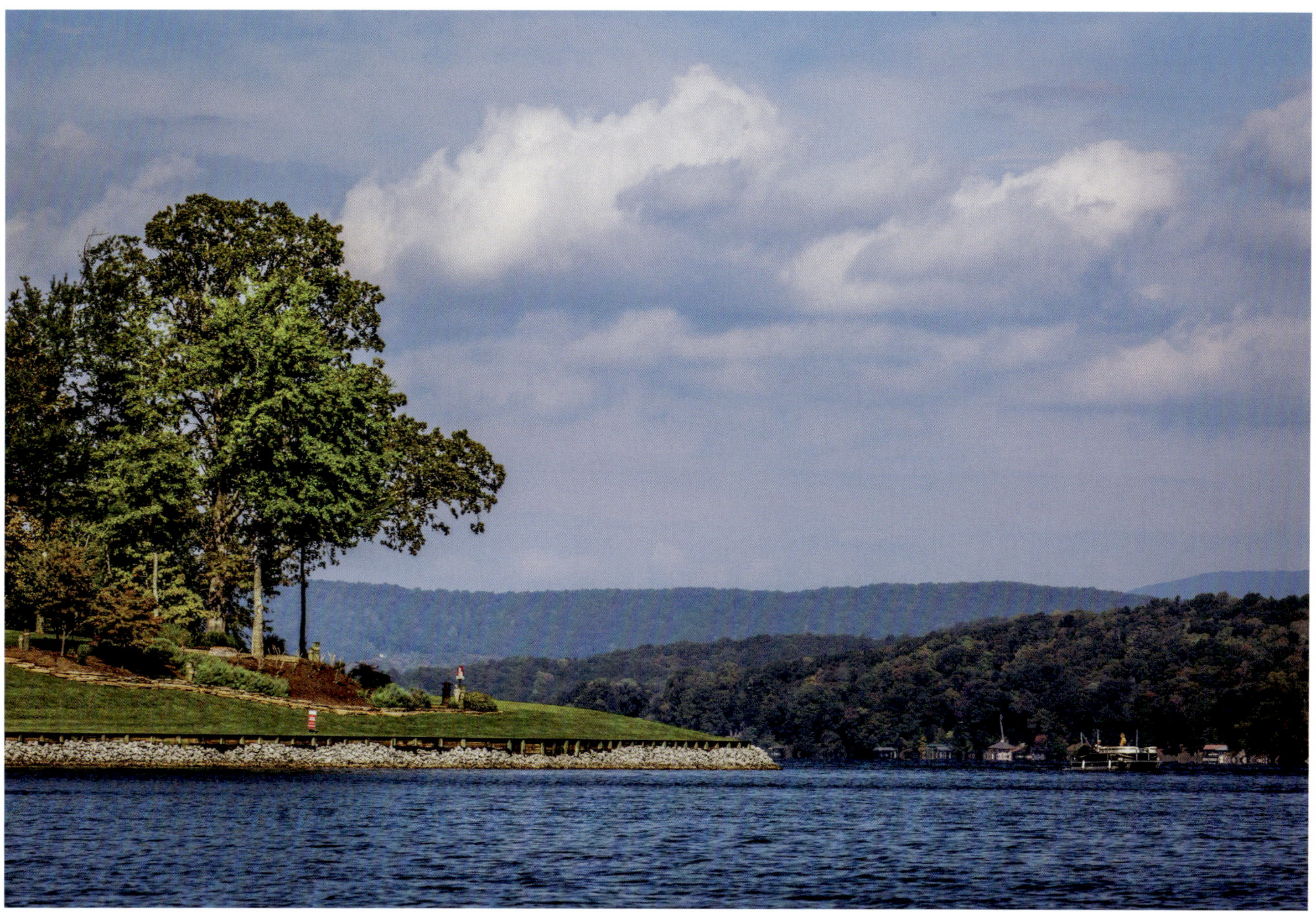

TENNESSEE RIVER, CONFLUENCE OF THE CLINCH RIVER, SEPTEMBER 17. The waters up the Clinch were the site of the notorious coal ash spill in 2008. Over 2.7 million cubic yards of coal fly ash inundated the waters, making it one of the worst environmental disasters in American history. Years later many locals still won't drink the water.

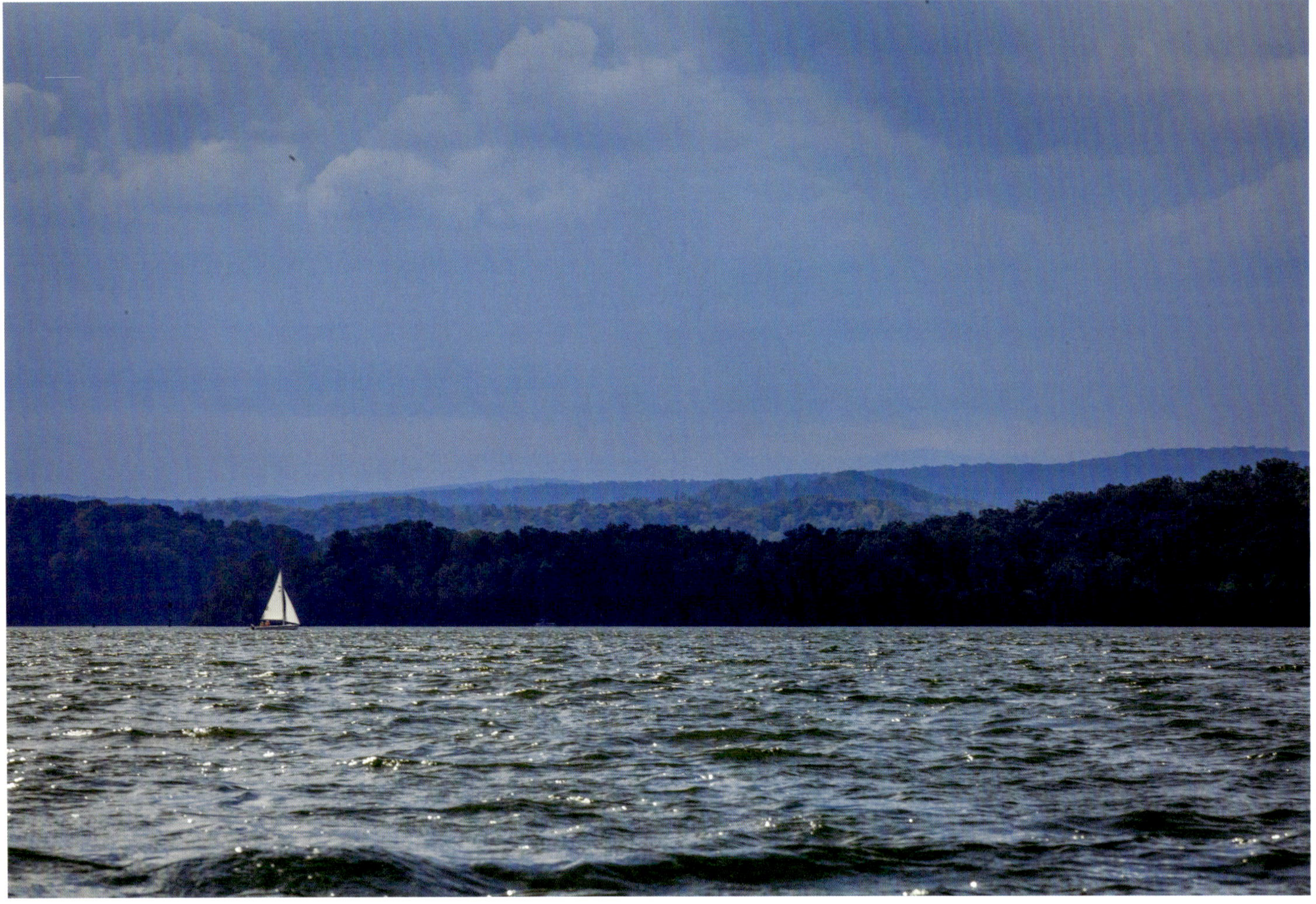

TENNESSEE RIVER, SEPTEMBER 17. Sailing the waters above the Watts Bar Lock and Dam. This is approximately where Donelson met up with another group of settlers referred to as the Clinch River Company. It is estimated that the flotilla had thirty flatboats along with other smaller craft with around three hundred men, women, and children on board; many were enslaved people of African origin.

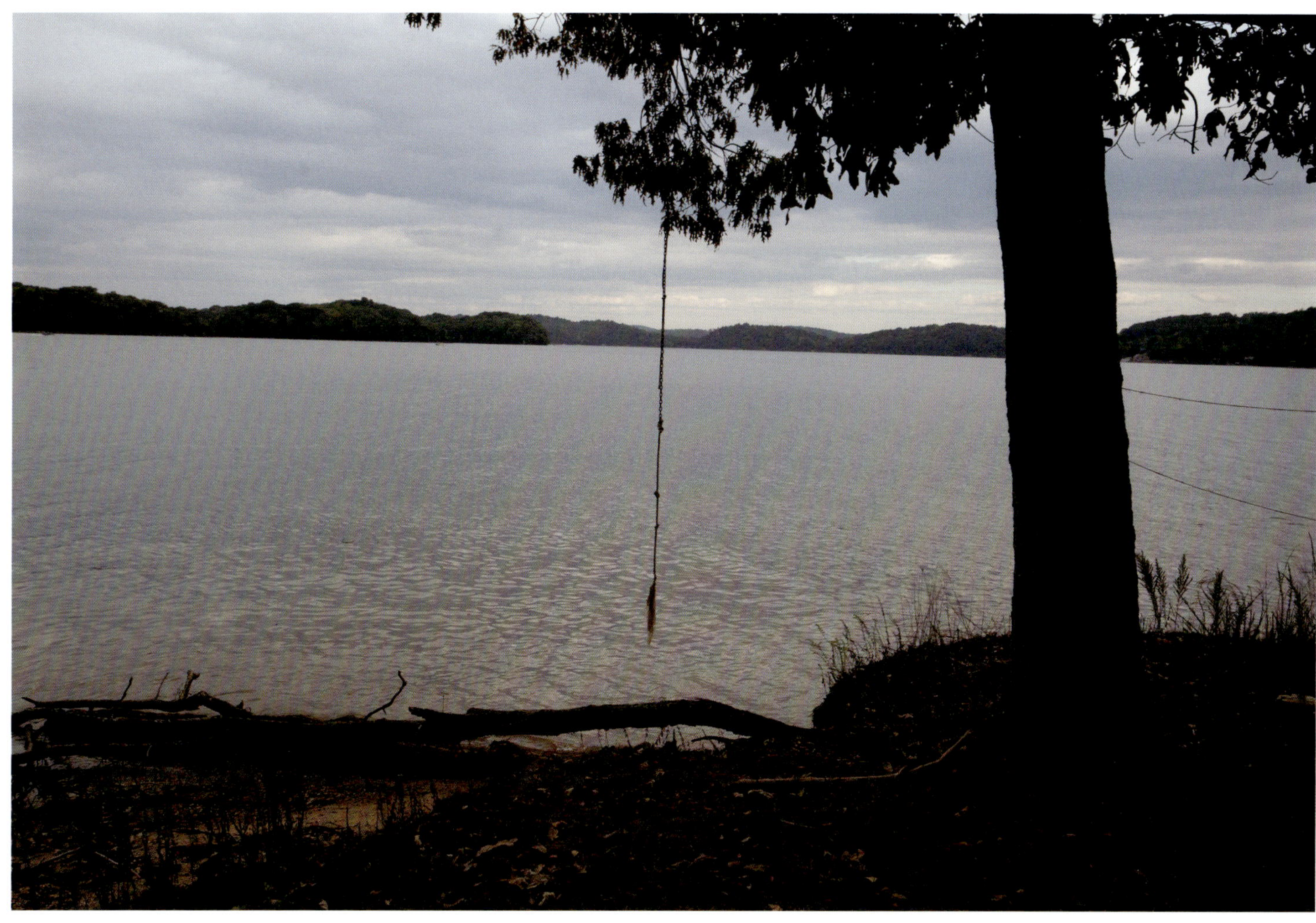

TENNESSEE RIVER, SEPTEMBER 17. Campsite on Half Moon Island. This is close to the site where Donelson recorded his first casualty, a slave. "Monday, March 6th (1780) . . . camped on the north shore, where Capt. Hutchings' negro man died, being much frosted in his hands and legs."

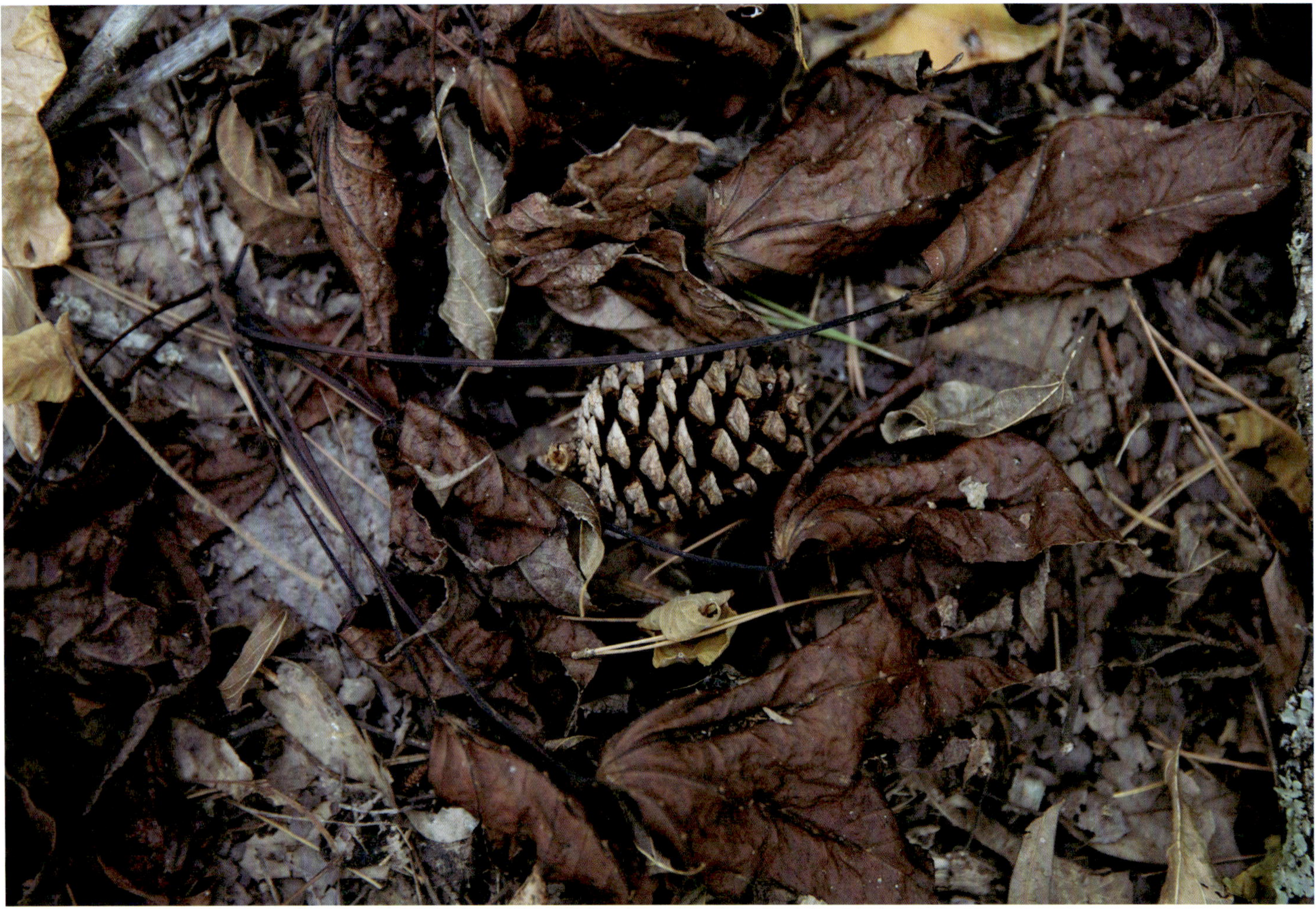

TENNESSEE RIVER, SEPTEMBER 17. An island still life. That evening I heard a bird gasp as it fell out of a nearby tree in the middle of its sleep.

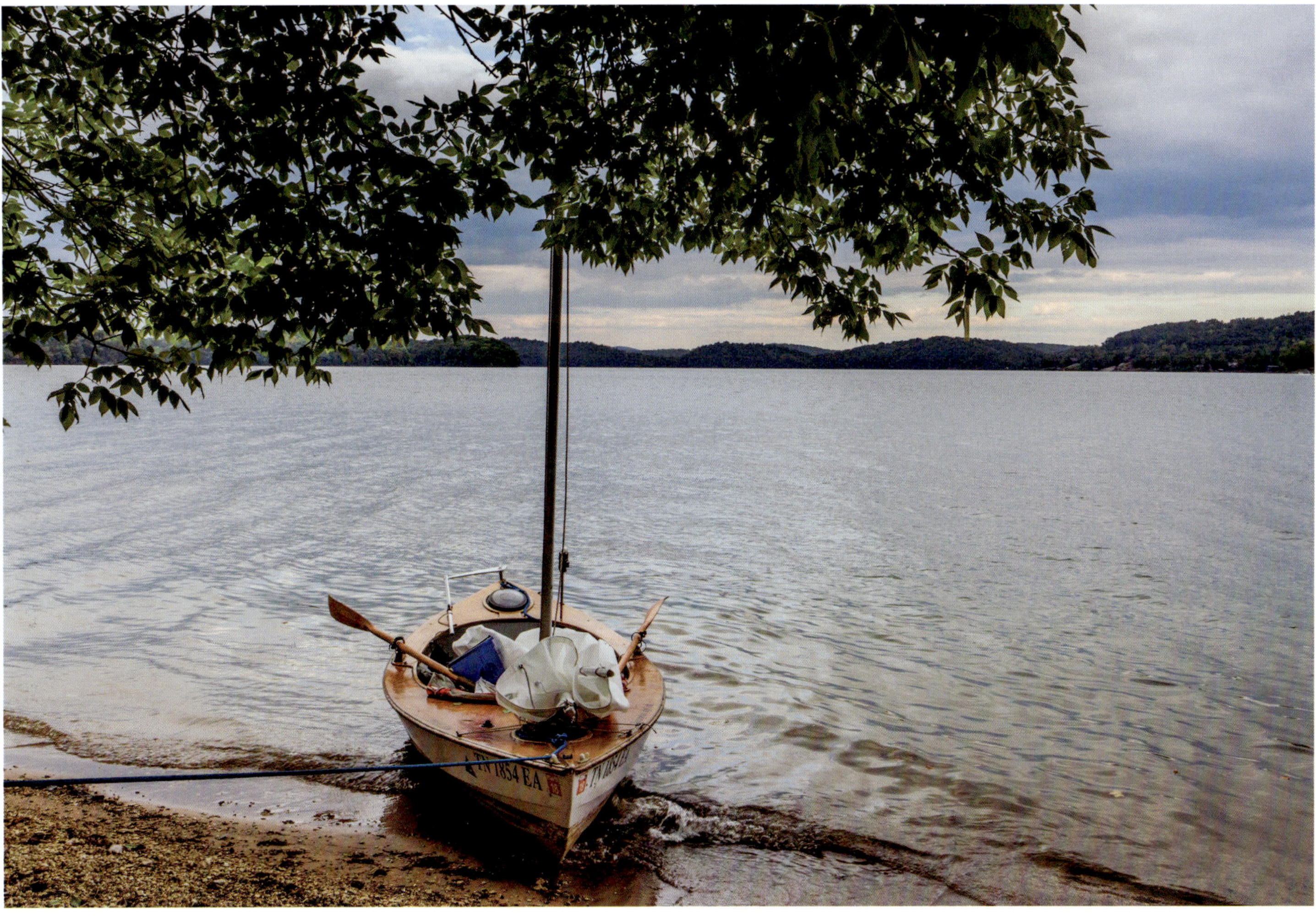

TENNESSEE RIVER, SEPTEMBER 17. The *Adventure II* at rest along the sandy shores of my island campsite. Secluded campsites are a rare find along the rivers. Between the privatization of the lands and the government control of the waters, I worry that someday journeys like mine may no longer be possible.

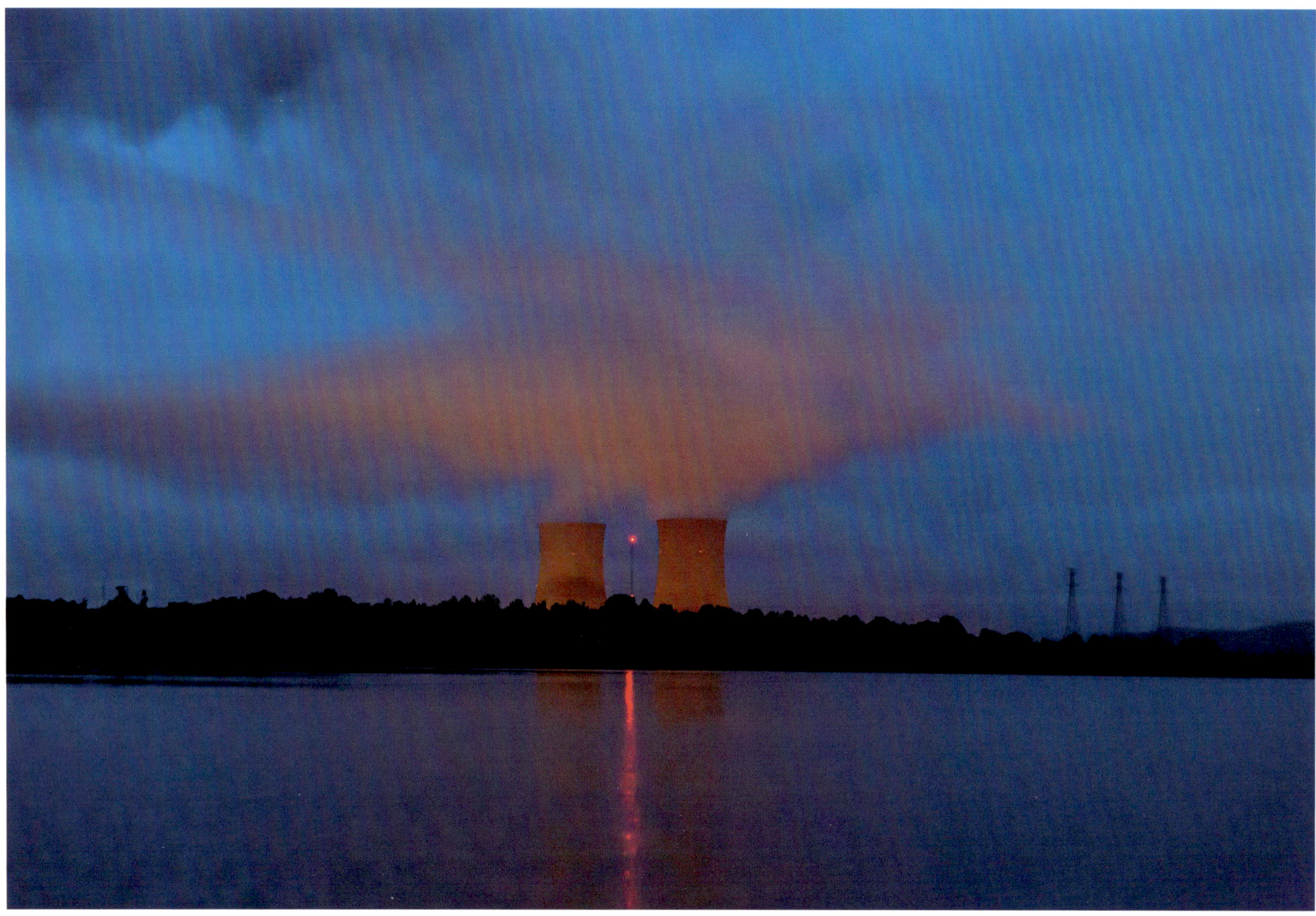

TENNESSEE RIVER, WATTS BAR NUCLEAR PLANT, SEPTEMBER 19. The red aircraft warning beacons atop the cooling towers cast an ominous scarlet glow on the dense mushroom-shaped steam that rose up to meet the storm clouds overhead.

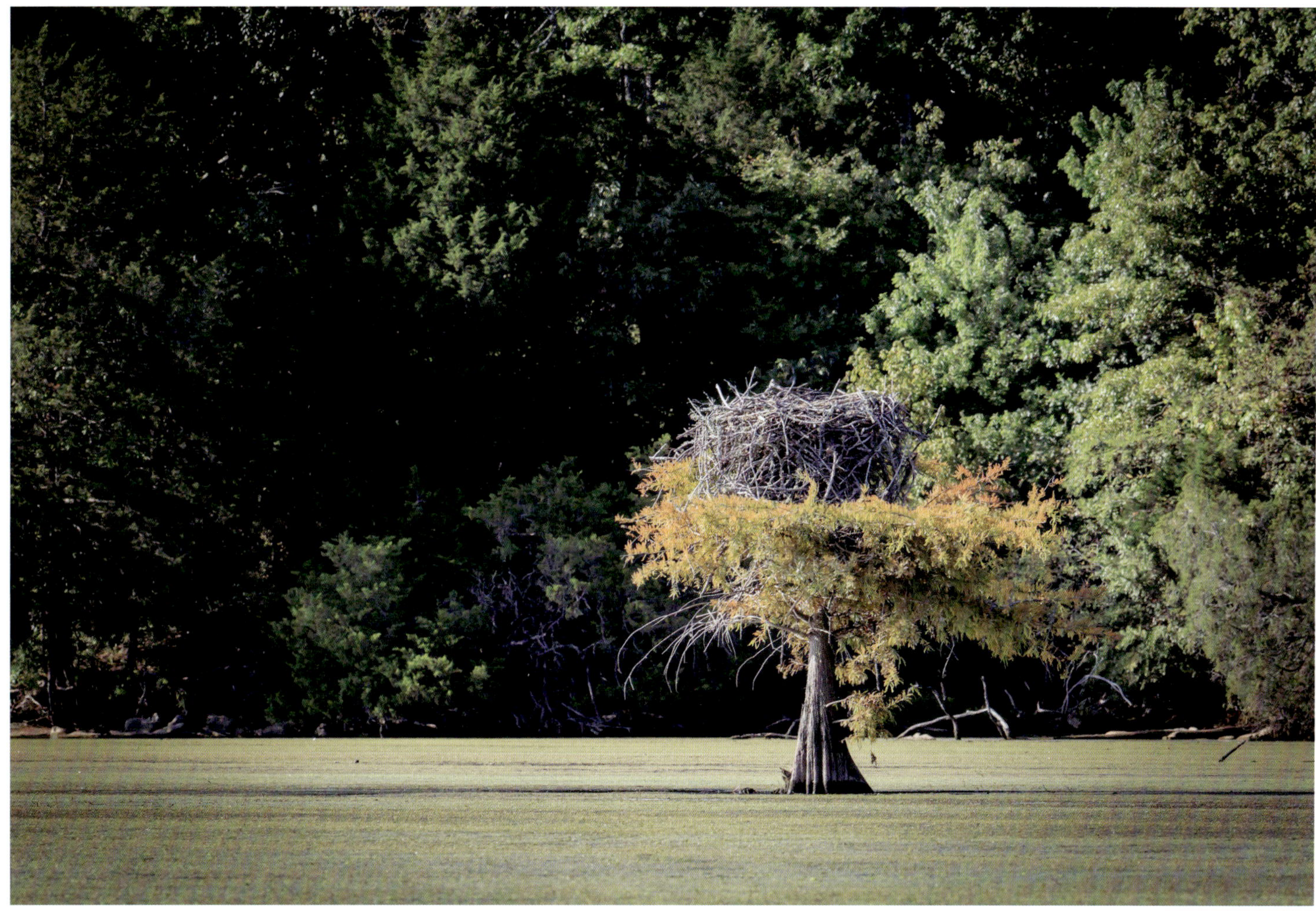

TENNESSEE RIVER, SEPTEMBER 19. Eagles nest on top of a small cypress tree. Cypress trees are unique in that they are one of the rare deciduous coniferous trees whose leaves actually turn brown and fall off in the winter.

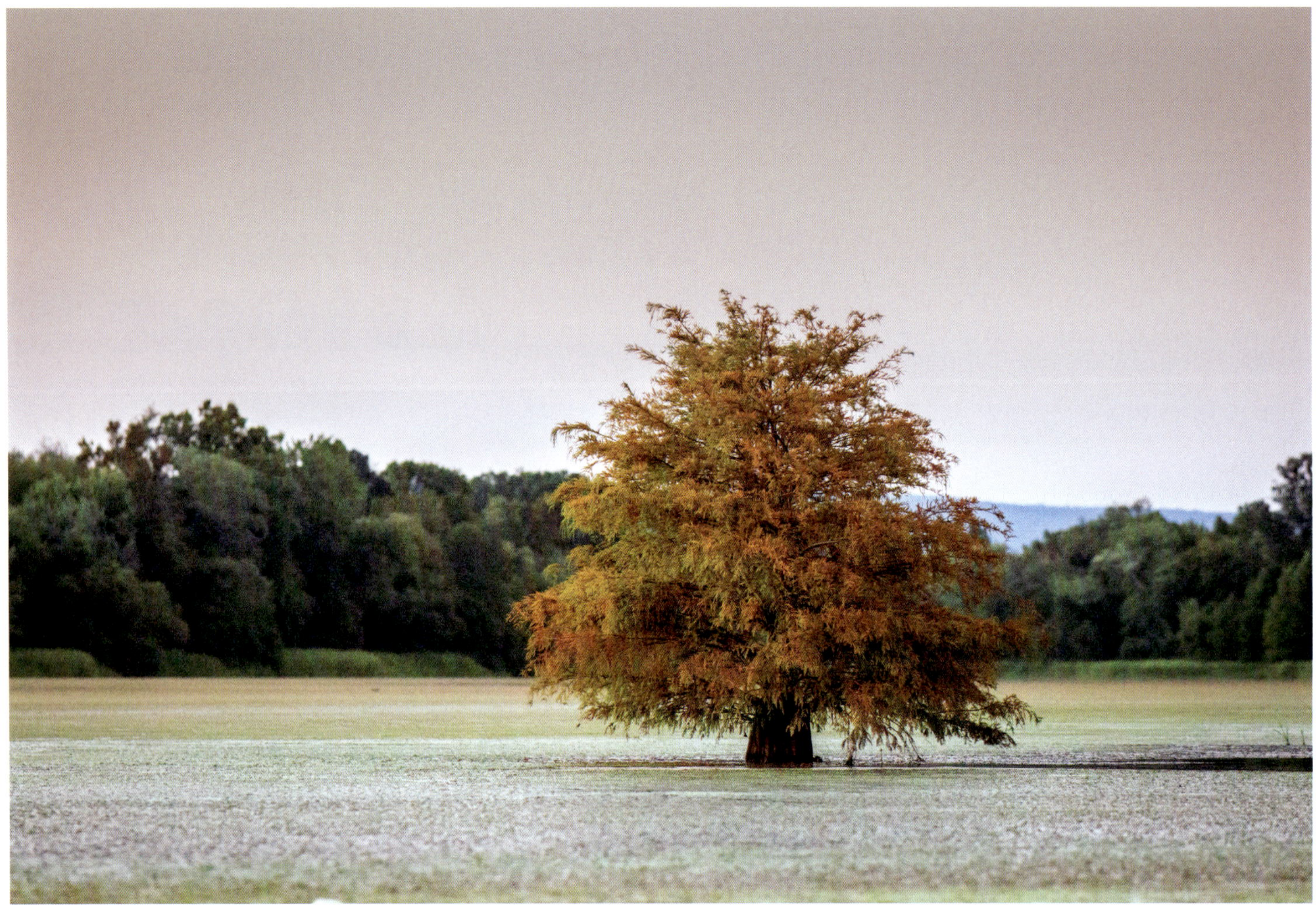

TENNESSEE RIVER, SEPTEMBER 19. Cypress tree in its fall colors surrounded by the invasive water plant known as hydrilla, which forms a nearly impenetrably dense carpet-like growth on the surface of the water, choking out all the other natural species that try to survive beside it. It is fed by the runoff from the farms and pastures that line the rivers.

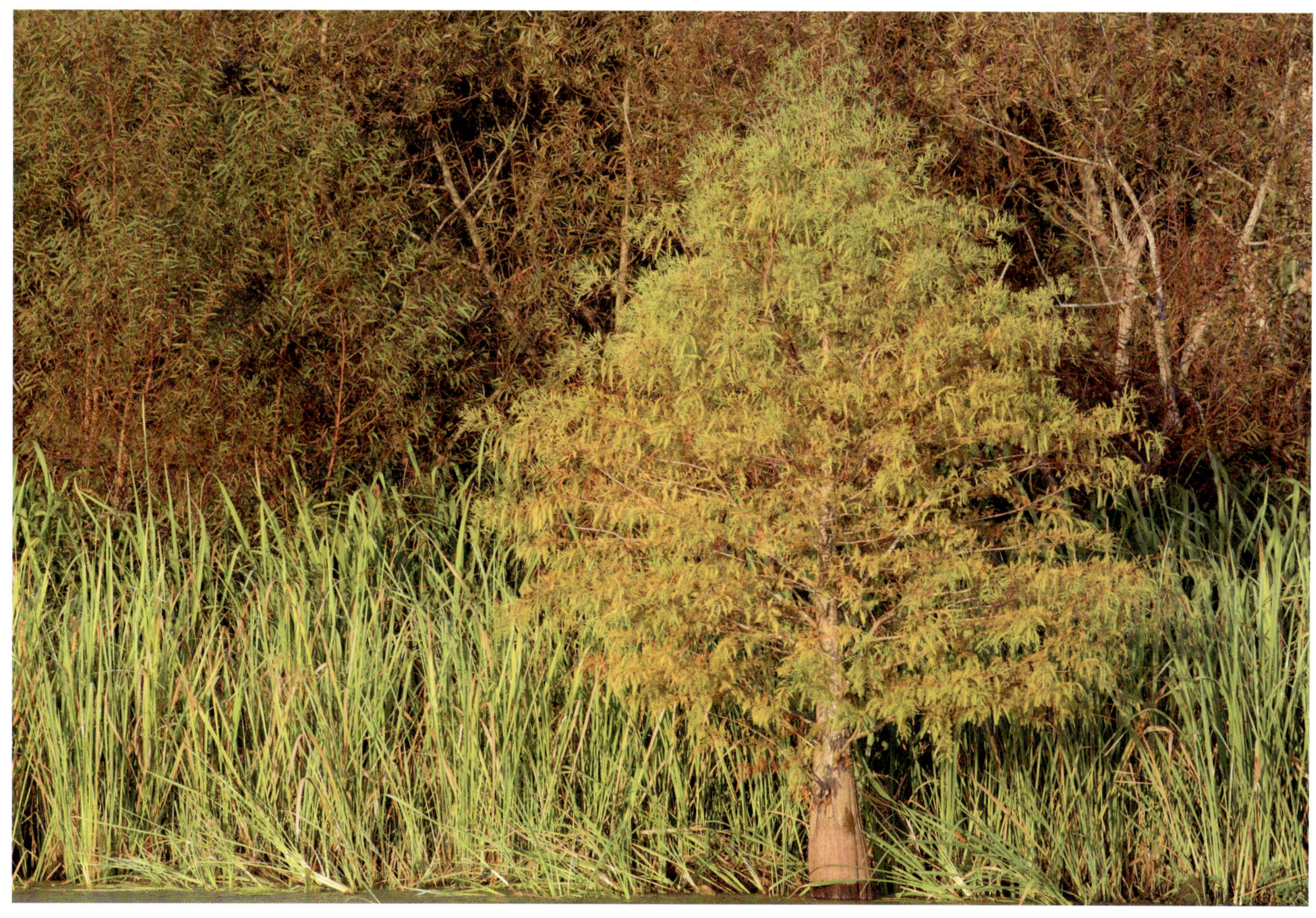

TENNESSEE RIVER, SEPTEMBER 19. Cypress tree nearly camouflaged along the riverbank.

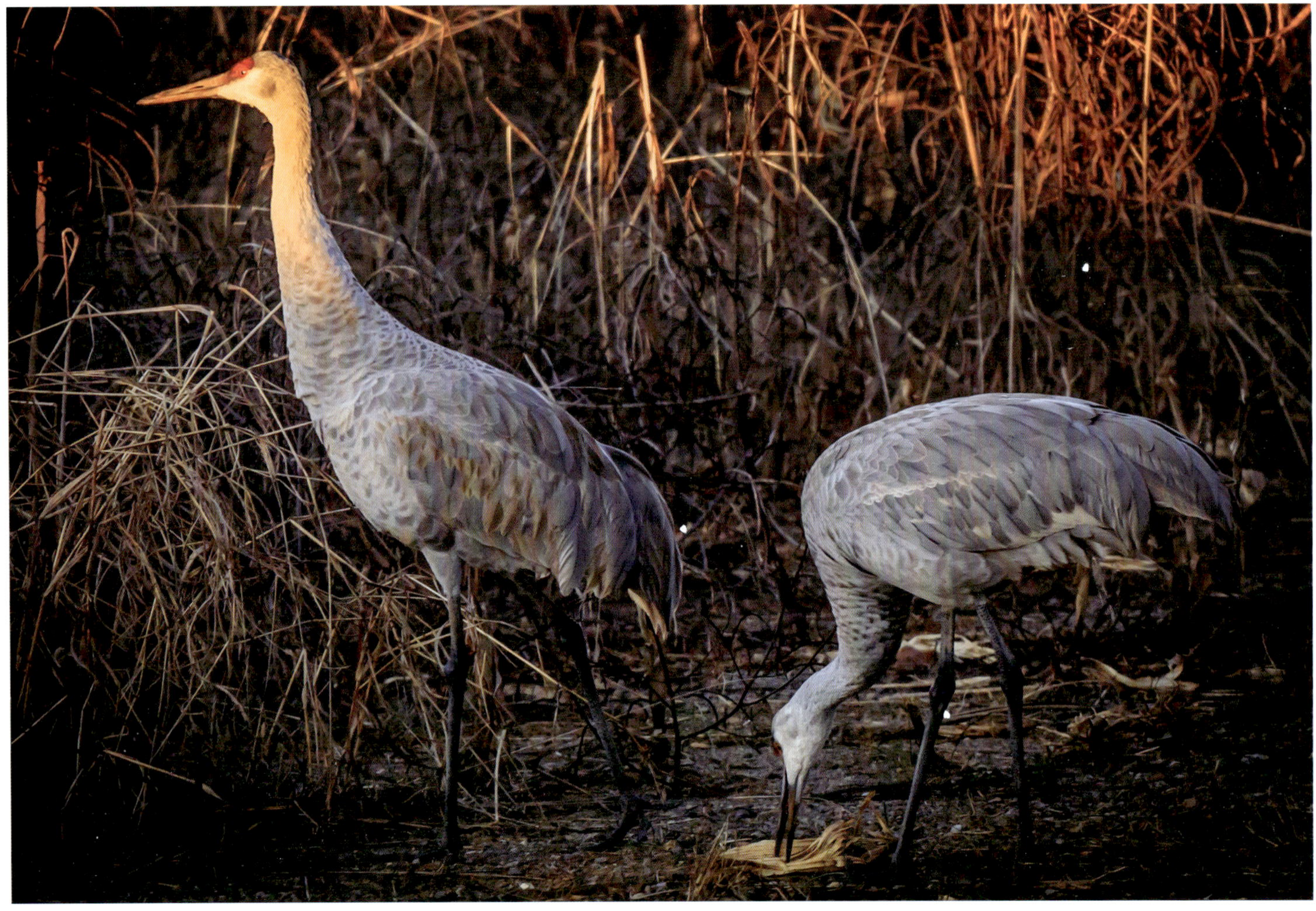

TENNESSEE RIVER, AT THE CONFLUENCE OF THE HIWASSEE RIVER. Sandhill cranes in migration across eastern North America. Tennessee recently passed a law making these lovely creatures fair game during hunting season.

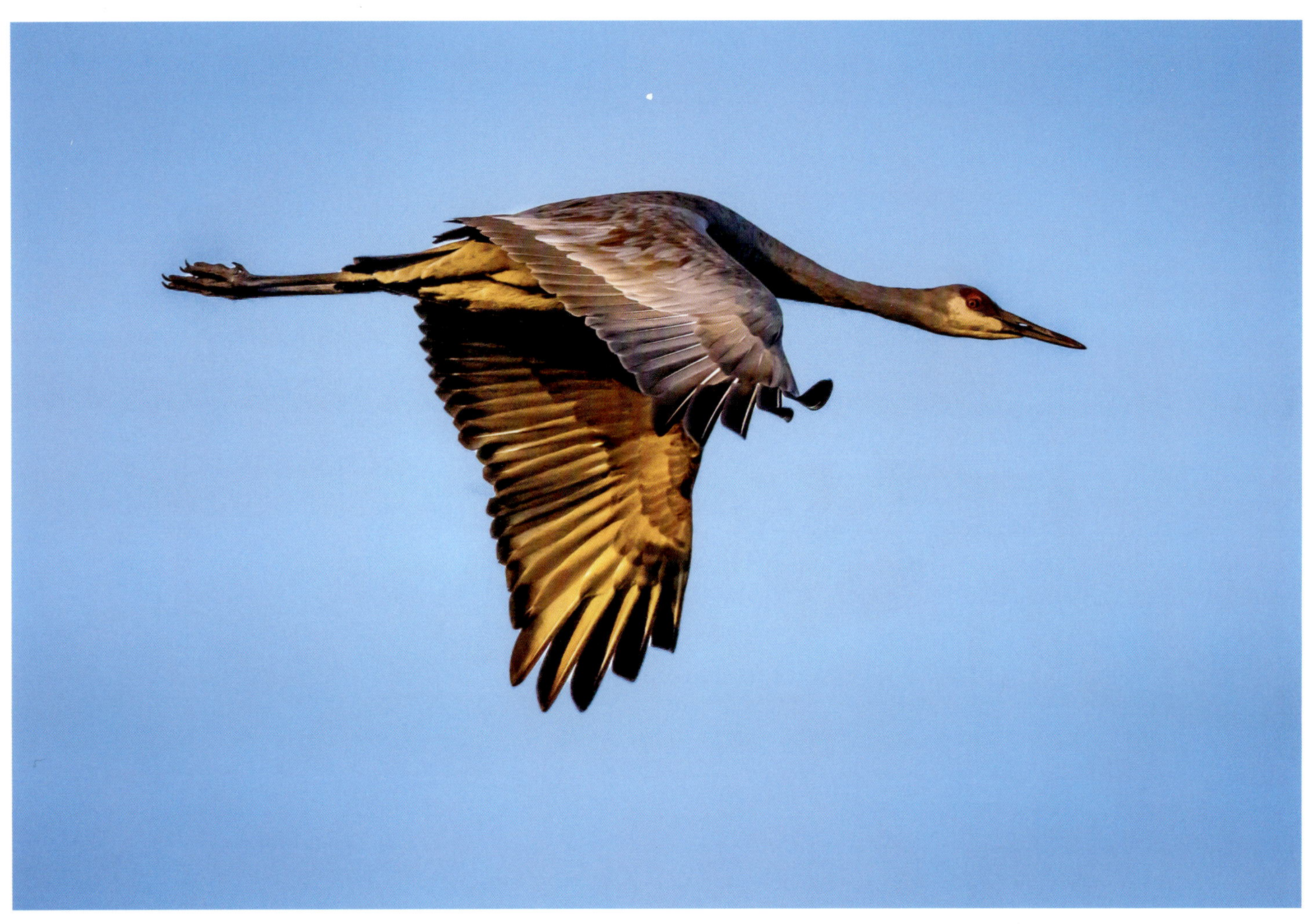

TENNESSEE RIVER, CONFLUENCE OF THE HIWASSEE RIVER. Sandhill crane in flight. Birds will never be contained by borders or walls.

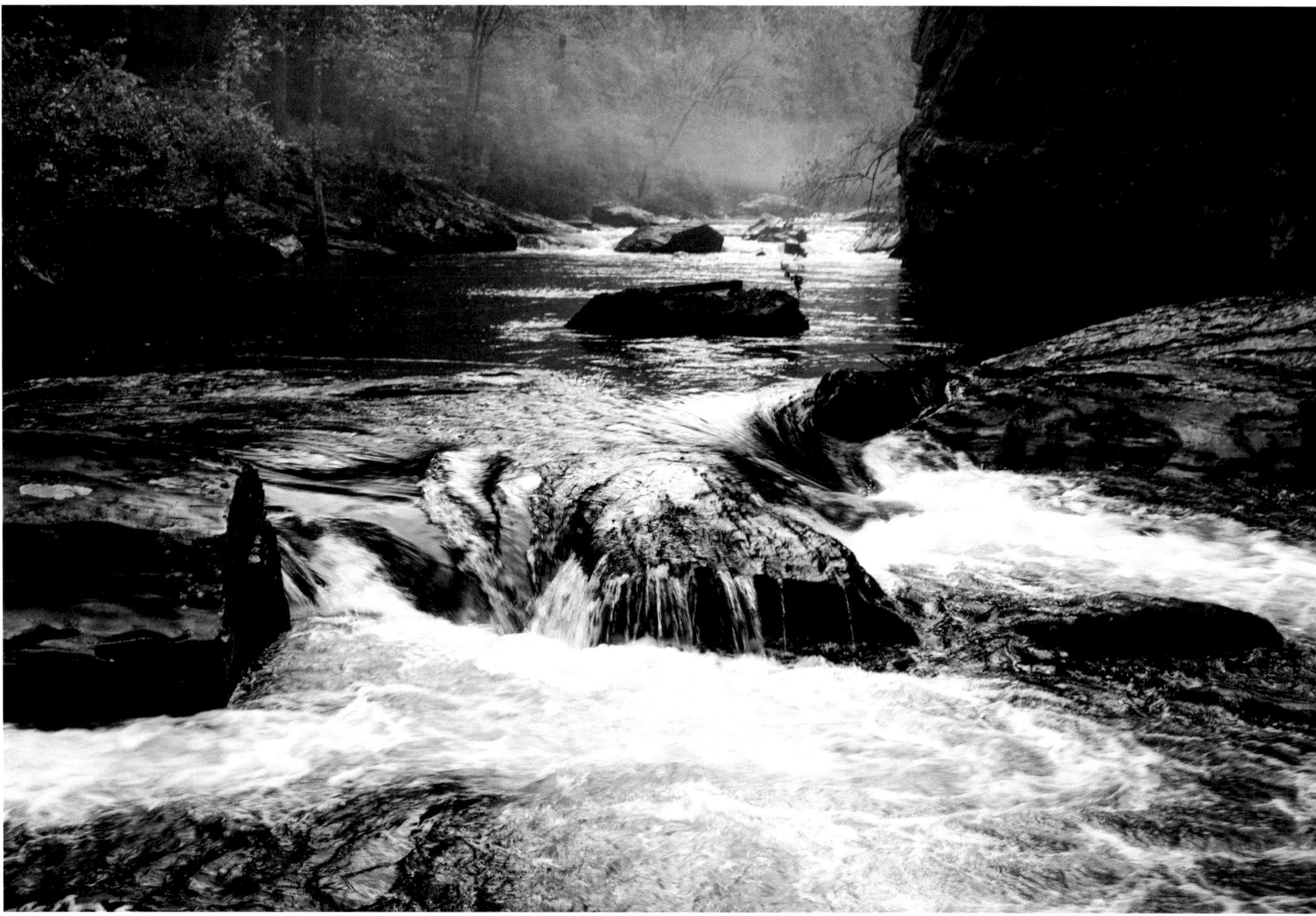

TELLICO RIVER. One of the many rivers that flow from the mountains to form the Tennessee River watershed. Tennessee has more water features per acre than any other state in the union. An environment worth protecting.

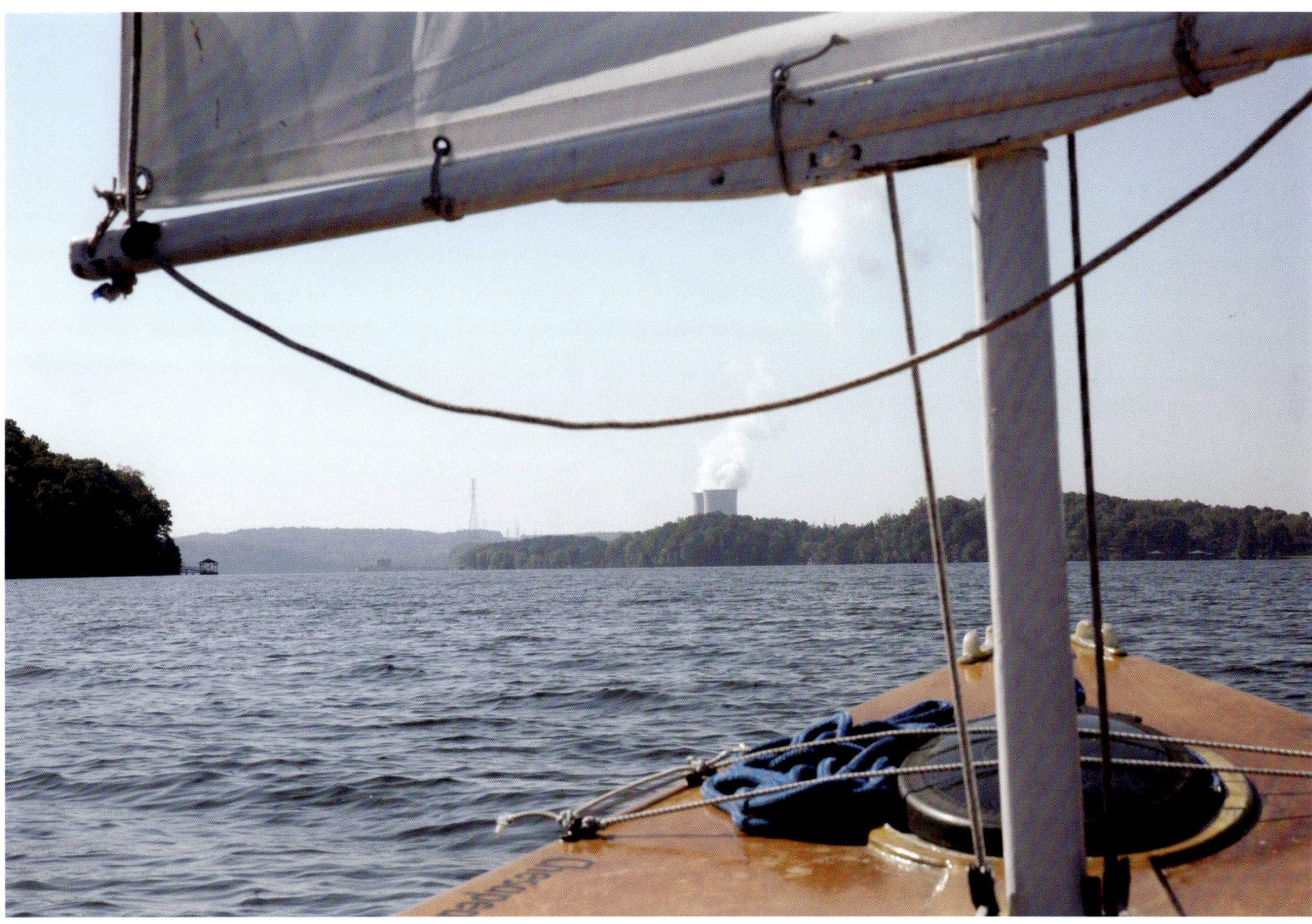

TENNESSEE RIVER, HAMILTON COUNTY, TENNESSEE, SEPTEMBER 21. Catching a following wind. Sailing toward the Sequoyah Nuclear Plant in the river broadened by the Chickamauga Lock and Dam that lay below.

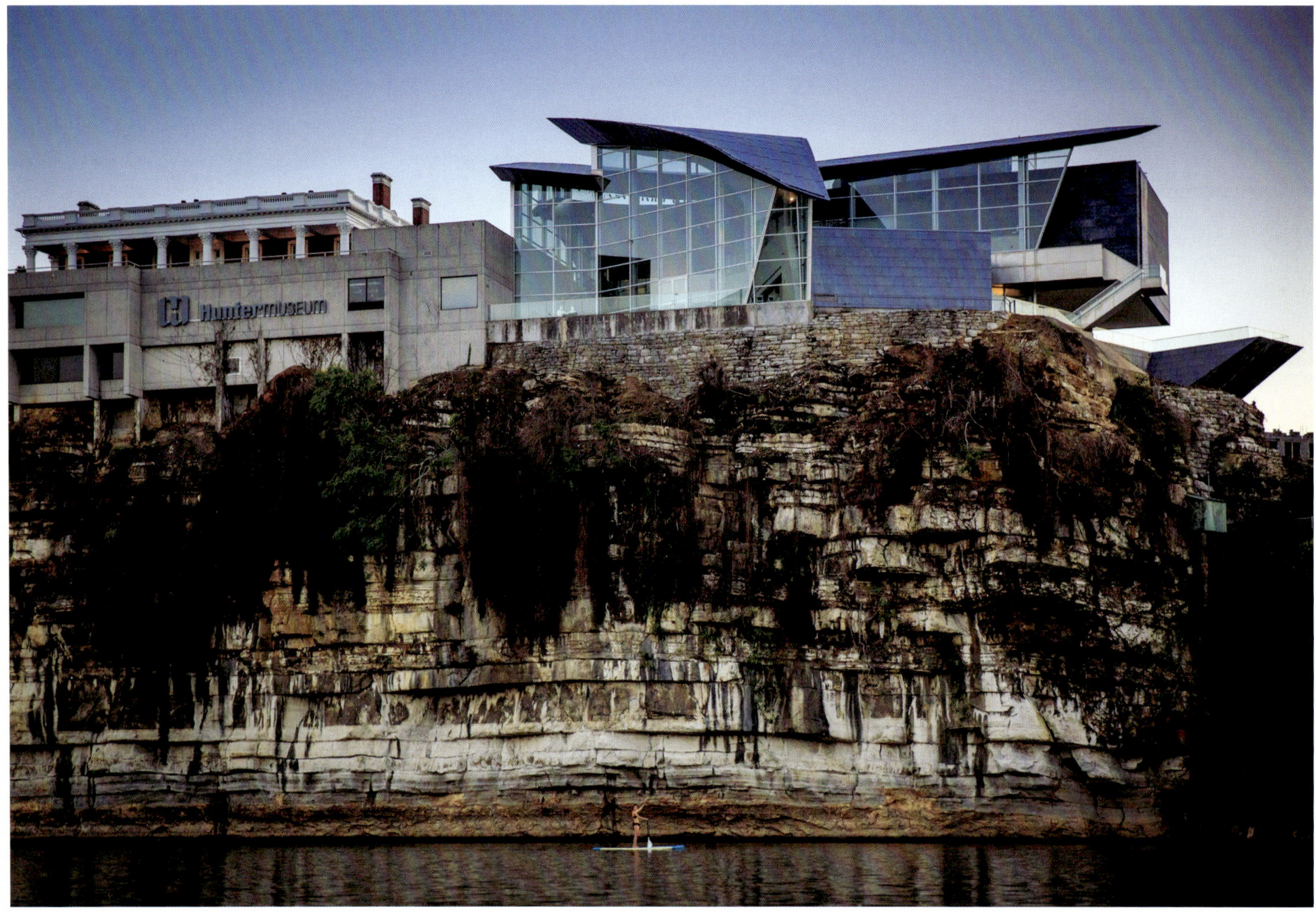

TENNESSEE RIVER, CHATTANOOGA, TENNESSEE, SEPTEMBER 21. Paddle boarder in front of the aquarium. Prior to Donelson's journey in 1779, a militia formed under the command of Evan Shelby and John Montgomery had raided all the Chickamauga towns along the Tennessee up to present-day Chattanooga, forcing most of them to relocate south into Georgia. To that point, the flotilla had been free of indigenous reprisal. That was about to change.

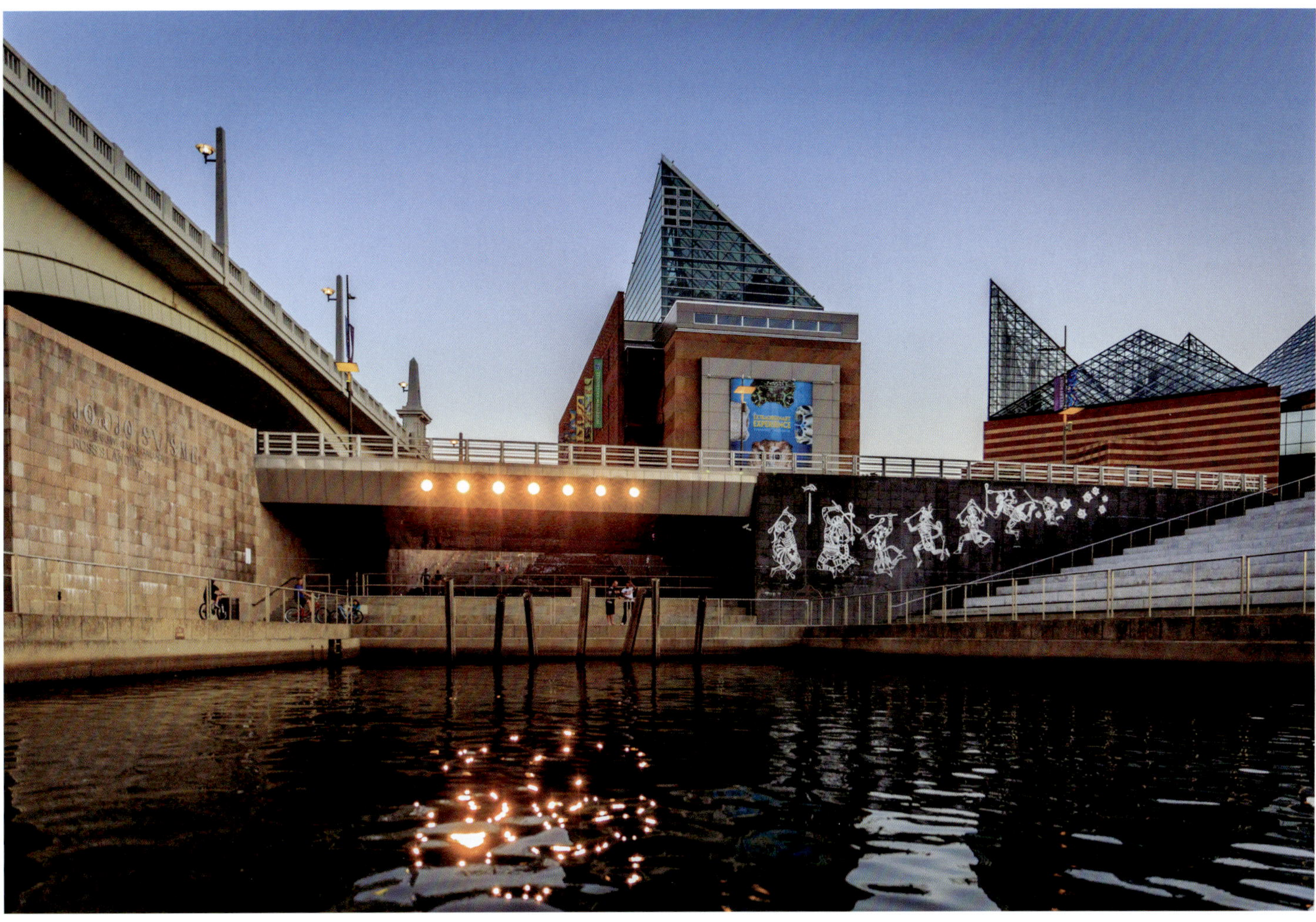

TENNESSEE RIVER, CHATTANOOGA, TENNESSEE, SEPTEMBER 21. It was nearby, on March 7, 1780, that a child was born to Elizabeth Peyton; her husband, Ephraim, had traveled by land with James Robertson. The birth barely delayed the flotilla and they moved forward quickly into the dangers ahead.

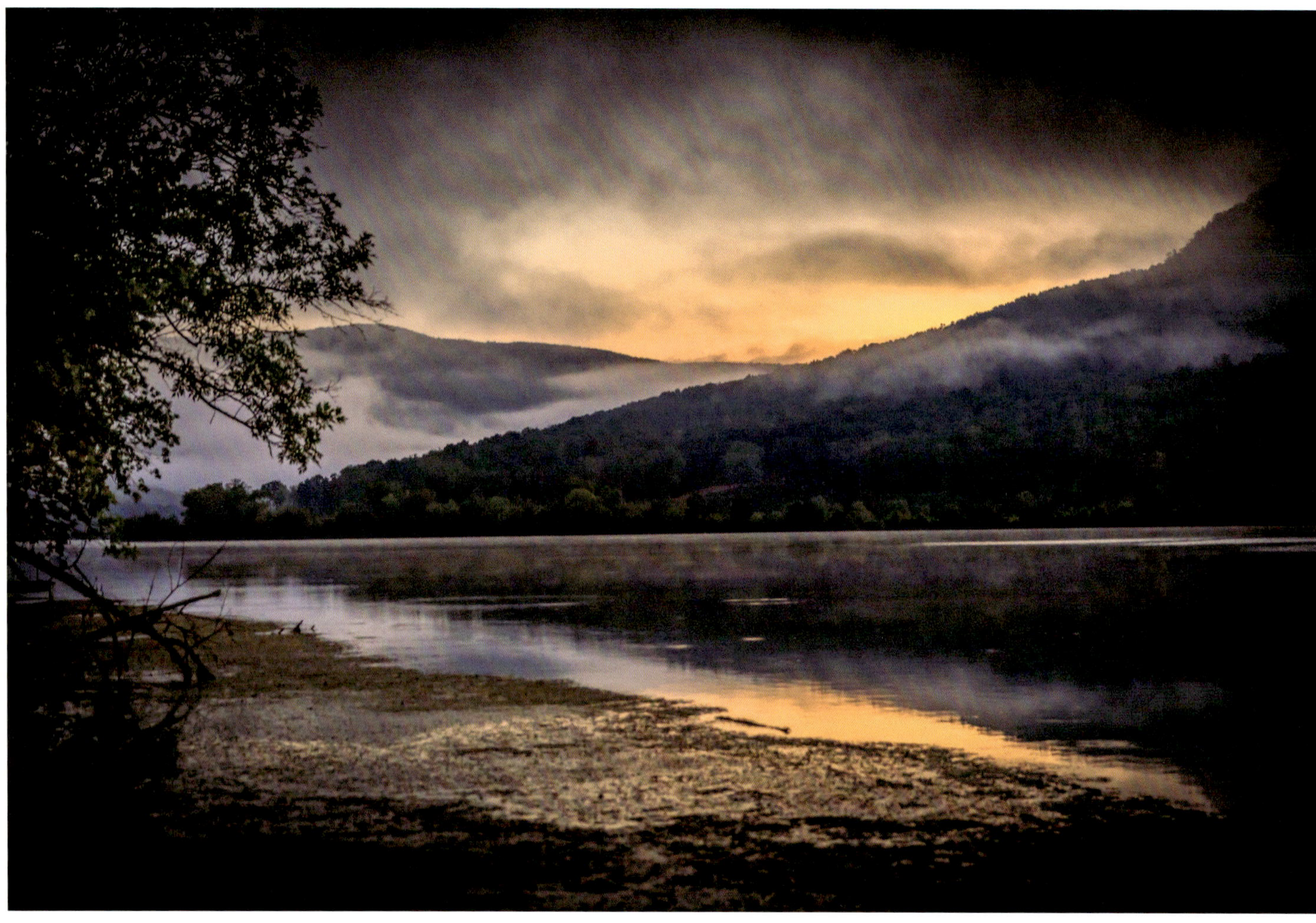

TENNESSEE RIVER, TENNESSEE RIVER GORGE, SEPTEMBER 23. Sunrise from my campsite in the Tennessee River Gorge. Before the dams raised the water levels, the narrow gorge was full of dangerous hydraulics and whirlpools that only the most experienced boaters could navigate. It was here that the Chickamauga, under the command of Chief Dragging Canoe, made their deadly stand. Thirty-one members of the Donelson party lost their lives, including the two-day-old baby of Elizabeth Peyton.

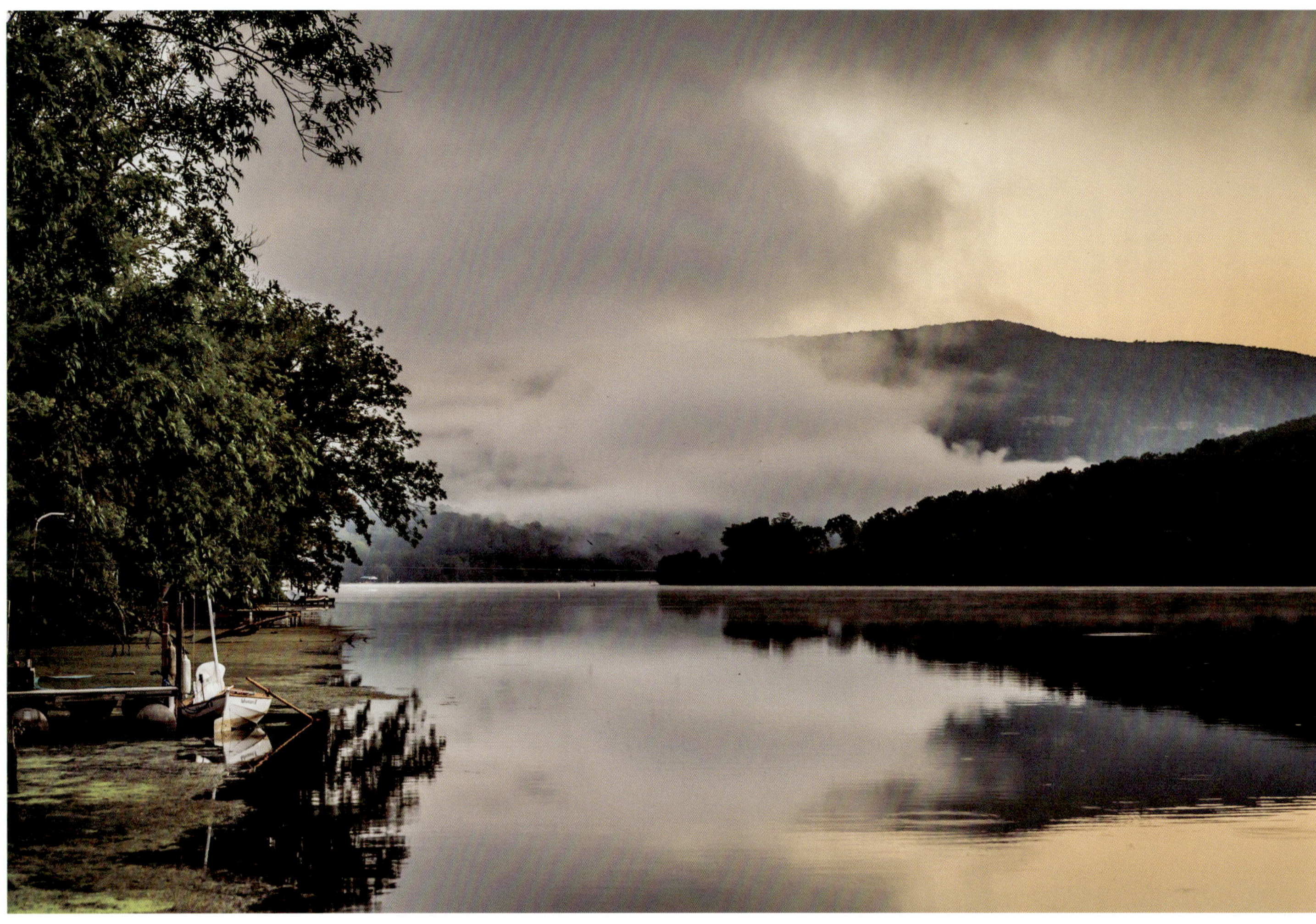

TENNESSEE RIVER, TENNESSEE RIVER GORGE, SEPTEMBER 23. Mist clearing the skies with my boat secure along the dock. The majestic river gorge is the fourth largest in the eastern United States and is flanked by sheer cliffs and forested mountains that rise as high as a thousand feet along the Cumberland Plateau.

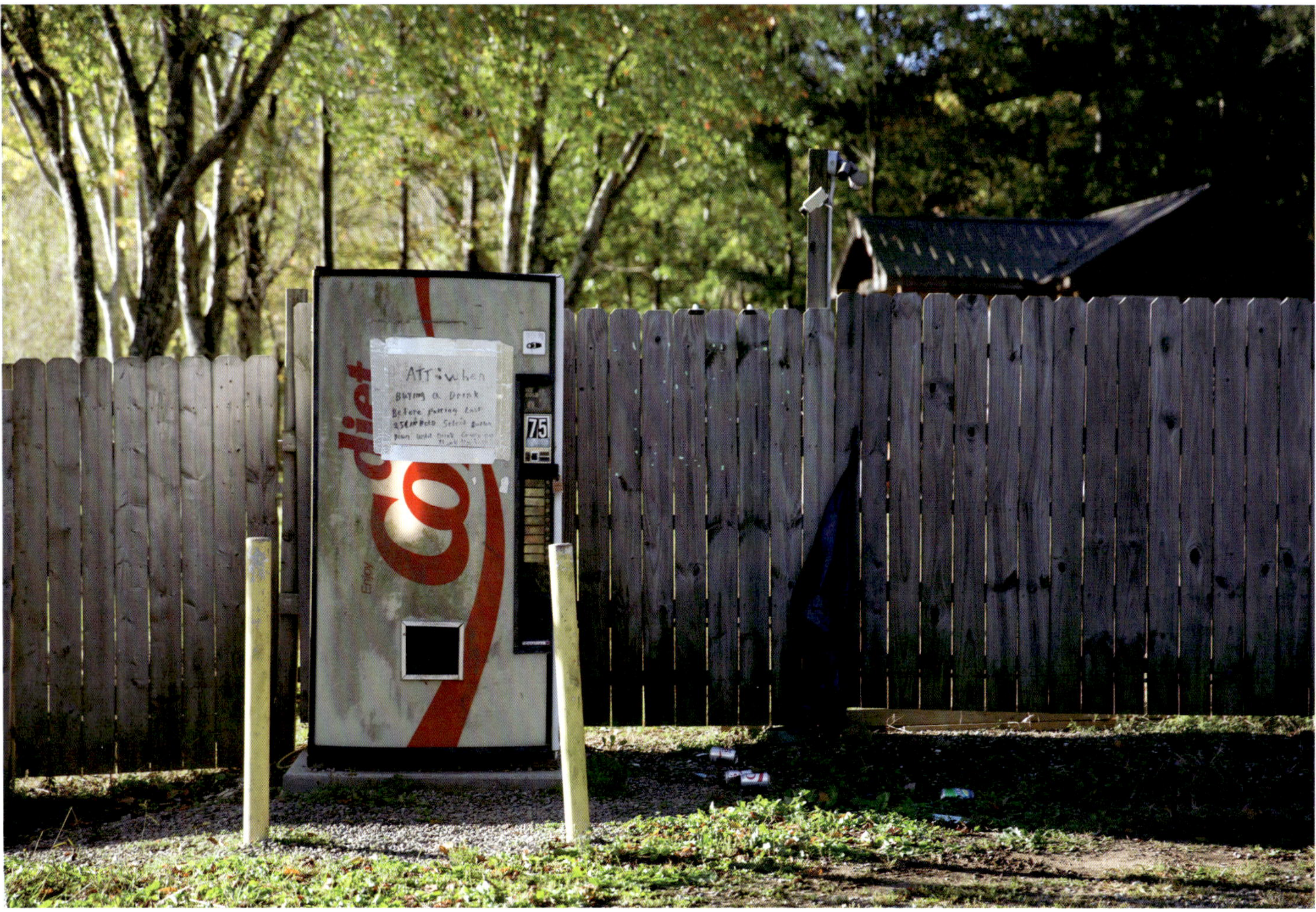

TENNESSEE RIVER, TENNESSEE RIVER GORGE, SEPTEMBER 23. Coca-Cola machine. The evening before, I was entertained by a group of locals who were enjoying the sunset. They had set up chairs along the bank next to their prized Coca-Cola machine. It was there that I learned about the growing divide between the haves of the urban dwellers and the have-nots of the rural communities and the marginalization it creates.

THE FURTHER I rowed toward the opposite end of the gorge, the more docks and cabins came into site. My best recourse was to find someone outside and ask to land for the night. I rowed back and forth along the opposite banks looking for a secure anchorage until I spotted a group of folks sitting in lawn chairs close to a private landing on the north side of the river. Around a dozen people sat, laughing it up while swatting mosquitoes. I rowed up and introduced myself, and before I knew it I was sitting with the group enjoying the conversation. By now it was dark and I saw shadows more than faces, however their kindness and generosity was clearly visible. One man bid his wife to go to the house for change to put in the vending machine for me. Even before she returned I had a lap full of Cokes. The dark of night and the incessant mosquitoes broke the party up not long after my arrival. Once again I was left alone to bask in the quiet chirrs of nature that marked the evening's arrival. One of the men said I could tie up my boat on his dock and pitch my tent on the grounds next door. For a moment I just sat in the comfort of the lawn chair and stared as the mountains faded into the star-lit sky, sipped my Coke, and reveled in my good fortune. I took my time setting up the tent and organized my gear. When I did finally lie down, my right hip and leg started to hurt and I knew sleep wasn't going to come easy. Around midnight I heard a car veer off the highway and come to a sliding stop on the gravel landing. With the engine still running, the cab door slammed shut, and a few moments later I heard someone cursing and banging hard on the sacred Coke machine. From the violence of the pounding I thought for sure it had to be one of the "meth heads" I kept hearing about, trying get at the money. My tent was away and hidden in the shadows of the trees. I felt sure he didn't see it. Maybe if I kept quiet I could call the police as soon as he took off and they could catch him.

But then I started to think of all the good people I had met and how they put their trust in me. I couldn't let their property be destroyed like that. I decided I owned the moment and had to act. I jumped out of the tent and yelled, "Hey! Can I help you with something?" The man mumbled incoherently and kept beating on the machine. I yelled again, "What's going on?" He turned around and started walking straight at me with the ferocity of the Incredible Hulk. I braced. "It's that damn machine!" he said. "It took my money! It's happened before." When he came shoulder to shoulder to me I recognized him as the only young man in the group I had met earlier. Even though he had school the next day, he had decided he wanted a Coke and drove all the way back to get one. "There aren't any stores around these parts."

In order to calm him and me down, I said, "Hey, no problem. I have two Cokes left over from earlier. Why don't you take them and not worry about that machine tonight?" "How much do you want for them?" the conversation continued.

"I don't want anything. Take them." "I have to pay you something." His voice was still upset and aggressive. "No, they were given to me as gifts. It wouldn't be fair for me to make a profit. Take them both, my pleasure." He would only take one, said little more, and then turned back to his car and pulled out with a screech. I returned to the tent. I was almost back to sleep when I again heard the sound of a truck pulling into the drive. This time as the door slammed shut I could hear the footsteps heading toward me. I stepped out of the tent for the second time. The same young man greeted me. He had a bottle of water in his hand and he said, "Here, I want you to have this." I thanked him and said it wasn't necessary. He said no, he wanted me to have it. I took it and thanked him again with a smile. He untensed a little and said, "You're nice. You're not like all the rest." I told him I didn't understand. All the people I met this evening had been kind as they could be. "Yes, they are. It's the outsiders. They treat us like dirt. You're not like that." We talked awhile. He told me his name was Jacob. He went to high school and thought he wanted to take up welding to make his living. I told him that would be a great profession and encouraged him to go forward. Jacob wasn't much for words, but the comfort in his stance spoke volumes. Finally he forced a slight smile as he anxiously made his way to leave, hopping into his pickup truck and speeding away for the last time into the night.

I was awake in plenty of time for the sunrise. I loitered about waiting for my tent and gear to dry, lost in my thoughts about the events of the previous evening. We talk openly about the divides between the races and the sexes and the resultant ill will that leads to discrimination and segregation. Less is said about the divides that lie within the races. Jacob's problem with outsiders had nothing to do with color or sex. It had to do with being treated as someone less than human. From his point of view, it seemed the cities were thriving. Everyone drove big cars and lived in beautiful houses while in his own community all they had to show for their effort was a soda machine.

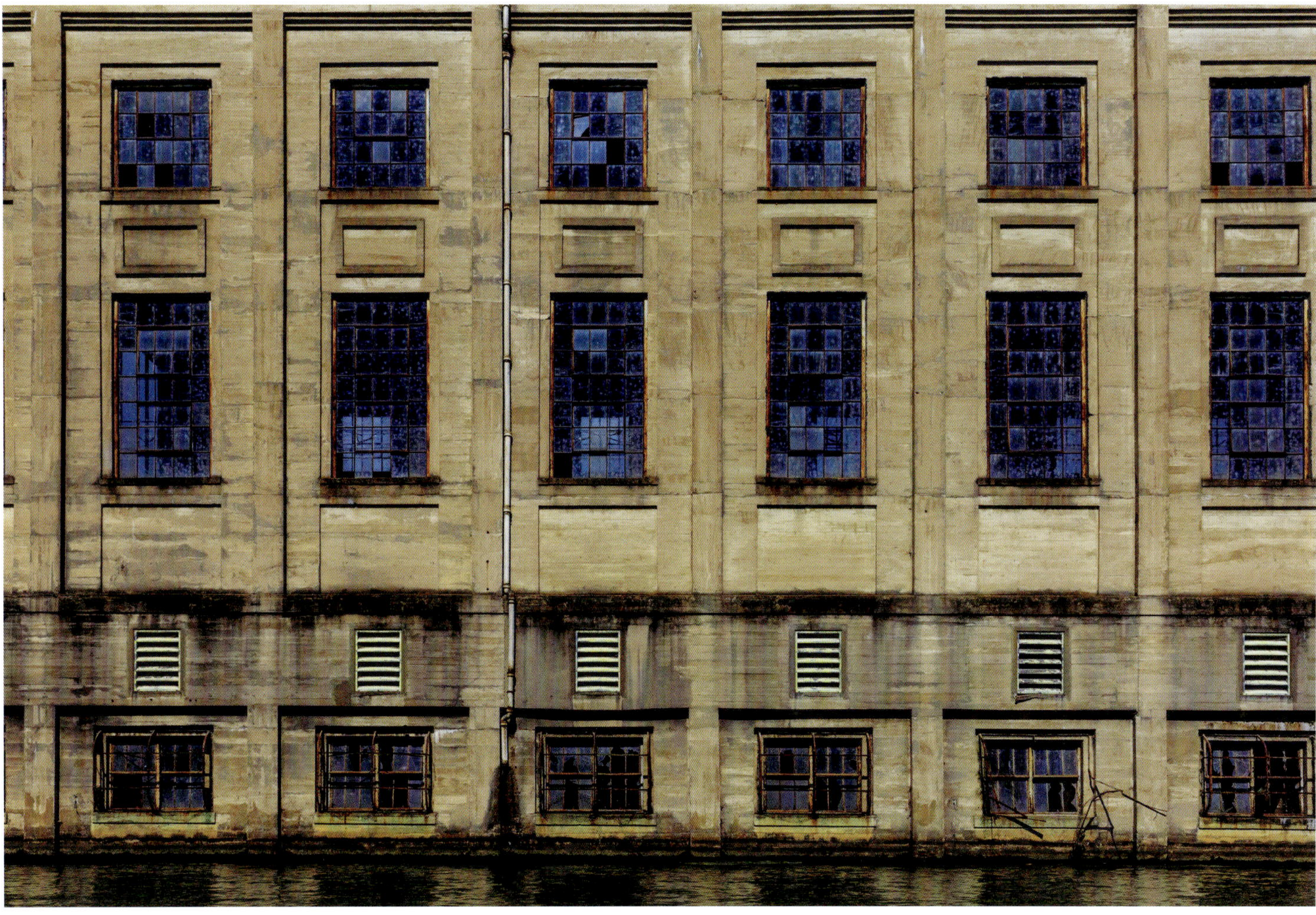

TENNESSEE RIVER, HALES BAR, TENNESSEE, SEPTEMBER 24. Facade of the old Hales Bar electric plant. Site of the privately funded lock and power dam built in 1913. Later the government used its powers of eminent domain to gain control of the dam in its desire to control the entire river system. The act continued to feed the locals' distrust of the overriding power of the government.

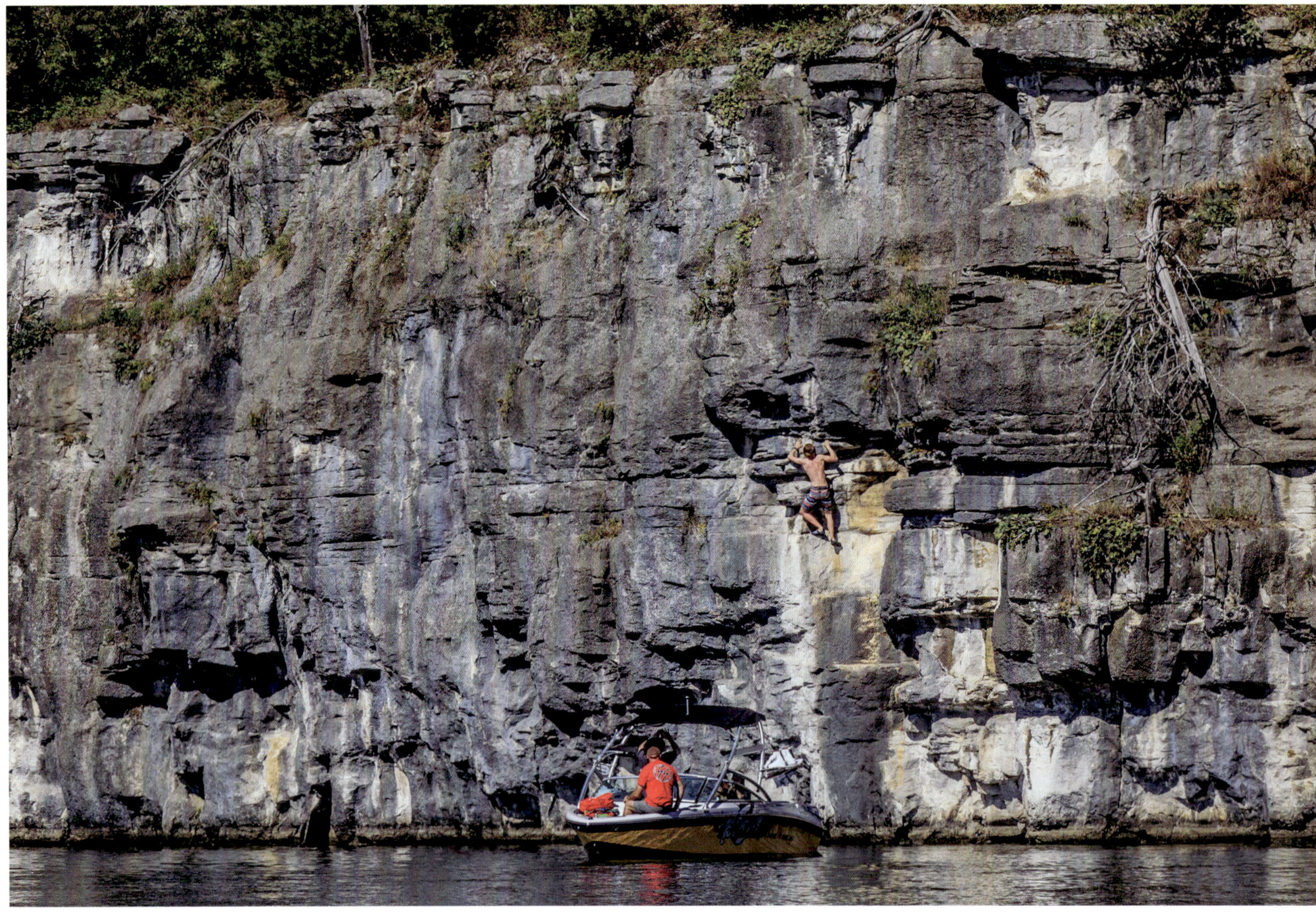

TENNESSEE RIVER, NICKAJACK LAKE, TENNESSEE, SEPTEMBER 23. Teenage boy scaling the cliffs while his family looks on. In 1968, TVA completed the Nickajack Dam and removed the dam at Hales Bar while impounding more waters and flooding the bottomland farms below.

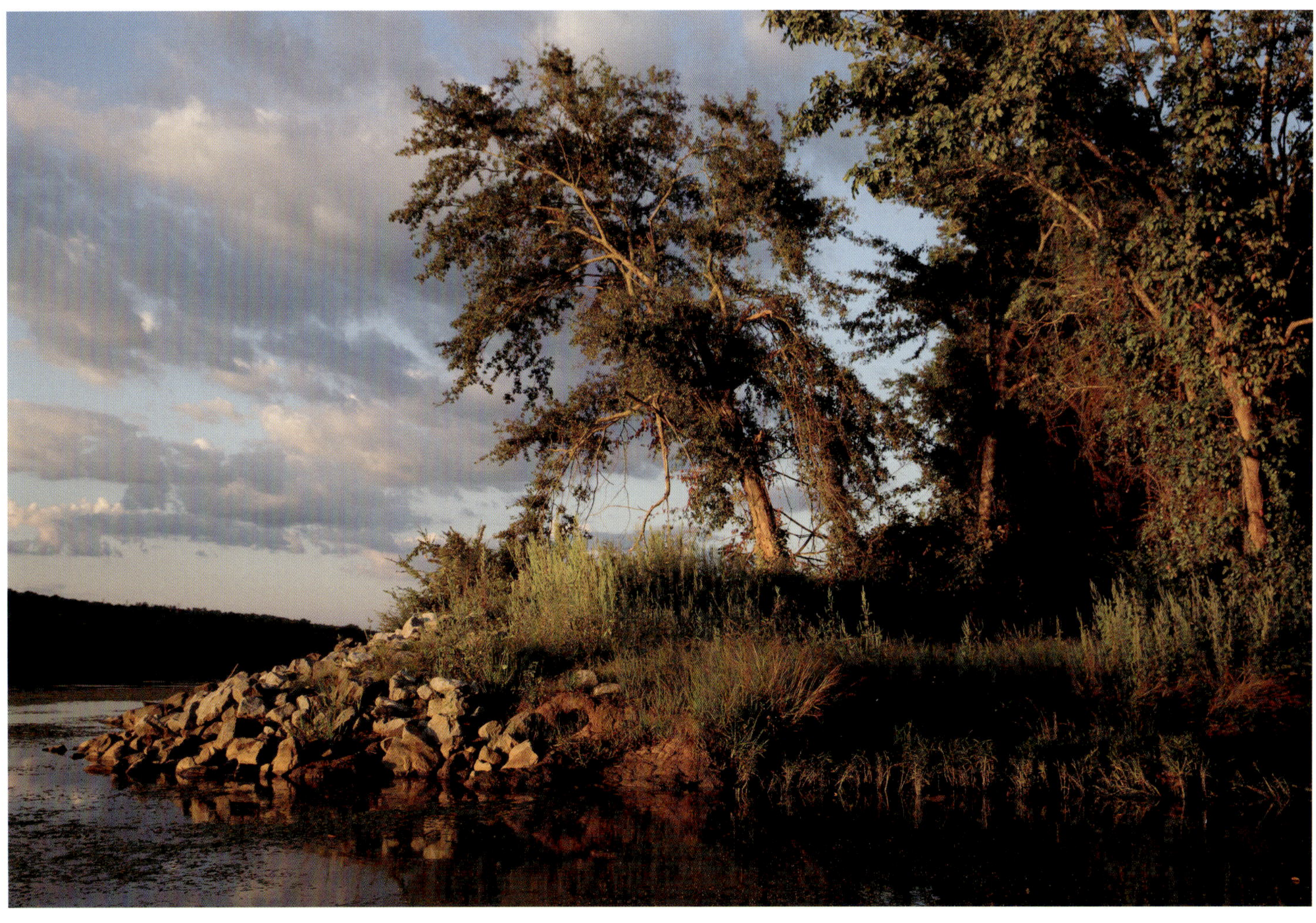

TENNESSEE RIVER, JACKSON COUNTY, ALABAMA, SEPTEMBER 24. Waning light along the waterway. It is said that the nine dams containing the Tennessee River have impounded over six hundred thousand acres of fertile bottomland, creating over ten thousand miles of shoreline.

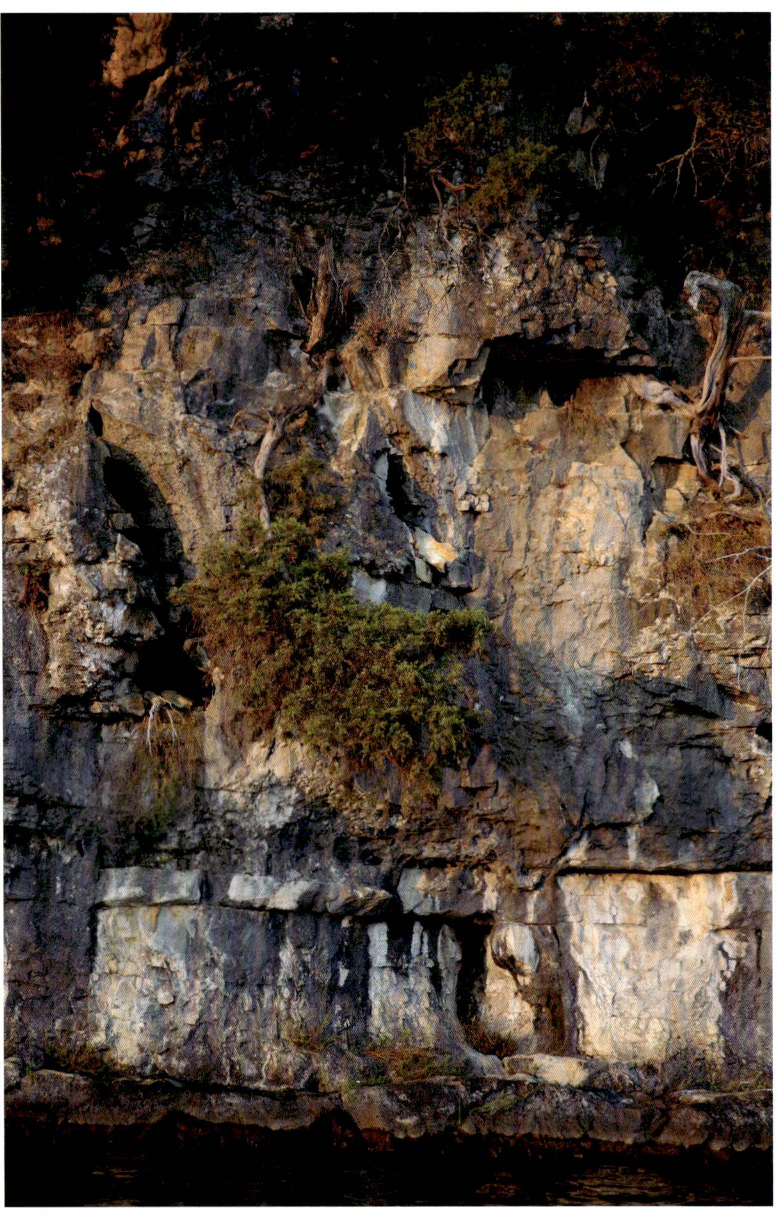

TENNESSEE RIVER, GUNTERSVILLE, ALABAMA, SEPTEMBER 27. The over two-billion-year-old rock cliffs continue to control the flow of the river. Bat caves lie nearby. I was tempted to wait until sundown to watch the creatures take flight.

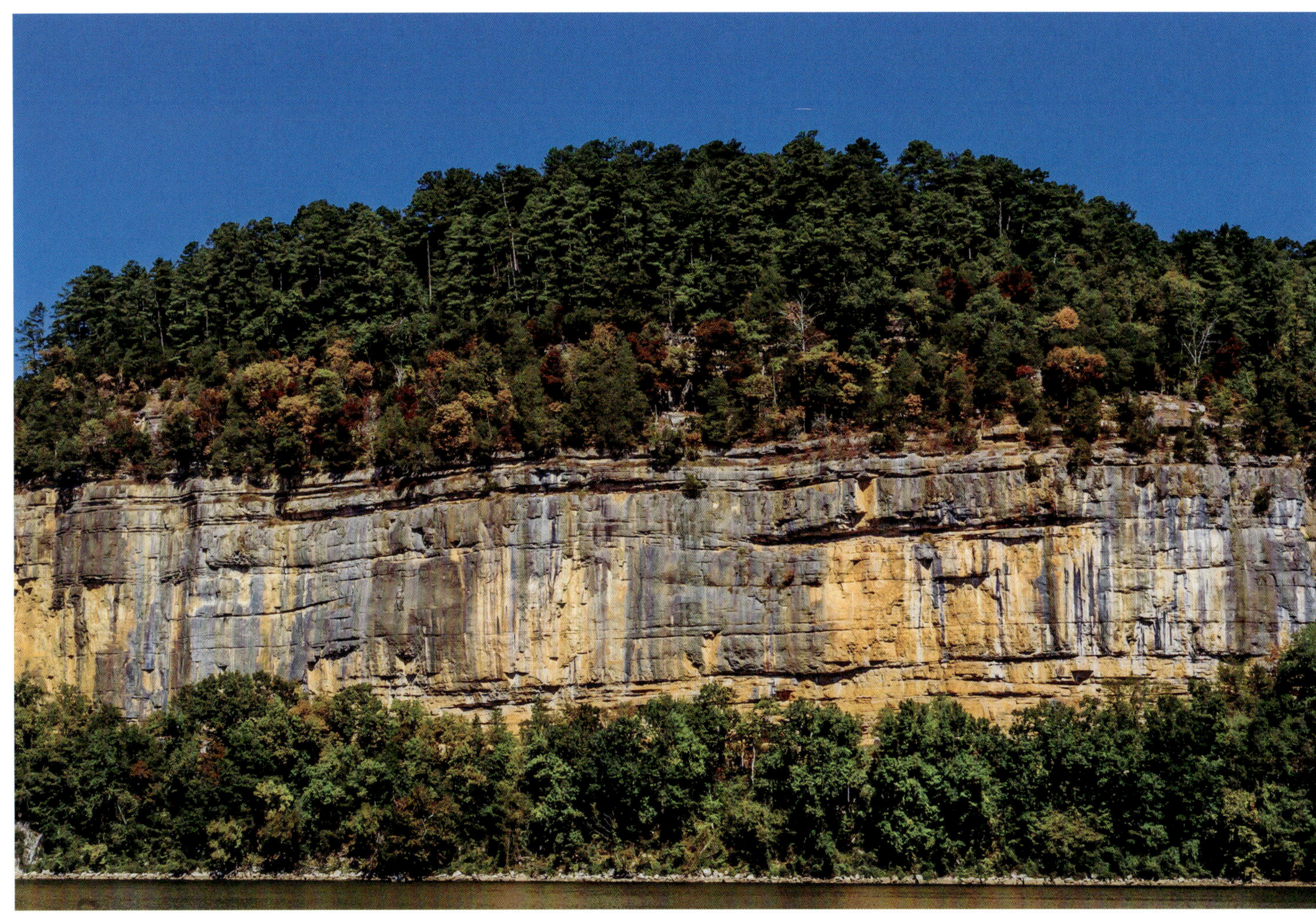

TENNESSEE RIVER, MADISON COUNTY, ALABAMA, SEPTEMBER 28. Painted Bluff, towering 485 feet above the water line, has the reputation of being the most photographed landmark on the Tennessee River. Donelson saw the exact same sight.

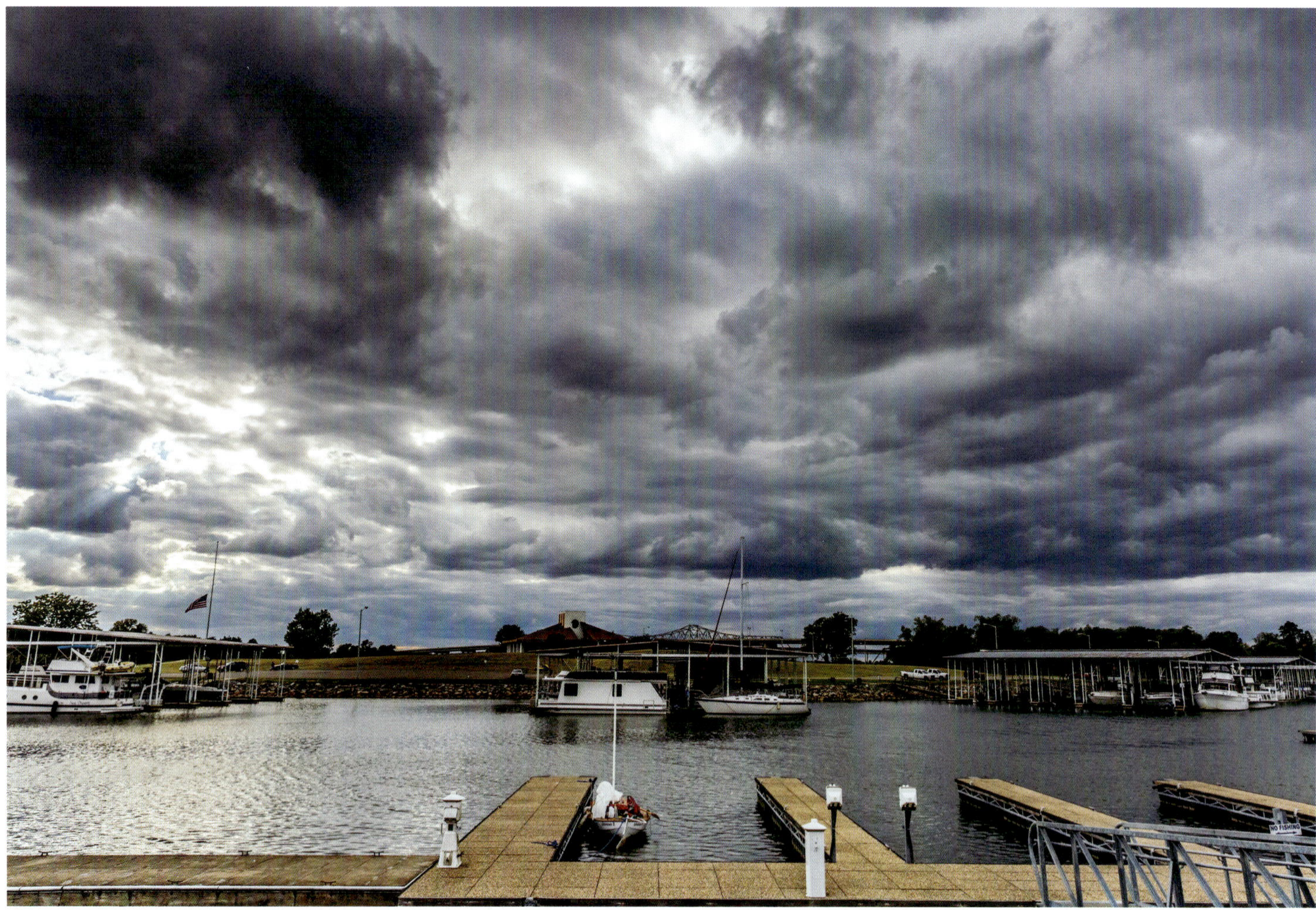

TENNESSEE RIVER, HUNTSVILLE, ALABAMA, SEPTEMBER 29. Storm clouds over the Ditto Landing Marina.

I HADN'T EATEN since South Sauty two days earlier. Once fully awake, I pulled my cooking gear from the boat and walked it over to one of the picnic tables in the adjacent park campground. After a full meal of boiled rice, soup mix, and packaged salmon, I washed out the pot and utensils and left it all to dry on the table. The campgrounds were all but empty so I just put my stuff in a neat little grouping and walked back to the boat. The campground had a laundromat and after three weeks on the water, I had some mighty soiled clothes. While waiting on the dryer, I walked back to the boat and noticed a city police car and a state police car driving past the parking lot. Later I walked back to check on my cooking gear. When I did, a maintenance man pulled away from his chores and trotted up to me saying, "Is that your belongings?" I replied, "Yes." He continued excitedly, "Why, I just had the police in here. Saw the cooking gear and just knew it was a meth lab! The police showed up in a hurry and rummaged through everything. Thought it was okay and left. One cop did say he wished he had your olive oil though." I laughed at the thought as he continued, "It happens. People sneak in at night, set up a tent, and cook meth until morning. Then they scurry off before anyone comes in. I've caught them doing it."

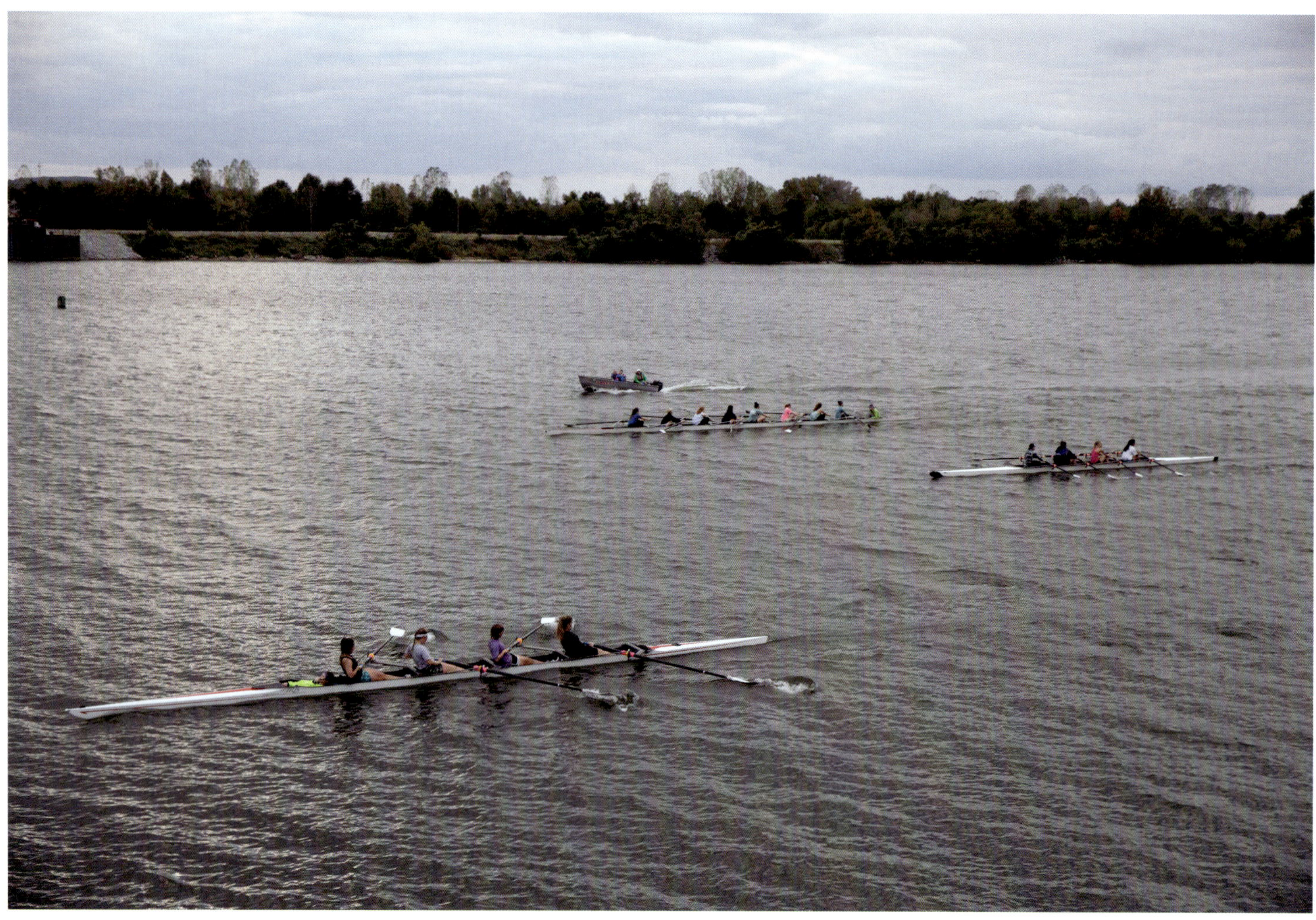

TENNESSEE RIVER, HUNTSVILLE, ALABAMA, SEPTEMBER 29. Women's rowing team practicing on the river.

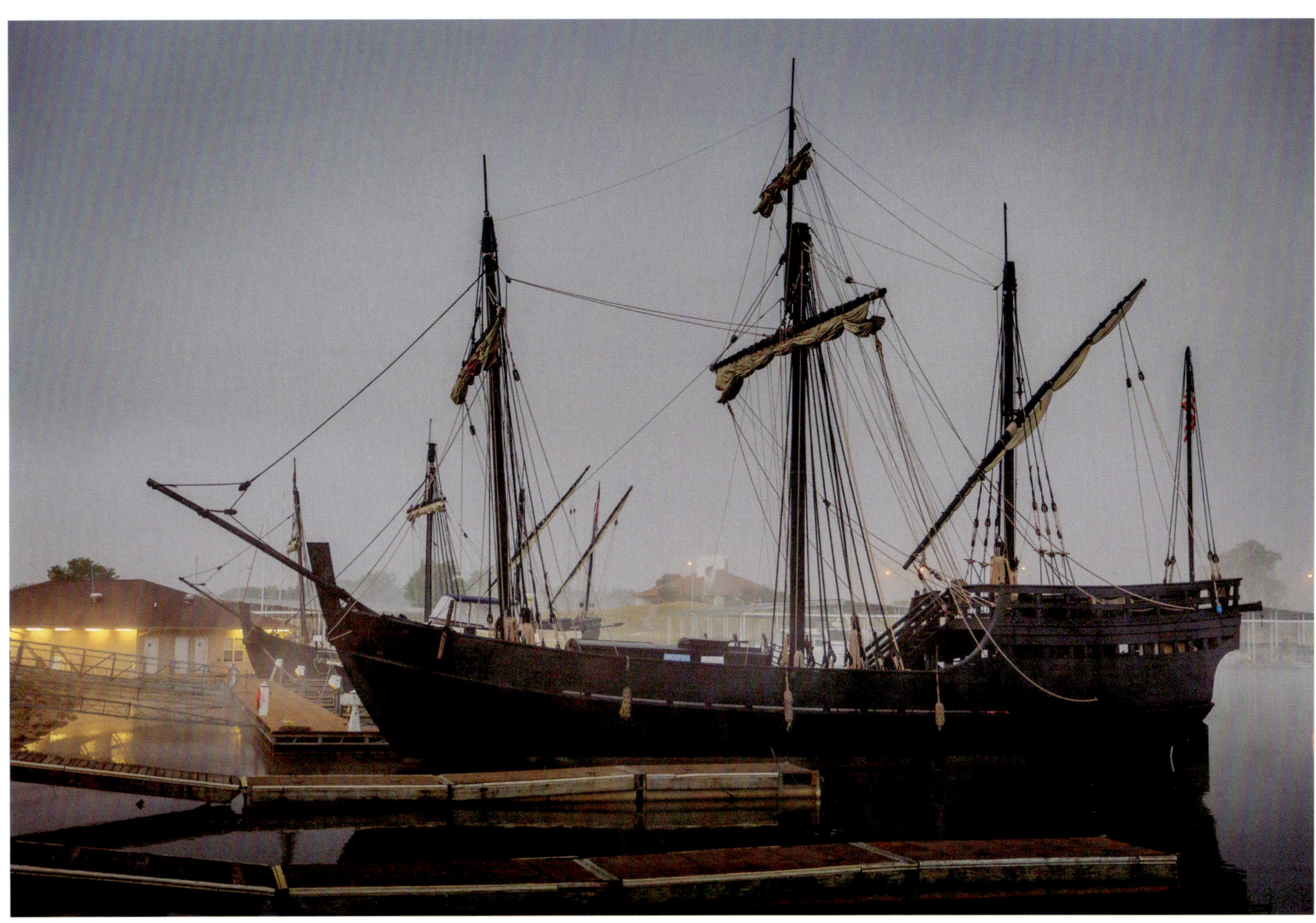

TENNESSEE RIVER, HUNTSVILLE, ALABAMA, SEPTEMBER 30. The *Niña* and the *Pinta*, replicas of two of Christopher Columbus's three vessels. The two ships travel the rivers, inviting tourists and school groups on for tours.

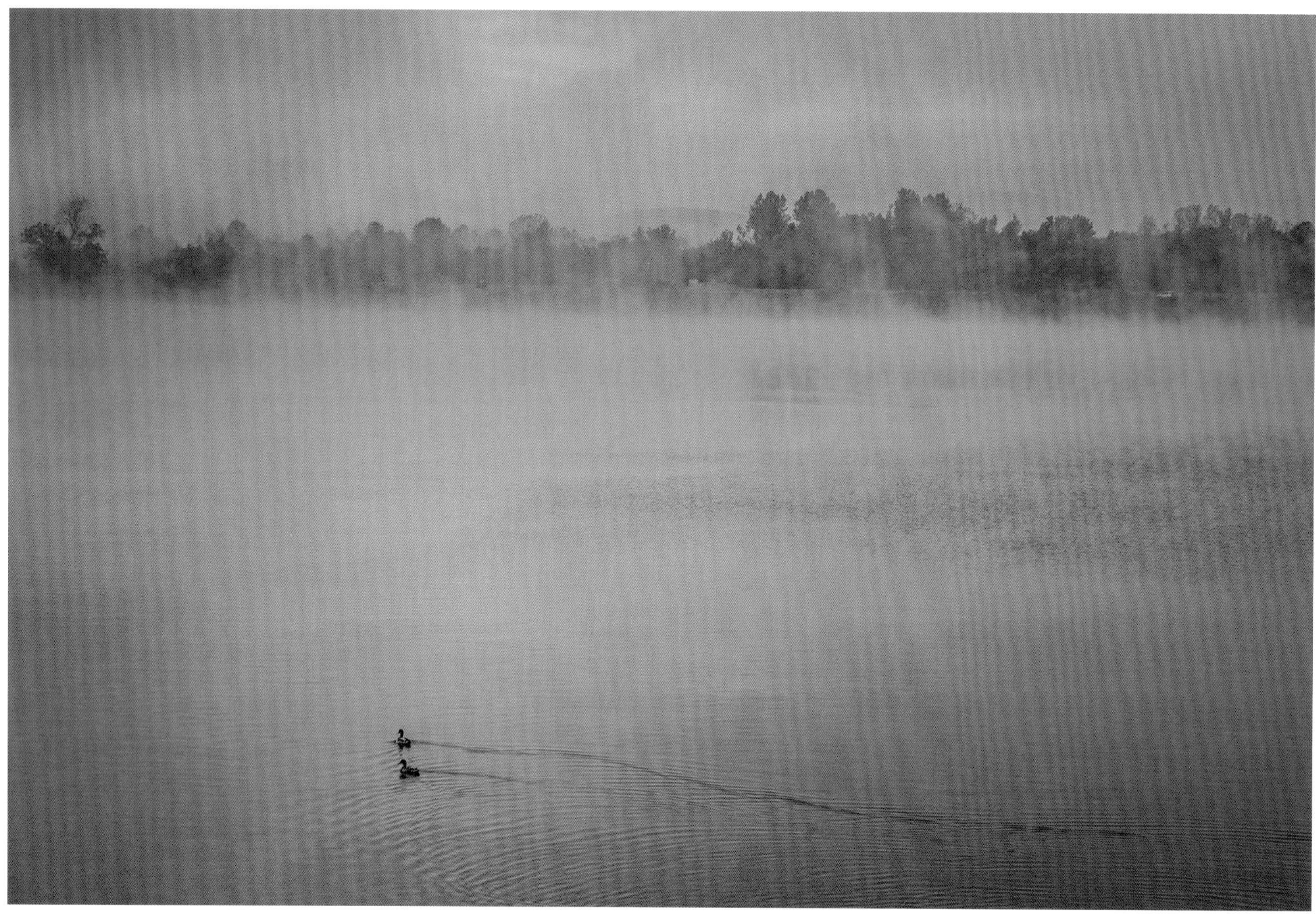

TENNESSEE RIVER, HUNTSVILLE, ALABAMA, SEPTEMBER 30. Ducks swimming through the mist. Not too far away, close to Florence, Alabama, lay the infamous Muscle Shoals. For Donelson, March 12, 1708, was another day of reckoning. The power of the rapids was legendary and there were no hundred-foot dams to ease the turbulence. After three hours of sheer terror, they made it through the dreaded shoals.

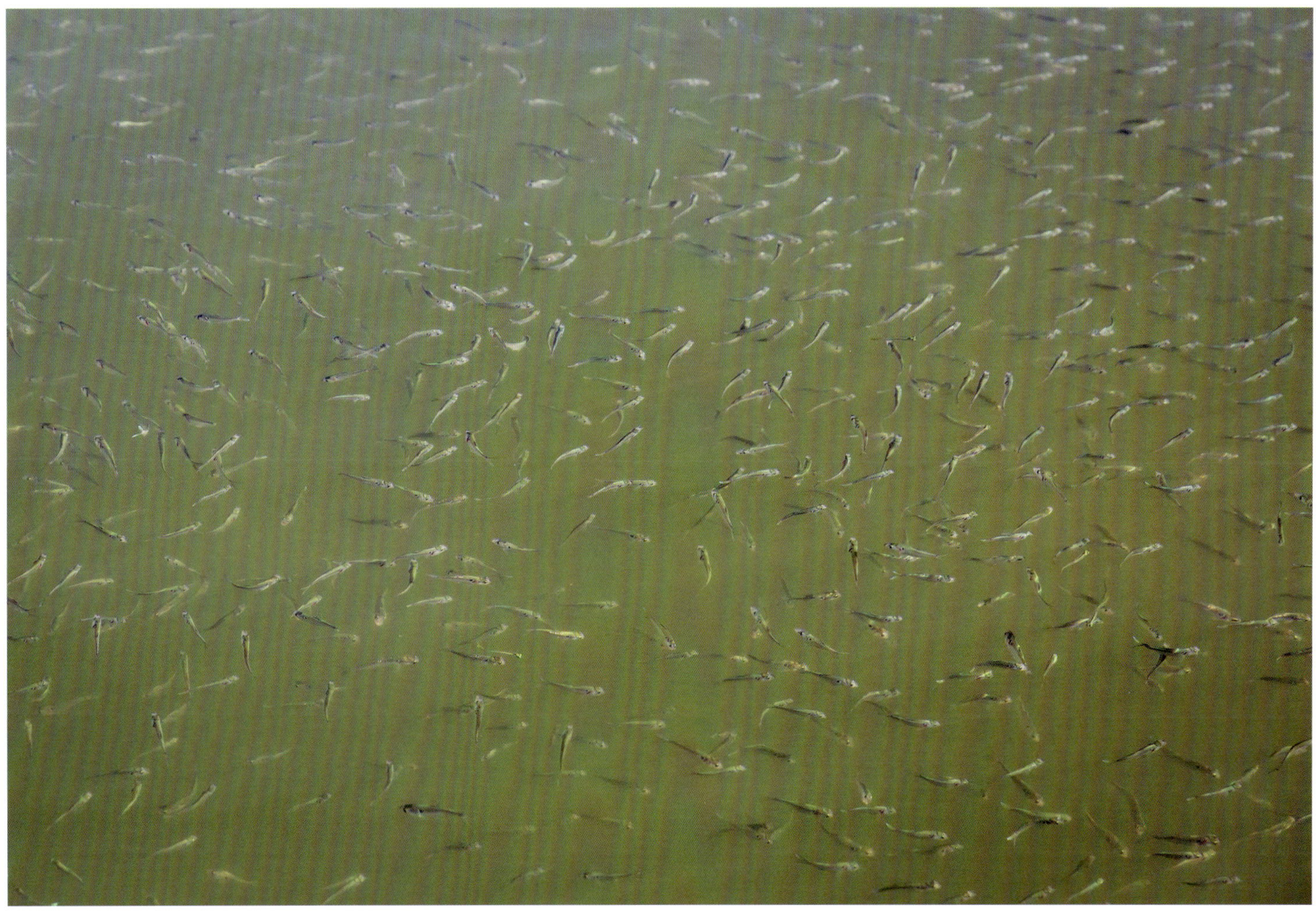

TENNESSEE RIVER, PICKWICK LANDING STATE PARK, OCTOBER 7. Minnows swarm the water. Fish were evident all along the river, but the warning signs posted at many of the public landings cautioned that ingestion could be hazardous due to contamination.

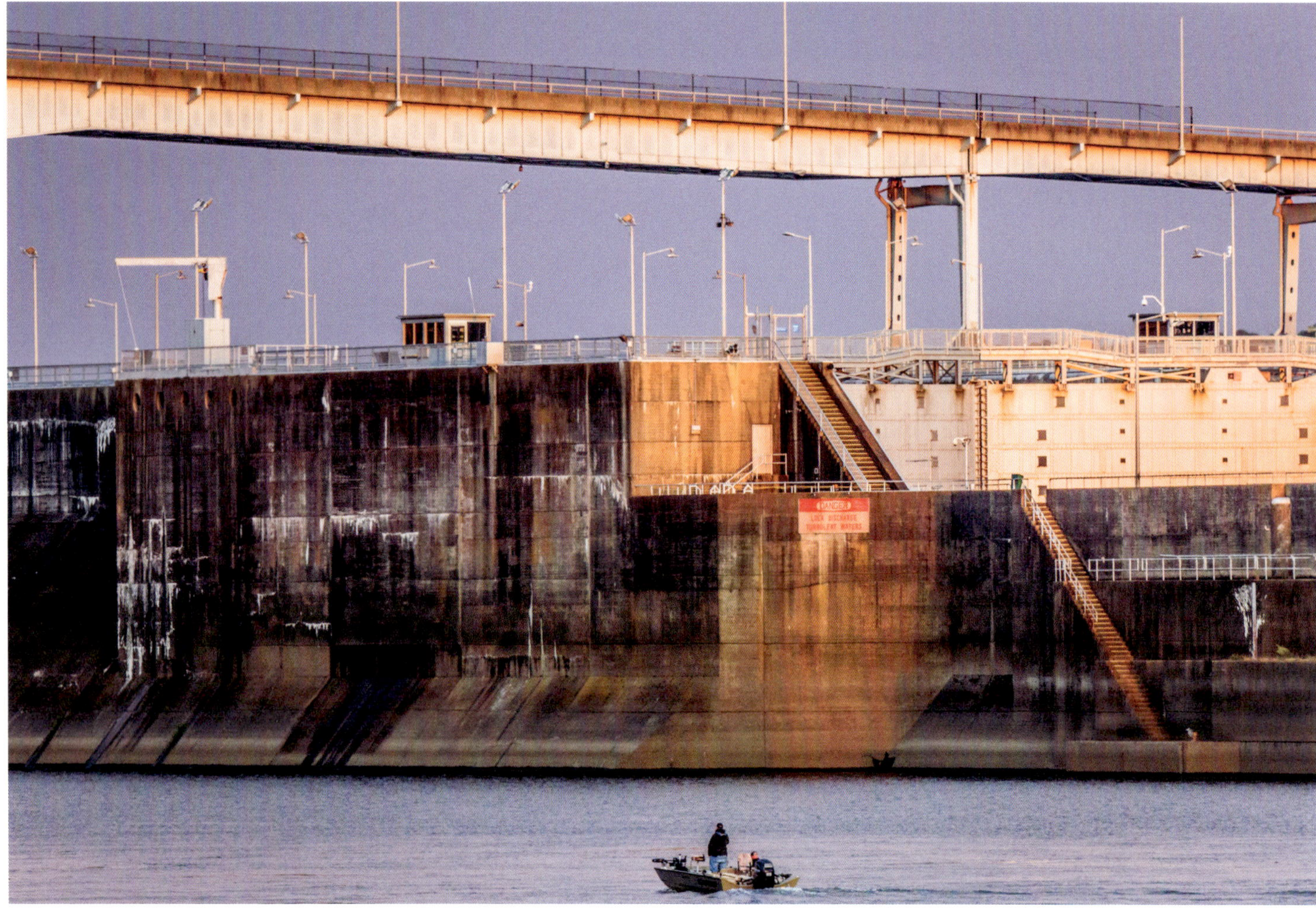

TENNESSEE RIVER, PICKWICK LOCK AND DAM, OCTOBER 7. Fisherman cruising the waters below. The warm waters coming off the hydroelectric generators attract fish.

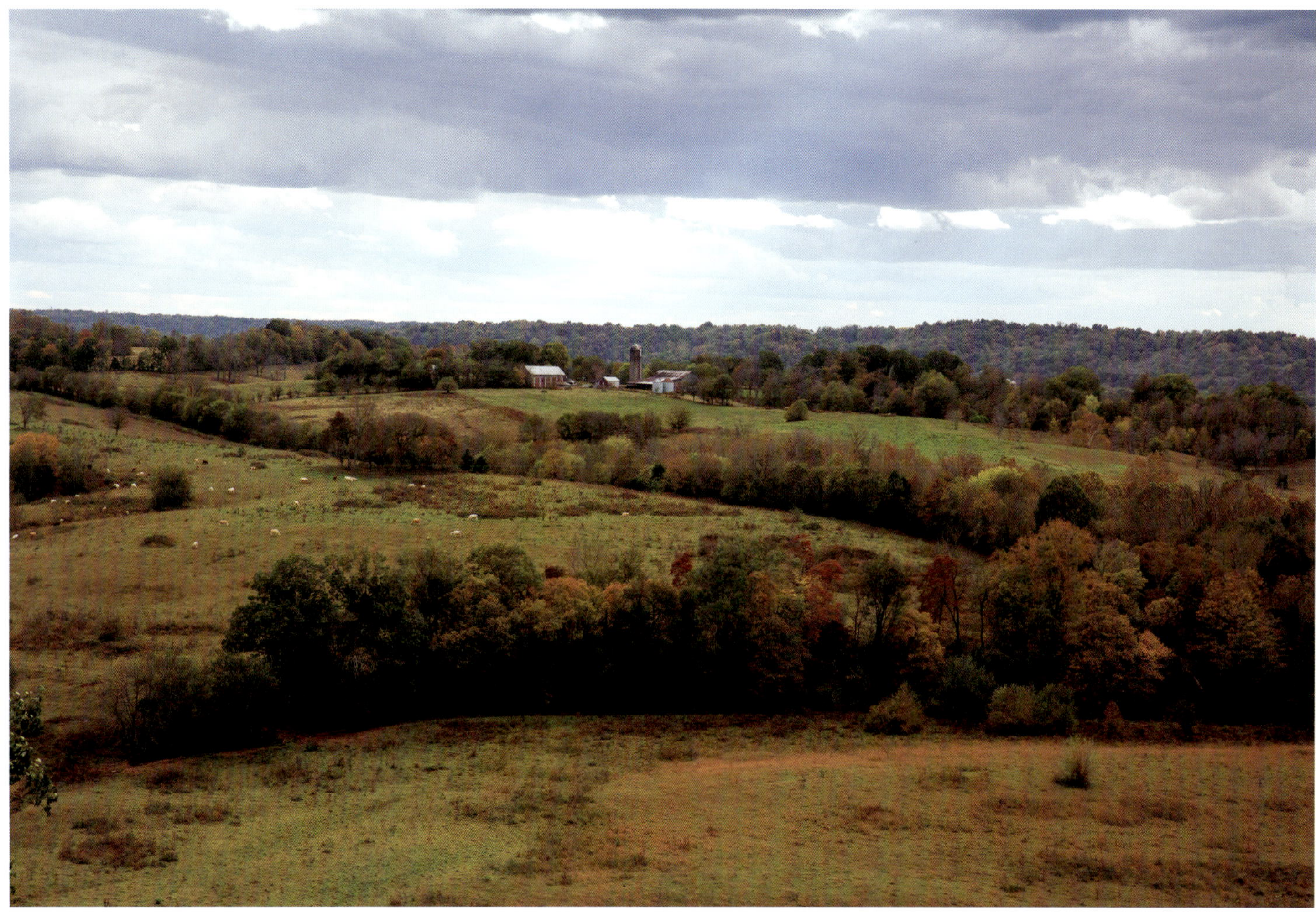

TENNESSEE RIVER, HARDIN COUNTY, TENNESSEE. Tennessee landscape close to Pickwick Landing.

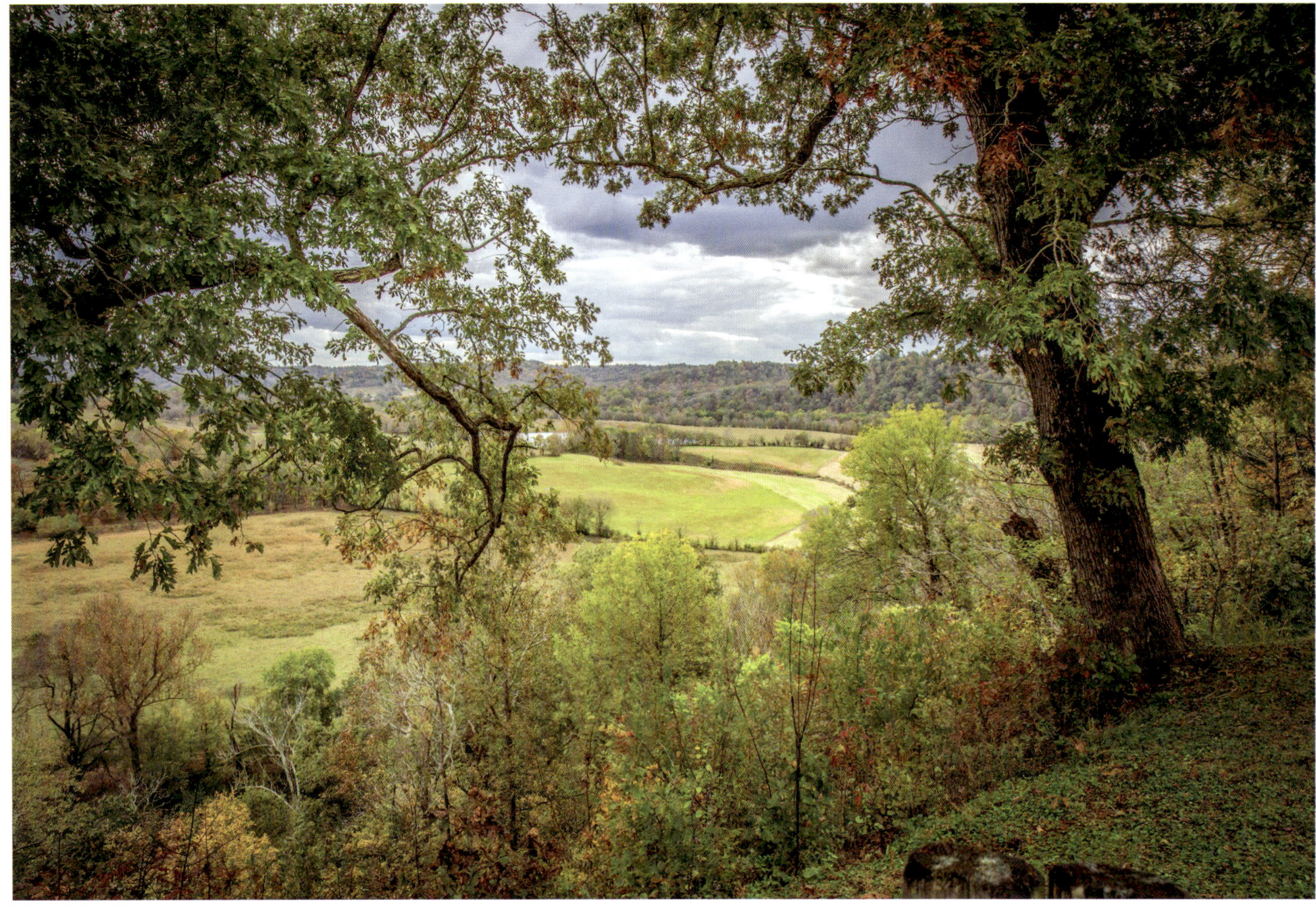

TENNESSEE RIVER, HARDIN COUNTY, TENNESSEE. Tennessee landscape close to Pickwick Landing.

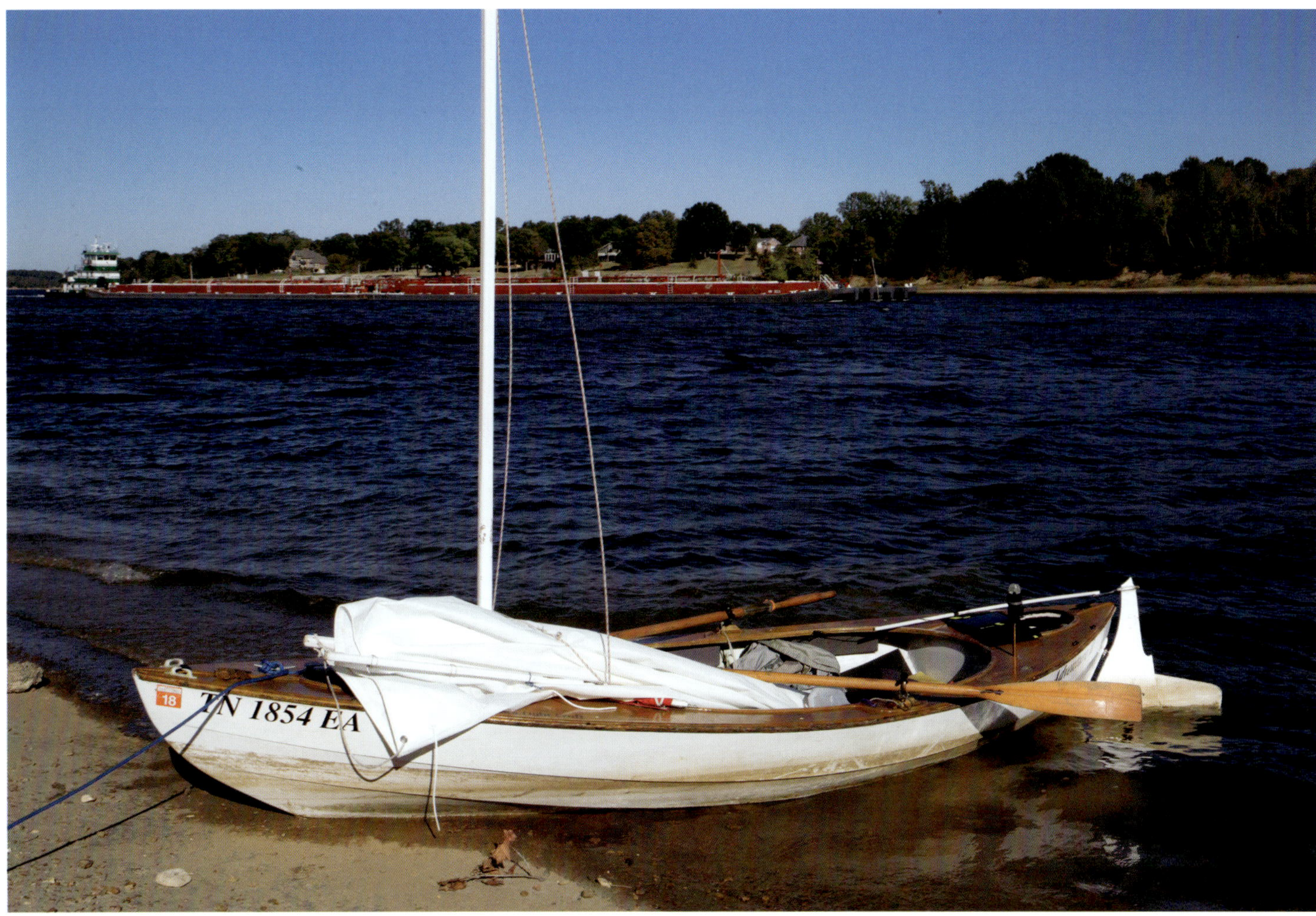

TENNESSEE RIVER, SAVANNAH, TENNESSEE, OCTOBER 8. High winds stalled my progress, forcing me to break for camp early. The shoreline that had been mostly rock and mud had turned to an inviting sand as the river headed through the lowlands of West Tennessee.

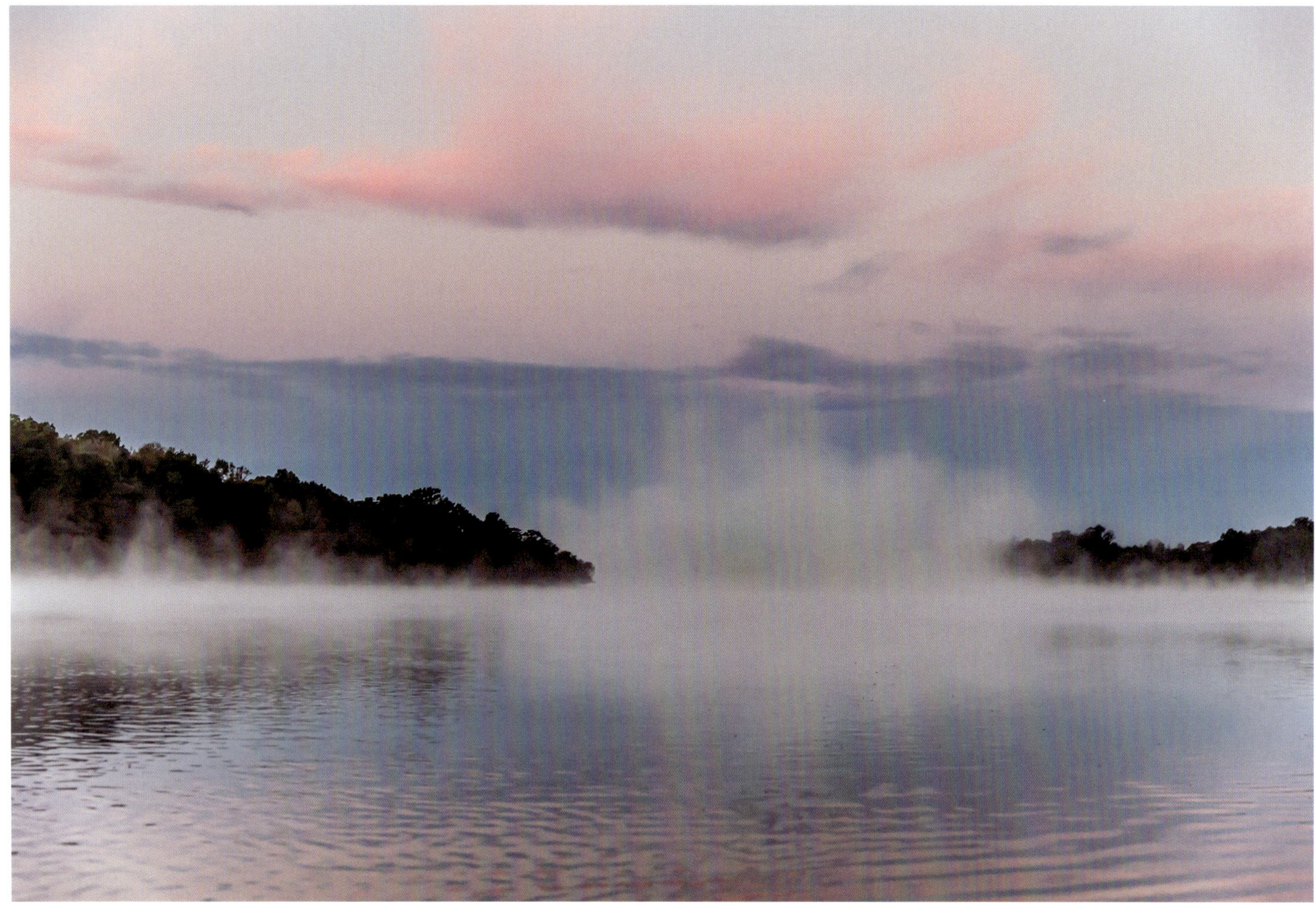

TENNESSEE RIVER. Sunrise after sleeping on my anchored boat. Like the mussels that lay so famously in the Tennessee waters, I myself was encapsulated in a shell of my own making, the *Adventure II*. During the day, the lid would open to reveal the spectacle of the outside world. At night the cover of my Bimini top would confine me to a universe of only a few square meters. The isolation and ignorance of what might be lurking could either be calming or frightening, as one's imagination has a way of running wild. The calming of the mind brought on by exhaustion is one of the true gifts of hard work.

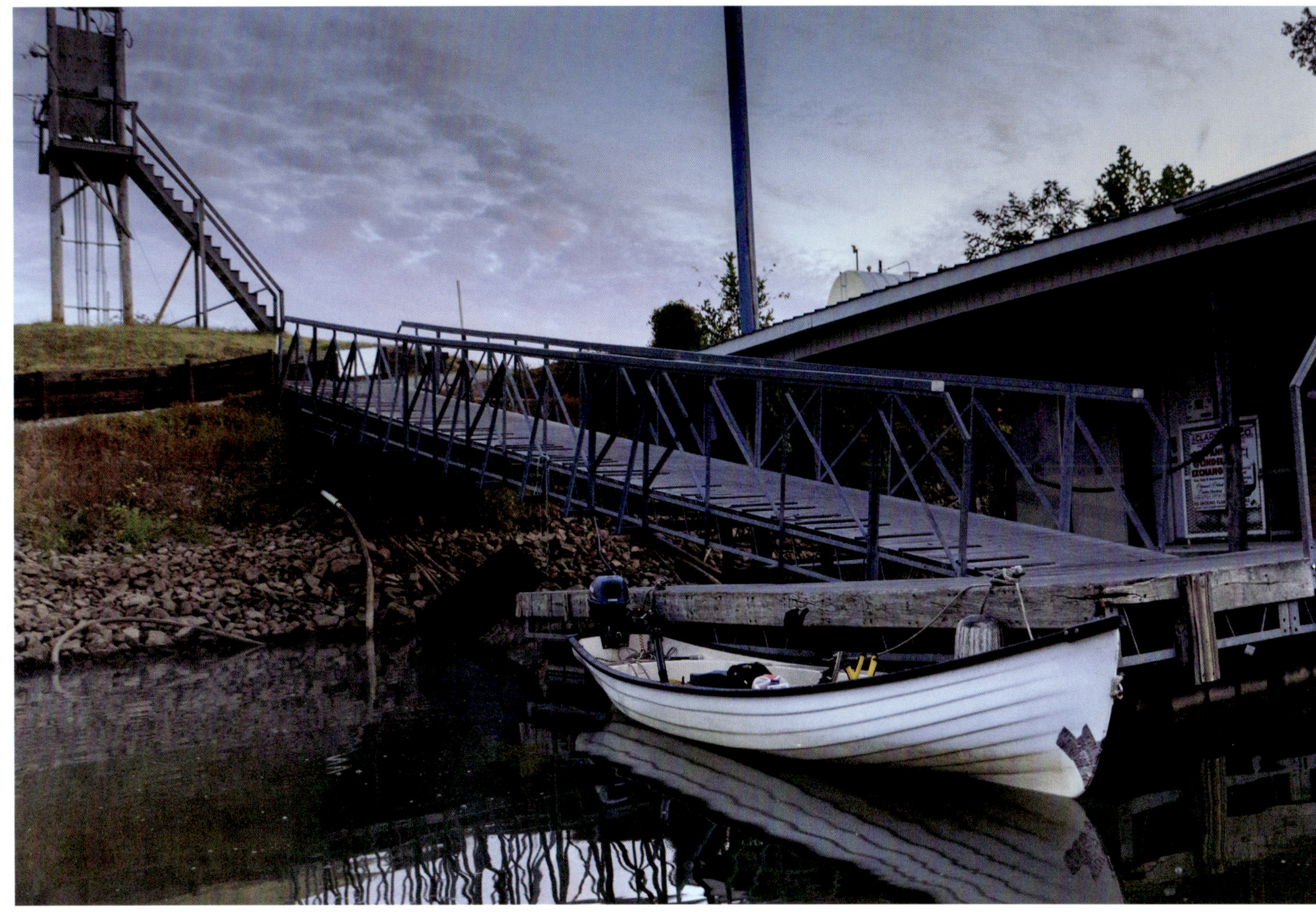

TENNESSEE RIVER, CLIFTON MARINA, OCTOBER 11. Treg Warner's boat. Made a new friend from Nashville. As happened at the marina in Huntsville, I was offered shelter from the storm. Donelson had no such comfort.

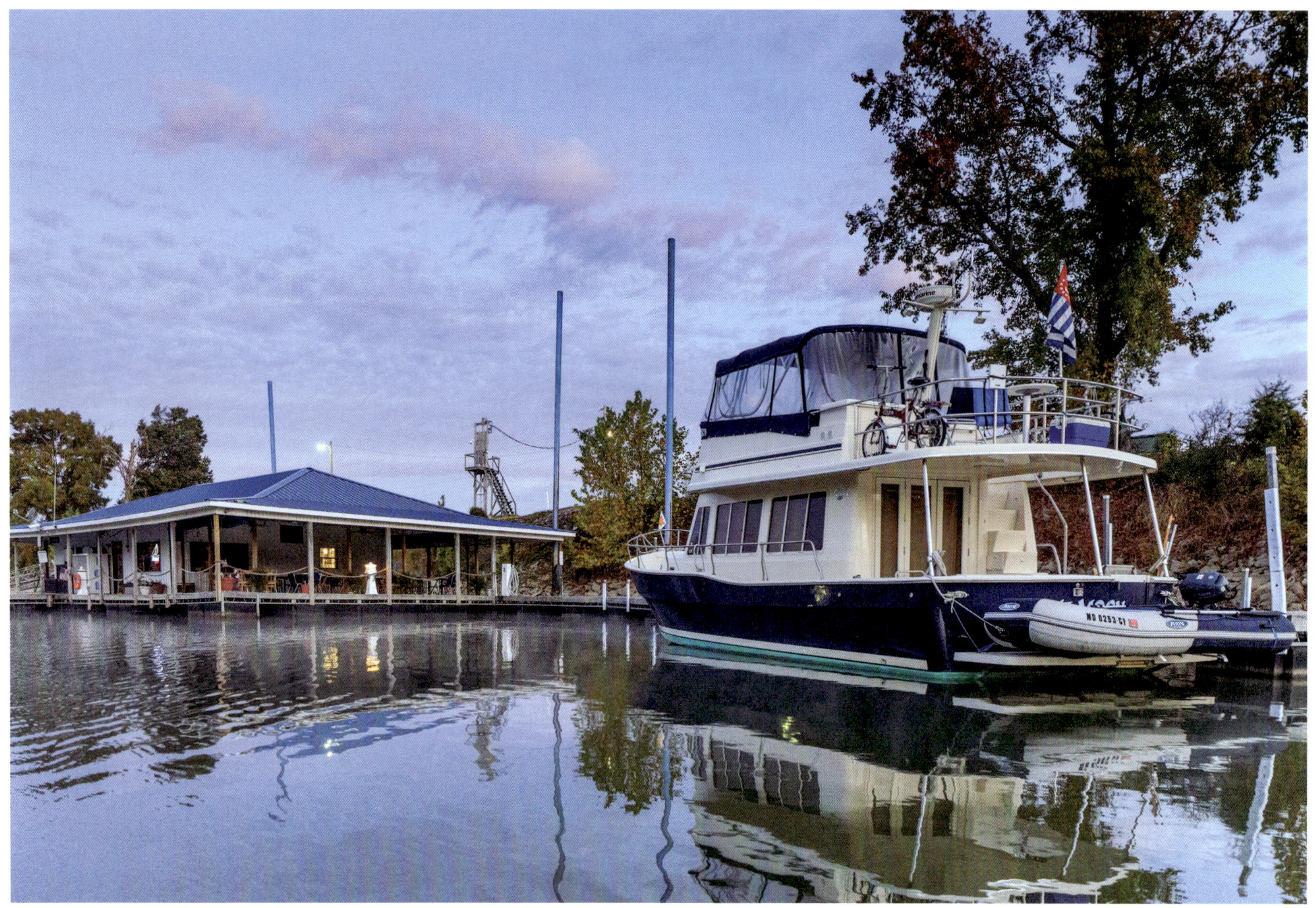

TENNESSEE RIVER, CLIFTON MARINA, OCTOBER 11. John and Barbra Locke—friends I had met a number of years earlier on my Great Loop voyage. Had I passed them on the street, I may have never recognized them, but their boat I knew.

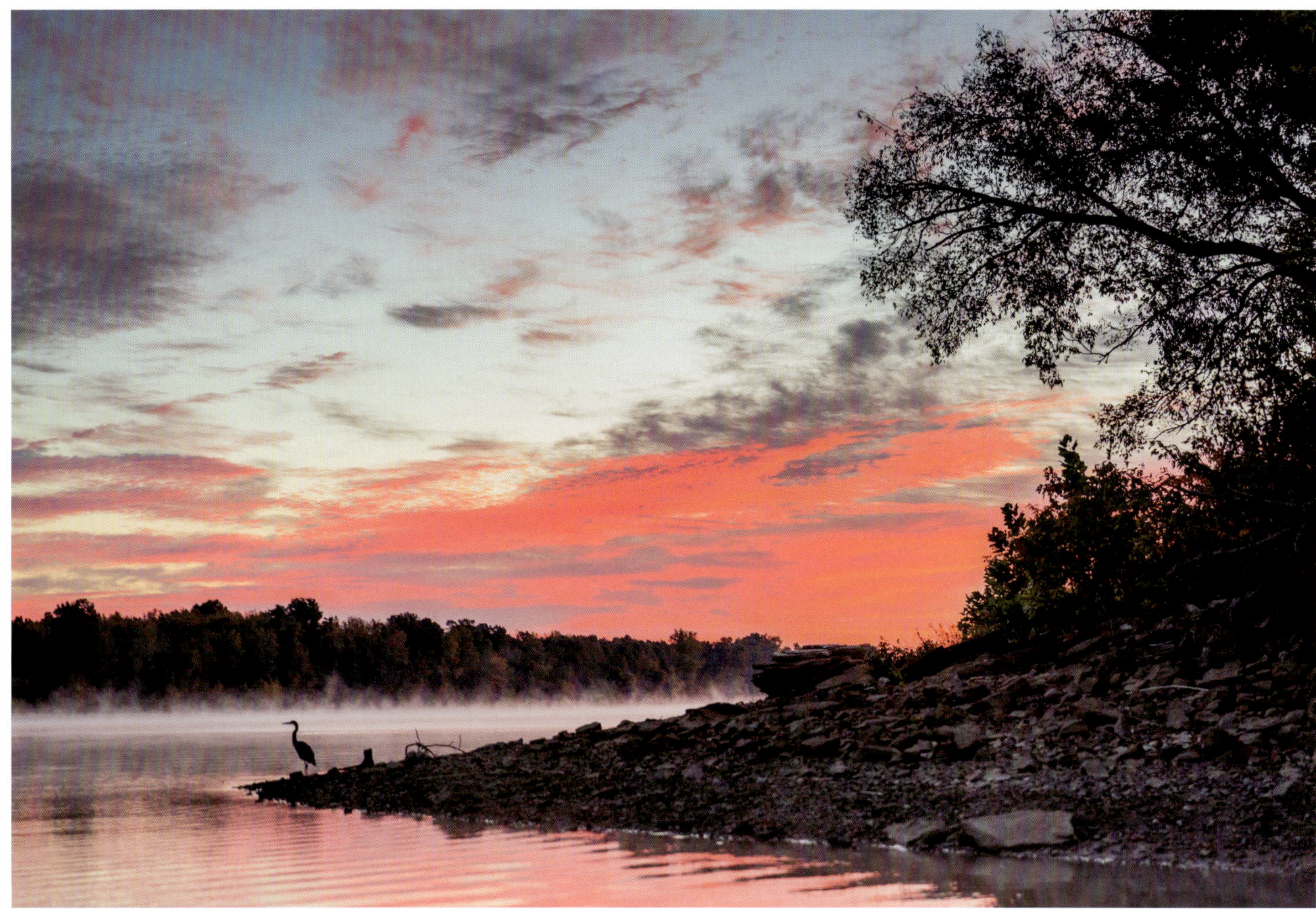

TENNESSEE RIVER, HUMPHREYS COUNTY, OCTOBER 11. Sunset along the Tennessee National Wildlife Refuge. “I believe there is a subtle magnetism in Nature, which if we unconsciously yield to it, will direct us right.” —Henry David Thoreau

A Cherokee Perspective on the Founding of Nashville and the Late Eighteenth Century

ALBERT BENDER
Cherokee activist, historian, political columnist, and reporter

THE LATE EIGHTEENTH CENTURY was a period fraught with dire circumstances and consequences for the Cherokee Nation. The voyage of the *Adventure* by the Donelson party and the founding of the settlements that became Nashville were part and parcel of this tragic historic epoch.

Considerable background to the period surrounding the voyage is necessary to appreciate the setting of this seminal series of events and developments. That setting was dominated by the struggle of the Cherokee Nation to survive; the specific milieu was the long and bloody Cherokee War, which raged for eighteen years, and the Treaty of 1777—made by the official Cherokee leadership with the colonial governments—which only fanned the embers of racial conflagration.

The Cherokee Nation, led by the great war chief Dragging Canoe, was at war with the encroaching white settlers. Part of the immediate background of this conflict was the Treaty of Sycamore Shoals of March 1775. An unscrupulous land speculator, Richard Henderson, headed up what was called the Transylvania Company. This early real estate company purportedly engineered the largest Indian land cession in American history, resulting in the transfer of twenty-two million acres of Cherokee land covering all of the present-day state of Kentucky and a large portion of Middle Tennessee. The transaction was illegal under the Proclamation of 1763, by which English settlers were forbidden by the British Crown from residing west of the Appalachians. Stepping even further back in time, the articles of agreement signed by the Cherokee Nation and the British government in 1730 mandated that only the Crown could purchase land from the Nation. Private transactions with British subjects, such as Henderson and his Transylvania Company, were illegal.

The Treaty of Sycamore Shoals was controversial from a myriad of perspectives. There are many different versions of what the parties understood was taking place. The Cherokee Nation was reputedly selling this huge amount of acreage for six wagonloads of trade goods and a cabin filled with more of the same. This seems incomprehensible—the Cherokees were known as very shrewd traders.

According to Cherokee accounts, the chiefs who negotiated the transaction later completely repudiated it, claiming their understanding was that they were only granting Henderson and his settlers limited grazing rights on certain tracts of land in Kentucky. The Cherokee leadership said they thought the trade goods were an indemnification for damages done to Cherokee towns by lawless white marauders. Dragging Canoe, in an eloquent speech, vehemently spoke against even considering the sale of any more Cherokee land.

Between March of 1775 and July of 1776, everything remained for the most part status quo. Since matters were in a state of political instability, Henderson made no moves to colonize the land in question.

But there were other whites who moved independently of Henderson's machinations; their settlements actually predated the Treaty of Sycamore Shoals. These white colonists had already settled in upper East Tennessee, which was itself part of the traditional Cherokee homeland. These settlements were begun in 1768. In 1772, wishing to avoid conflict with the Cherokee Nation, the settlers negotiated a lease agreement with the Cherokee leadership under which they would make yearly payments in trade goods and agricultural produce.

However, as the year 1776 approached, these settlers—prominently the Robertsons, the Beans, and the Browns—told their relatives, friends, and other whites that they weren't just leasing the land but had bought it outright from the Nation, thus they had the authority to sell tracts themselves. Further, they began fencing the land. This encouraged a large influx of illegal tenants, more than ever anticipated by the Nation. The earlier settlers had been offered the olive branch of peace by the Nation, and they gave back a perfidious, treacherous stab in the back.

Word of the illicit sales reached the Nation, and Dragging Canoe and his supporters approached the official leadership to demand the termination of the lease. The settlers were given forty days to move; instead, they started building forts.

In the meantime, the American Revolution broke out. The upper East Tennessee settlers hoped that the revolutionary government would legalize their illegal land transactions.

At the end of the forty-day period, Dragging Canoe and his supporting war chiefs began military actions to remove the defiant settlers. This preemptive military action had the support of the official leadership; the colonists were building fortifications and there were rumors that colonial armies were already massing to invade the Nation. As open warfare broke out between Cherokee forces and settlers, the colonists appealed to the American revolutionary government for assistance. The American government responded, "We will send forces to utterly extirpate the Cherokee Nation." *Extirpate* of course means *exterminate*.

The revolutionary government dispatched an invasion composed of several thousand troops from the states of Virginia, North and South Carolina, and Georgia. In the initial stages of this war, despite the valiant, heroic resistance of the Cherokee people, the Nation was devastated. The Lower, Middle, and Valley towns were utterly destroyed. Thousands of Cherokees were sent fleeing into the woods with little to eat as the colonial armies conducted a scorched earth policy. Only the Overhill towns were not completely razed. The Cherokee capital of Chota was not burned, as the colonist commanders said "We are only destroying towns that have been hostile American settlers." This was a shoddy attempt to divide the Nation.

Let's step back a bit to further discuss the colonial armies that invaded the Cherokee Nation in the late summer of 1776. This was the start of the Second Cherokee War (the first being the Anglo-Cherokee War of 1760–61). Many histories written by white writers assert that there was little or no resistance by the Cherokee forces. Nothing could be further from the truth. There were major pitched battles and skirmishes everywhere. There were major battles at Cowee Gap, the Black Hole, Eseneca, Neowee Pass, the Ring Fight, Sugartown, Tomasse, Tugaloo, and Wayah Gap; in all of these, invading American forces sustained heavy losses. Further, when the colonials camped at night, sentries were often attacked and killed or carried off by groups of Cherokees or by lone Cherokee warriors. The flanks of the colonial armies were constantly harried by Cherokee sniper fire.

All four states that mounted the invasion had considered such a campaign for some time before the actual start of hostilities in late July of 1776. In early July, an official of North Carolina had stated bluntly, "If such a campaign can be mounted I have no doubts of the destruction of the Cherokee Nation."[1] Whenever possible the colonial soldiers acted with genocidal barbarity, savagely killing men, women, children, and the elderly. Accounts abound of women being tied up and burned alive in their flaming homes, children swung by their heels against trees and boulders until their brains were bashed out, and women decapitated as they ran from soldiers swinging broadswords (this was reportedly a form of sport for the troops). South Carolina, in order to raise a large volunteer army, offered seventy-five English pounds for every Cherokee scalp taken and one hundred pounds for every live prisoner delivered. Live prisoners, including women and children, were sold into Caribbean slavery.

Some attention should also be given to the so-called Indian fighter, the first governor of Tennessee, John Sevier, and the writing of the Tennessee history of this period. According to Tennessee history, Sevier fought thirty-five battles with Cherokees and won every battle. This is simply not true. It is racist mythology. In one instance, research disclosed that one so-called battle never took place at all. The account was a complete fabrication.

The formation of the Five Lower Towns by Dragging Canoe, according to some histories, was the result of John Sevier leading a frontier army and destroying the resistant Cherokee towns in 1782. But the so-called Five Lower Towns, the core of the resistance (actually more than five towns because the resistance encompassed the majority of Cherokees in 1782), were formed in response to an invasion by Evan Shelby in April of 1779—after the formation of the militant war towns north of the Chattanooga area. (As a side note, Shelby only invaded those Chattanooga towns when he found out that most of the warriors were absent, off fighting in South Carolina and Georgia.) Sevier and the frontiersmen he led, though they wanted to strike Dragging Canoe's towns, always ended up attacking what was left of the peaceful Cherokee towns in East Tennessee. They were afraid to even venture into the area occupied by the resistant Cherokee forces.

Tennessee history is filled with spurious stories of frontiersmen's victories over Cherokee war companies. There are even historical markers attesting to these "triumphs." Many of these accounts were "developed" (and I use the word charitably) in the 1930s in an attempt to lure tourists to Tennessee to bolster a flagging state economy during the Great Depression. This was an attempt to mythologize a superiority of white settlers over Indigenous peoples on the field of battle.

In response to the devastation inflicted by the colonial armies, Dragging Canoe advocated that

Tennessee history is filled with spurious stories of frontiersmen's victories over Cherokee war companies.

the entire Cherokee Nation move south and continue the war from more geographically defensible locations. He could not persuade most of the elder Cherokee leadership to abandon the towns in upper East Tennessee (however, it is worthy of note that some prominent elder chiefs, including Ostenaco and Willenawah, did follow him south). But Dragging Canoe was able to convince the majority of the Cherokee people to adhere to his plan by moving to the area of southeast Tennessee centered around present-day Chattanooga, the Chickamauga Creek area and the surrounding region.

The Nation was decimated in August and September of 1776; in March of 1777 the Great Migration took place. Thousands of Cherokee men, women, children, the elderly, and some of the official leadership moved with Dragging Canoe. It was a massive migration of Cherokees vowing to continue the war against the genocide-bent American colonial armies.

Because the first Cherokee refugees settled near Chickamauga Creek, the white frontiersmen called the resistant Cherokees *Chickamaugas*. But these displaced resisters called themselves the "true Cherokees," *Ani-Yun-wiya*, the "Real People," and considered all who dared to cooperate with the hated American colonists "traitors, rogues and dogs."

Thus, a state of acute war existed in the year 1779. This was the year in which, strange as it may seem, the Robertsons and the Donelsons—prominent leaders of the settlers of upper East Tennessee and largely responsible for the then raging Cherokee-American War—decided to invade Middle Tennessee, knowing full well they were heading into, at best, disputed Indian land. What makes this even stranger is that there was still plenty of stolen Cherokee land in upper East Tennessee on which they might live and thrive. On the face of it the move made no sense. There was no shortage of land.

It must be speculated that simple greed was a factor. The Robertson-Donelson emigrants wanted large acreages worked by slaves. These settlers dreamed of large plantations in the Cumberland basin, and they could not advance further down the Tennessee River because of the strength of Cherokee resistance.

But wait! This would also make sense from a military standpoint. With settlers on the Cumberland, the Cherokee forces led by Dragging Canoe would have to fight on two fronts. The first front was the settler entrenchment from the northeast, from upper East Tennessee. With settlers established in Middle Tennessee, Cherokees would also face a war front the northwest. Moreover, it must be kept in mind that the Robertson-Donelson incursion eventually turned Middle Tennessee into a "militarized zone" with more than thirty forts spread across the region. Keep in mind that the Ore expedition that destroyed the Cherokee war towns of Nickajack and Running Water in September of 1792 was dispatched from Nashville.

Moreover, the Middle Tennessee white settlements were strategically placed to obstruct communication between the northern and southern Native nations, for example between Cherokees and Shawnees. Several Indigenous roads important for military and trade purposes passed through the Middle Tennessee region that were hundreds if not thousands of years old.

At any rate, Robertson set out with an overland party and arrived at the site of present-day Nashville on Christmas Day of 1779. The Donelson party started down the Tennessee River in December to connect with the Cumberland River to bring settlers by flatboat to the same area.

The Donelson party, in coming down the Tennessee River from upper East Tennessee, would have to pass the Cherokee war towns commanded by Dragging Canoe. The first town they would have encountered was that of Tuskegee Island Town, located on what is now Williamson's Island. At this town the Donelson flotilla would have encountered a very surprised Cherokee community.

A great flotilla of flatboats and pirogues, crammed with men, women, children, and household goods, coming out of nowhere and heading down the Tennessee, must have been quite a shock. Their objective was the French Lick (present-day Nashville) on the Cumberland River, where they would disembark after traversing the entire length of the Tennessee River, then navigating the difficult upstream passage by way of the Ohio, and finally travelling down the Cumberland. The advance party of pioneers led by James Robertson had already started for the same destination by the overland route known as the Wilderness Road, across the Cumberland Plateau by way of Kentucky. It was their responsibility to build cabins and prepare the site for habitation. The Donelson company was the nautical component of this mass migration from the illegal East Tennessee settlements to what is now Nashville.

Historical speculation is that John Donelson could not have known the strength of the Cherokee war towns on the Tennessee River. He was aware that Evan Shelby had invaded the area with an army of about six hundred frontiersmen and destroyed about eleven towns (because most of the warriors were away fighting in other areas, as previously mentioned) in April of that year. It was an extremely cold winter, one of the coldest ever known. This was considered a protection, as it was believed that war parties were unlikely to be afoot. Winter was also considered the season for high water and swift travel on the river.

The *Adventure*, Donelson's flatboat, was the flagship for this expedition and carried at least thirty settlers. Thirty flatboats began the journey and more would join them downriver. The pirogues were dugout canoes; some may have been covered.

The first Cherokee towns they passed were still in ashes from the Shelby expedition of the preceding spring and were obviously not going to be rebuilt. The first inhabited town the flotilla passed was Tuskegee Island Town. It too had been destroyed by Shelby, but had been rebuilt. The whites saw Indians crowding the riverbank. There was an attempt to intercept the voyagers, with warriors crowding into canoes and giving chase, but the expedition made its escape without losses. At this point they had to know they were entering a war zone. The word was out—there were whites on the river! At the next town, probably Nickajack, the settlers were fired upon and one person was killed. But the fleet went by so swiftly that no other losses were sustained from gunfire.

However, the Cherokee warriors were able to capture the last boat in the line. The Stuart boat, with twenty-eight people onboard, was lost. Smallpox had broken out in this group a few days before and on Donelson's orders this boat was last in line and kept at a distance. No attempt was made at rescue because such an effort could jeopardize the entire flotilla. Some in the flotilla took grim satisfaction in knowing that the capture of the smallpox-infected voyagers would precipitate countless Cherokee deaths. History records that this indeed did happen.

The fleet next entered a section of the river known in settler terms as the Suck, where there was a sudden narrowing of the river lined with large bluffs. These bluffs were ringed with warrior marksmen firing down upon the unwary travelers. The settlers again escaped, but when the danger was over they discovered that Jonathan Jennings's flatboat was missing. It later caught up with the nautical cavalcade.

The flotilla pressed on. In early March they passed the last of the Cherokee towns and were fired on again. By the end of March, nearing the end of their journey, they encountered the often controversial and always infamous Richard Henderson and a party of surveyors. It is doubtful that this was a meeting by happenstance. At any rate, Henderson gave the voyagers useful information and they arrived at the French Lick on April 24, 1780. They climbed the bluffs to reside in the collection of cabins that spawned the city of Nashville.

Out of the original two hundred plus voyagers, at least thirty-three were lost, most killed or captured by Cherokee warriors, though a few may have been drowned. Many others were wounded by Native marksmen.

After the Donelson party arrived, sentinels were on guard twenty-four hours a day for the rest of the long and bloody Cherokee War. Dragging Canoe blockaded the Tennessee River for the entire period of the conflict. Upon sighting any whites attempting to traverse the river, sentinels would send runners to alert the downriver towns. Dragging Canoe's military strategy, called a "Defense in Depth," would go into effect. The further an invading force went down the river, the more and more combined Cherokee war companies they would have to combat. Dragging Canoe is now considered by many historians to be a military genius and his tactics are studied at West Point.

But back to the Donelson invasion. The flotilla was able to get past the Cherokee war towns because at the time Dragging Canoe and the rest of the war leadership had not envisioned that white settlers from upper East Tennessee—who were already sitting on stolen Cherokee land—would consider planting settlements in the Cumberland River Valley. The blockade had not been set up at that time and Donelson was able to get through, although with considerable losses.

After Donelson, Dragging Canoe blockaded the river for the next sixteen years so effectively that no white settler expedition could get through. So fearsome was the defense that with the exception of one foolhardy attempt led by the Brown family in

1788, no settlers even attempted to run the Cherokee gauntlet. The Brown attempt ended with all of that party either killed or captured.

This was a firm blockade by Dragging Canoe and his warriors, so firm that there could be no mass migration of the white colonists who spilled down the Ohio and its tributaries in Shawnee country. Settlers whose destination was Middle Tennessee had either to take the Wilderness Road through the Cumberland Gap and Kentucky or to rendezvous at Southwest Point Blockhouse (now the site of Kingston, Tennessee) for a military guard (also subject to Cherokee attack) to escort them over the wagon road across the Cumberland Plateau to Nashville. Many simply sought regions north of Tennessee.

Dragging Canoe chose the town of Running Water for his headquarters. It was on the south bank of the Tennessee about thirty miles below Chattanooga. The town of Nickajack was a few miles north of Running Water. It was backed by a huge cave, the mouth of which is mostly underwater today. Issuing from the cave is Nickajack Creek. The town spread out in front of the cave. The corn fields beyond were between the cave and the river. Nearby was the ancient village site now called Shellmound. (This writer has been to Nickajack and it is indeed awe inspiring to reflect on the history that took place there.)

Nickajack and Running Water fulfilled all the requirements of military astuteness. To the east, the approach was secured by the rugged promontory of Lookout Mountain and its surrounding elevations. No attacking force could advance from that direction without getting lost in mountainous defiles or becoming subject to deadly ambush, even if a trail to the town was found. To the northwest was the mighty Tennessee River, which had to be crossed before any attack could be mounted. The colonists knew of no shallow place to ford the water near the Cherokee towns, and south of Dragging Canoe's strongholds were his Muscogee Creek allies.

For purposes of a military offensive, the location of the war towns was in close proximity to both the illegal white settlements in upper East Tennessee and the transgressing colonists on the Cumberland. From these impenetrable bases Cherokee warriors, often accompanied by their Creek allies, could march in small war companies or in armies of several hundred to two thousand to scourge the white frontier. The objective of Dragging Canoe was to pursue this war until the original boundaries of the Nation that predated the Revolutionary War had been reestablished.

Under the purported Treaty of Sycamore Shoals, which the colonists claimed as the legal foundation for their incursion, all white settlements on the south side of the Cumberland were prohibited. Yet the first settlement the Robertson-Donelson party founded was on the south side of the river. As soon as Dragging Canoe concluded that the Cumberland colonists were planning to make a foothold in Middle Tennessee he determined to wipe them out before they became stronger with the accretions of other land-greedy white settlers. He bitterly remembered what had happened in upper East Tennessee.

This was changing the lives of Native people to an extent never seen before.

On April 2, 1781, a huge Cherokee war force of over one thousand warriors attacked the main fort, later known as Fort Nashborough, in the Battle of the Bluffs. The fort sustained heavy losses and by some accounts came close to being wiped out. In fact, the colonists were so shocked by the number of warriors attacking the settlement that many considered abandoning the area altogether. Word got around among the colonies that the Cumberland was not the place to go. Many whites were simply afraid to venture to the region because of the reputation of the Cherokee war companies and the battles that Dragging Canoe fought to stop the settlement of Nashville.

The epilogue of the voyage of the *Adventure* was relentless warfare conducted by the Cherokee war companies against the invading settlers. The strategy of Dragging Canoe, to destroy the Cumberland settlements, was one of attrition, with constant sorties by small groups of warriors to inflict casualties, terrify the invaders, and break their morale. Many survivors were left to consider abandoning the region for some place safer. Once weakened, a decisive blow could be delivered, completely destroying the illegal settlements.

But it must be remembered that the Cherokee Nation was still fighting settlers pouring over tribal boundaries in East Tennessee; hence, warrior power was limited. Addressing the wider matter of demographics, the hundred-year period covering 1600 to 1700 saw a veritable population collapse of many Indigenous nations east of the Mississippi. It is estimated by many authorities that the Native population of what is now the United States was over 60 million in pre-Columbian times. Between 1600 and 1700 it is estimated that 95 percent of the Native population east of the Mississippi went extinct primarily because of European diseases—measles, influenza, cholera, scarlet fever, and even the common cold were fatal, with smallpox being the most deadly. These diseases advanced far beyond the footfalls of European explorers and settlers because the Indigenous peoples had vast trading networks that transmitted the maladies from nation to nation. Native nations who traded with Europeans passed these infectious diseases to other Indigenous peoples, wiping out entire populations who had never even seen a white man. The mortality in many instances was 100 percent. Entire towns and villages had no survivors. By the year 1700, only 5 percent of the Indigenous population was left from what existed one hundred years before. The demographics changed rapidly and radically, resulting in a change in the balance of power, one that was to have severe consequences for the Indigenous peoples.

The hundred-year period from 1700 to 1800 was filled with so much conflict and bloody turmoil that many historians have called it a hundred years of war for Indigenous nations east of the Mississippi. But it was also transformative in a material sense because of the trade goods being brought from an industrialized Europe. This was changing the lives of Native people to an extent never seen before. Some tribal leaders envisioned an ongoing trading relationship and an absence of conflict between Native people and the newcomers.

Further, during times of peace between the Indigenous nations and the colonial government and its citizens in the eighteenth century, Native people were everywhere in colonial America—on the streets of the villages, towns, and cities. Native people would visit to do shopping; they came in diplomatic delegations; they came as tourists. Many Nations were allies and commercial partners of various European nations at times during this tumultuous time. For example, the Cherokee Nation was allied with Great Britain for most of the century.

But notwithstanding a change in the material life of the nations, the trade goods system was also fraught with territorial jeopardy. To begin with, most of the fur-bearing animals in Europe had been hunted out of existence by this time. European traders and settlers wanted to trade the manufactured goods of an industrialized Europe for the furs that could be provided by Native hunters. These new conveniences were much in demand by Native families. But this engendered intertribal conflict. When the fur-bearing animals of one region had been overhunted for trade goods, tribal hunters would have to look to the territory of another tribe for hunting.

This was in part the economic and demographic context of the late eighteenth century for all of Indian country east of the Mississippi. But because of the drastic change in demographics, the Cherokee Nation had considerably fewer warriors to muster than one hundred years earlier. Nonetheless, the Cherokee War continued unabated with Dragging Canoe fighting the colonists to a standstill. He kept in communication with the British in Detroit through diplomatic missions conducted by his brothers Little Owl and the Badger. Munitions were supplied by the Spanish in Florida. Dragging Canoe had a strong military alliance with the northern nations, in particular the Shawnees, who were also involved in a life-and-death struggle for survival. In the South he worked tirelessly to bring all of the other nations—the Chickasaws and the Choctaws—into an intertribal confederacy to resist American expansion.

The Muscogee Creek Nation, led by their powerful chief Alexander McGillivray and supported by the trading firm of Panton and Leslie at Pensacola, stood firm in their support of Cherokee efforts to stop the settlement of the Cumberland River region and to reclaim upper East Tennessee. The trading firm was in Spanish-controlled Florida, but Spanish interests in Florida and Louisiana coincided with Cherokee objectives in that the Spanish policy was to maintain an Indian buffer zone to stop American expansion into the lower Mississippi Valley. Hence, the Spanish were more than happy to furnish arms to the Cherokees to continue to fight the settlers.

The epilogue to this period in the history of Nashville must include the passing of the indomitable Dragging Canoe on March 1, 1792. Historical speculation is that had he lived there would have been no Nashville. Taking his place was the subordinate war chief John Watts (his English name). Although brilliant and visionary, Watts was no Dragging Canoe.

Watts followed the strategy of attrition developed by Dragging Canoe until the Cumberland settlers were weakened sufficiently for a decisive death blow. He led a tribal force of several hundred warriors composed in the majority of Cherokees (with a smaller component of Creeks and Shawnees) in the fall of 1792. They were defeated at the Battle of Buchanan's Station on September 30, due to a combination of unfortunate circumstances. They were unable to take the fortification, which was manned by the settlers shooting from behind stockade walls.

The original plan was to attack the main fort and then wipe out the smaller settlements. At that time the colonists did not live inside the fort itself, but in scattered homesteads. They only sought refuge inside the stockade in times of real or perceived danger. Hence, it would have been relatively easy to decimate the vicinity of present-day Nashville and later attack the smaller stockades. But a disagreement arose between Watts and other war leaders on where to strike first, and he conceded to a plan to take Buchanan's Station on the way to Nashville. Clearly, this was an error in military judgment. It would not have happened had Dragging Canoe been alive. There would have been no Nashville.

This was the last major battle between Cherokees and whites before peace was declared at the Treaty of Tellico Blockhouse in November of 1794. Even after the Treaty of Tellico Blockhouse there was still some desultory warfare for a short period of time, carried on by small, scattered war parties of Cherokees and Creeks, but for all practical purposes the long and bloody Cherokee-American War was at an end.

As for John Donelson, the leader of the flotilla and commander of the *Adventure* had been killed by Cherokees ten years earlier, in Kentucky in 1785.

NOTE

1. All quotes in this essay come from John P. Brown, *Old Frontiers: The Story of the Cherokee Indians from Earliest Times to the Date of Their Removal to the West, 1838–1938* (Kingsport, TN: Southern Publishers, 1938).

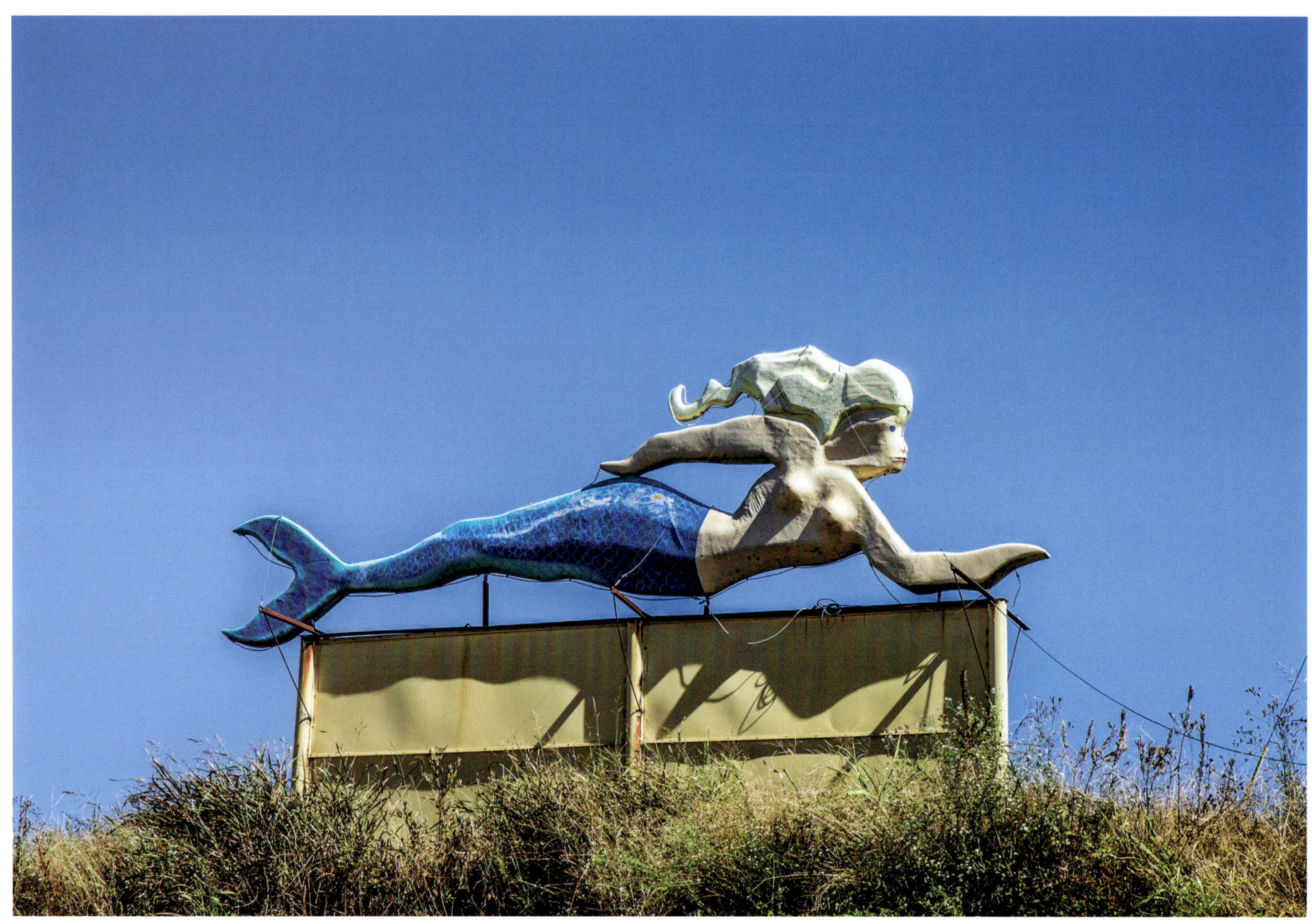

TENNESSEE RIVER, DECATUR COUNTY, OCTOBER 11. Billboard for the Mermaid Marina.

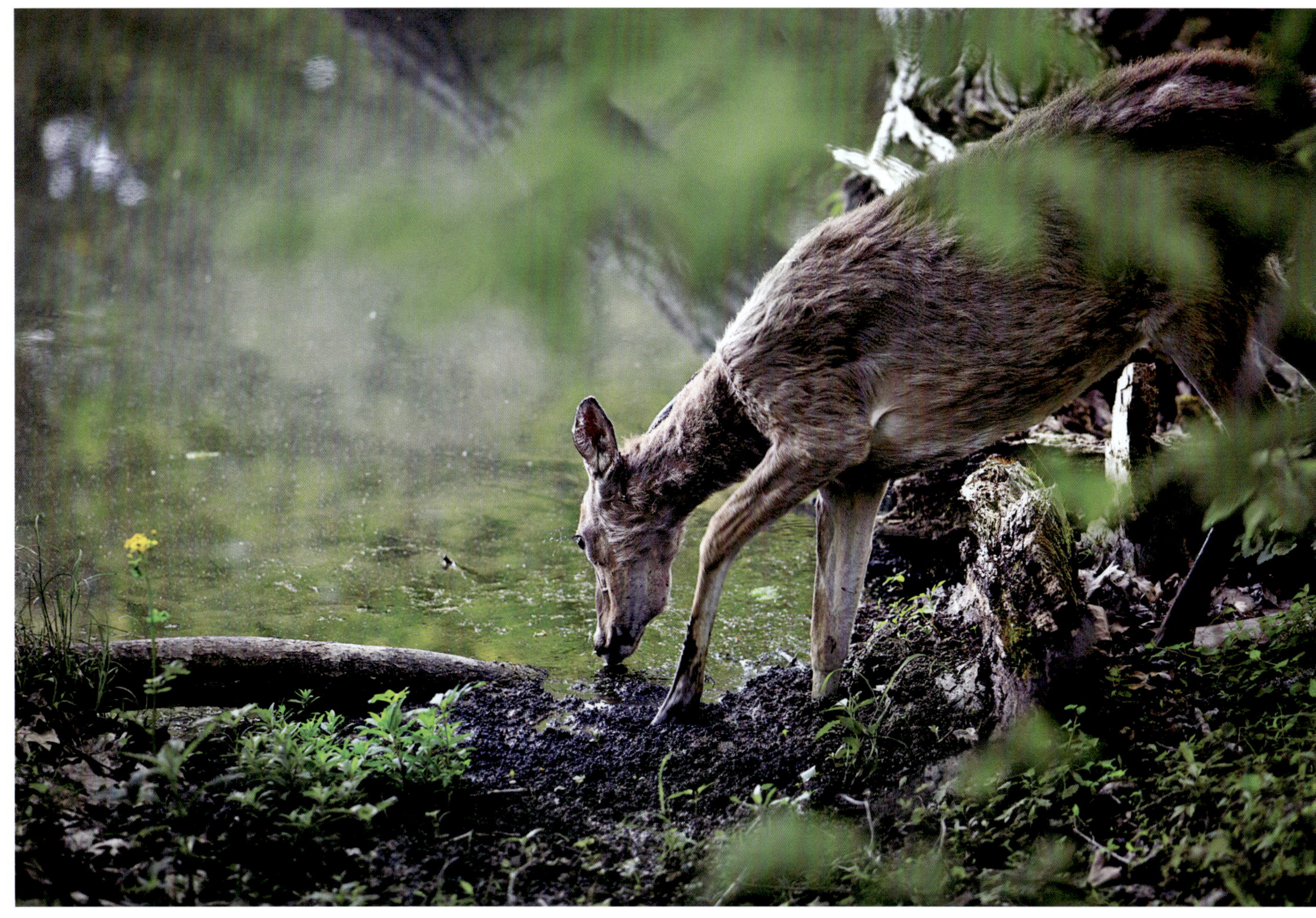

Deer at water's edge. After over seventeen years of traveling the waterways and quietly observing nature, I have come to learn that many of the woodland creatures express emotions similar to ours.

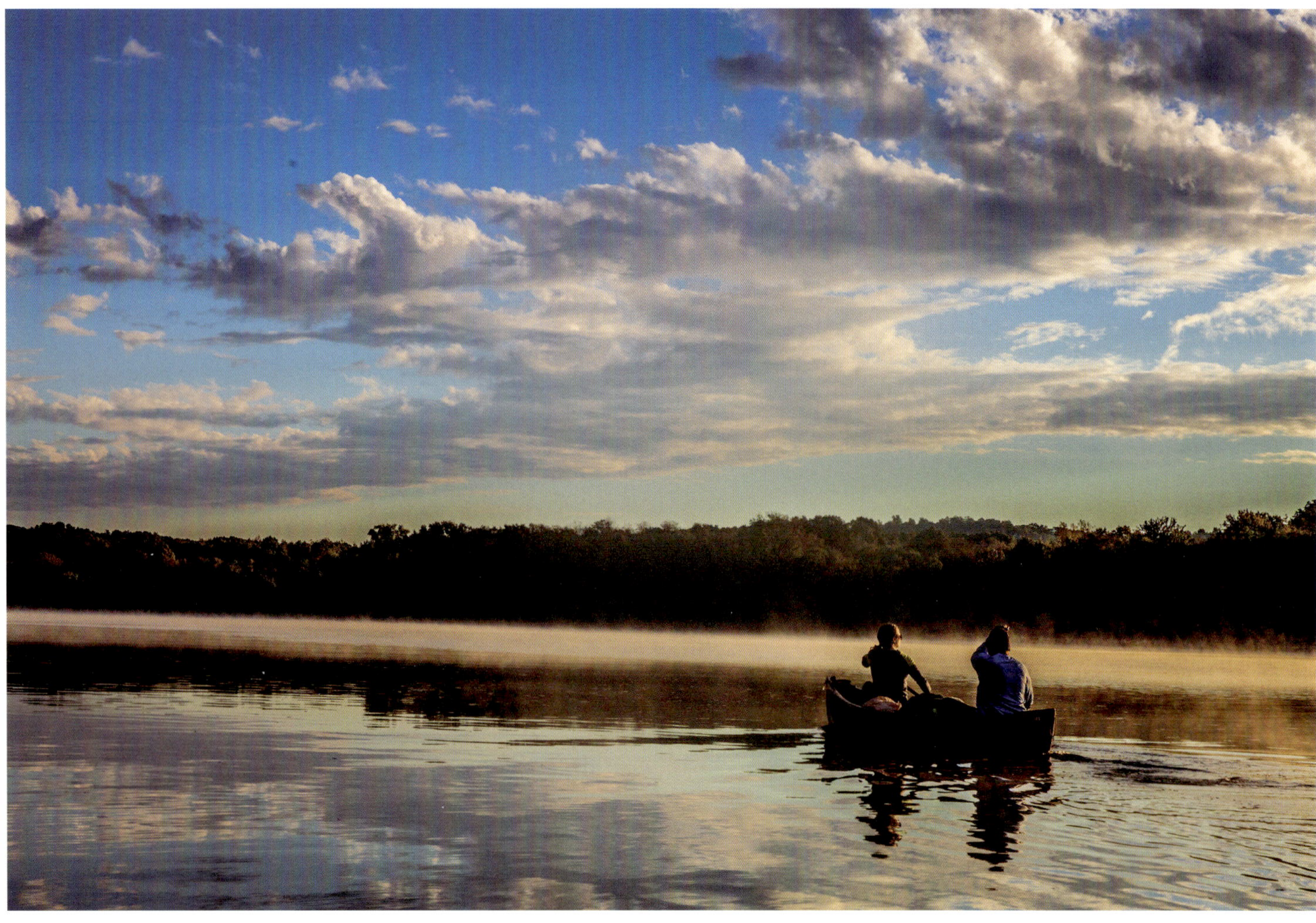

TENNESSEE RIVER, PERRYVILLE, TENNESSEE, OCTOBER 12. Jessica Bliss and George Walker from the *Tennessean* newspaper came up to spend a night with me on the banks of the river.

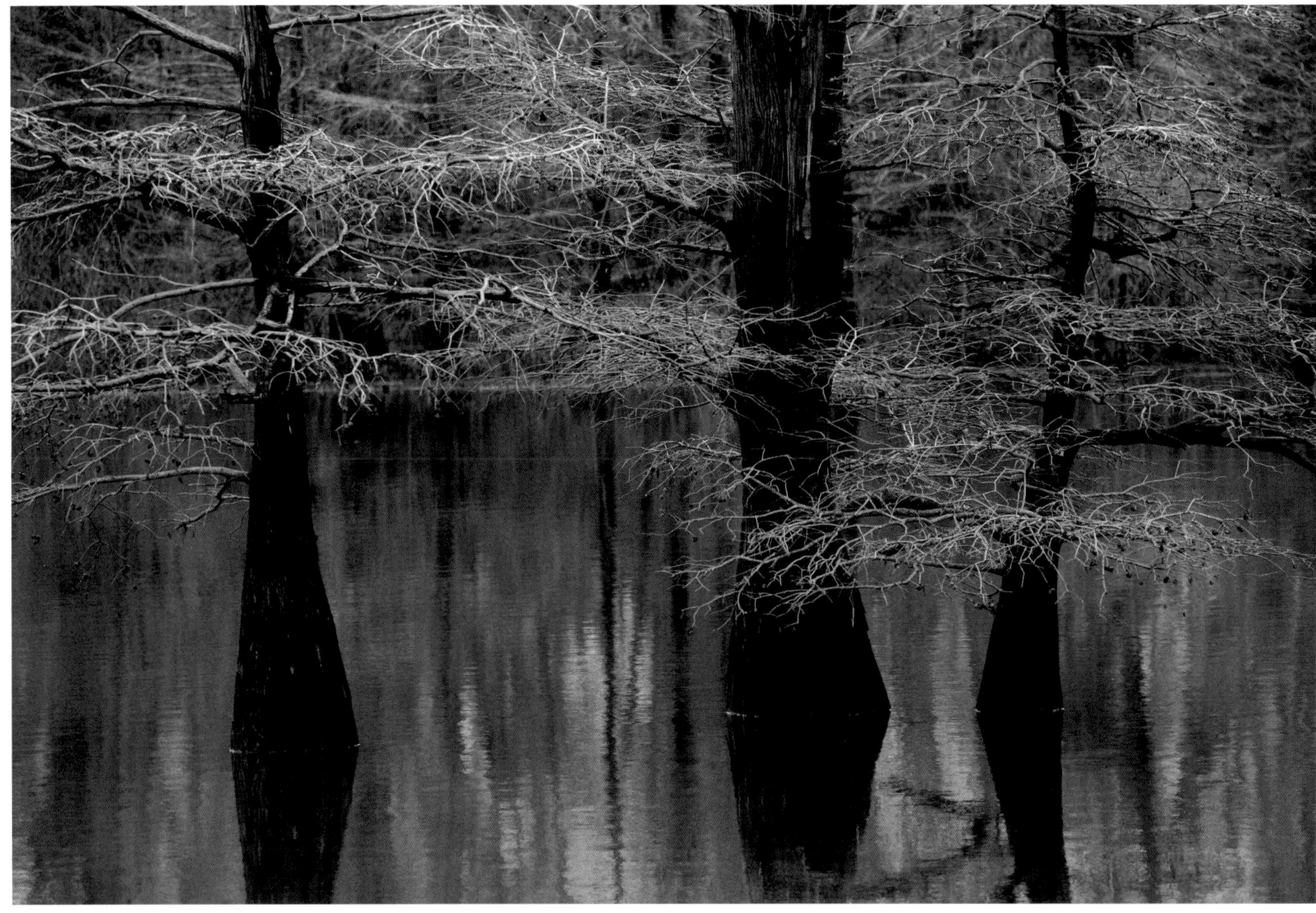

DUCK RIVER LANDSCAPE. The Duck River has been named one the most biologically diverse rivers in the United States. A river worthy of protection.

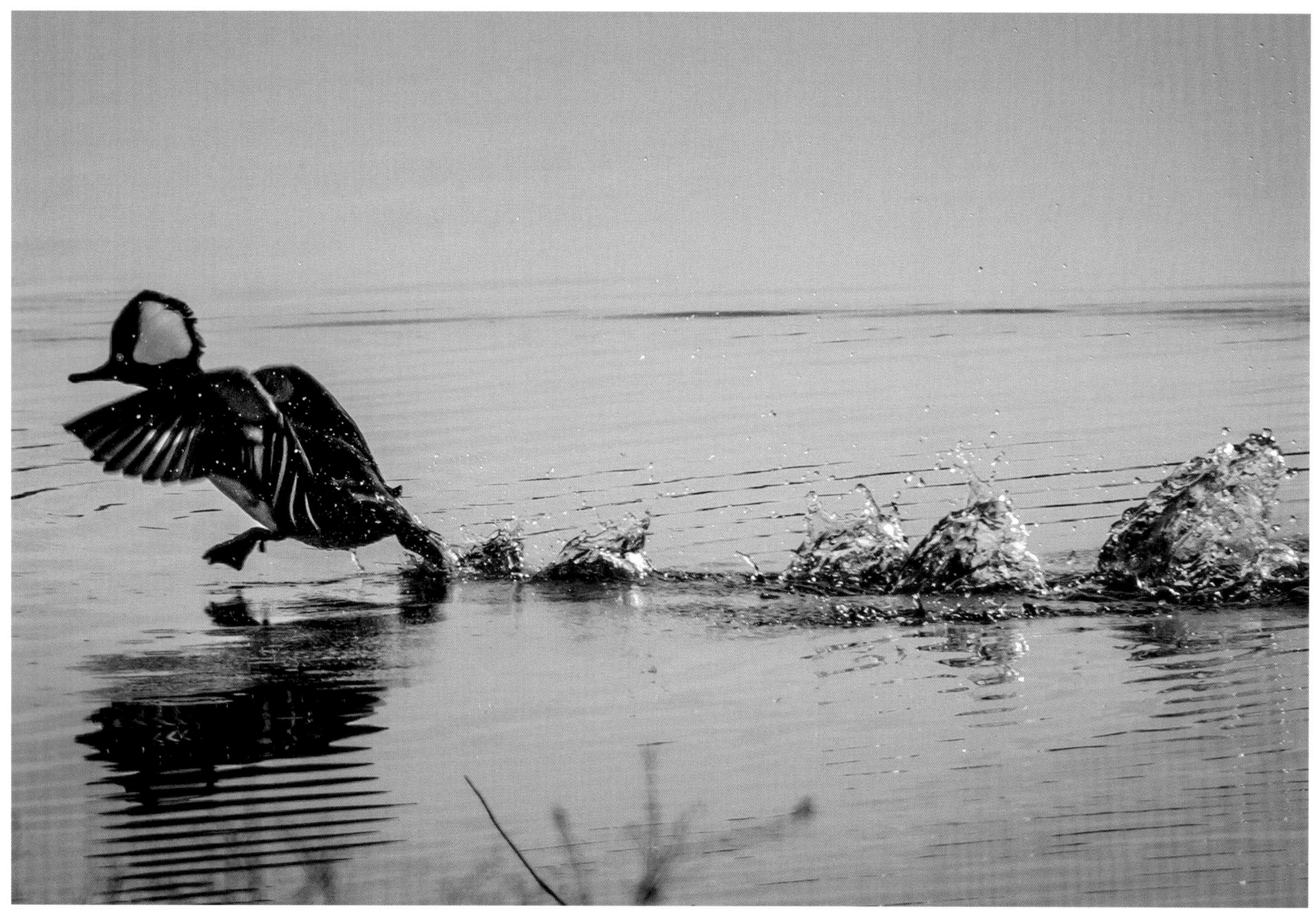

TENNESSEE AND DUCK RIVER CONFLUENCE. Hooded Merganser taking off.

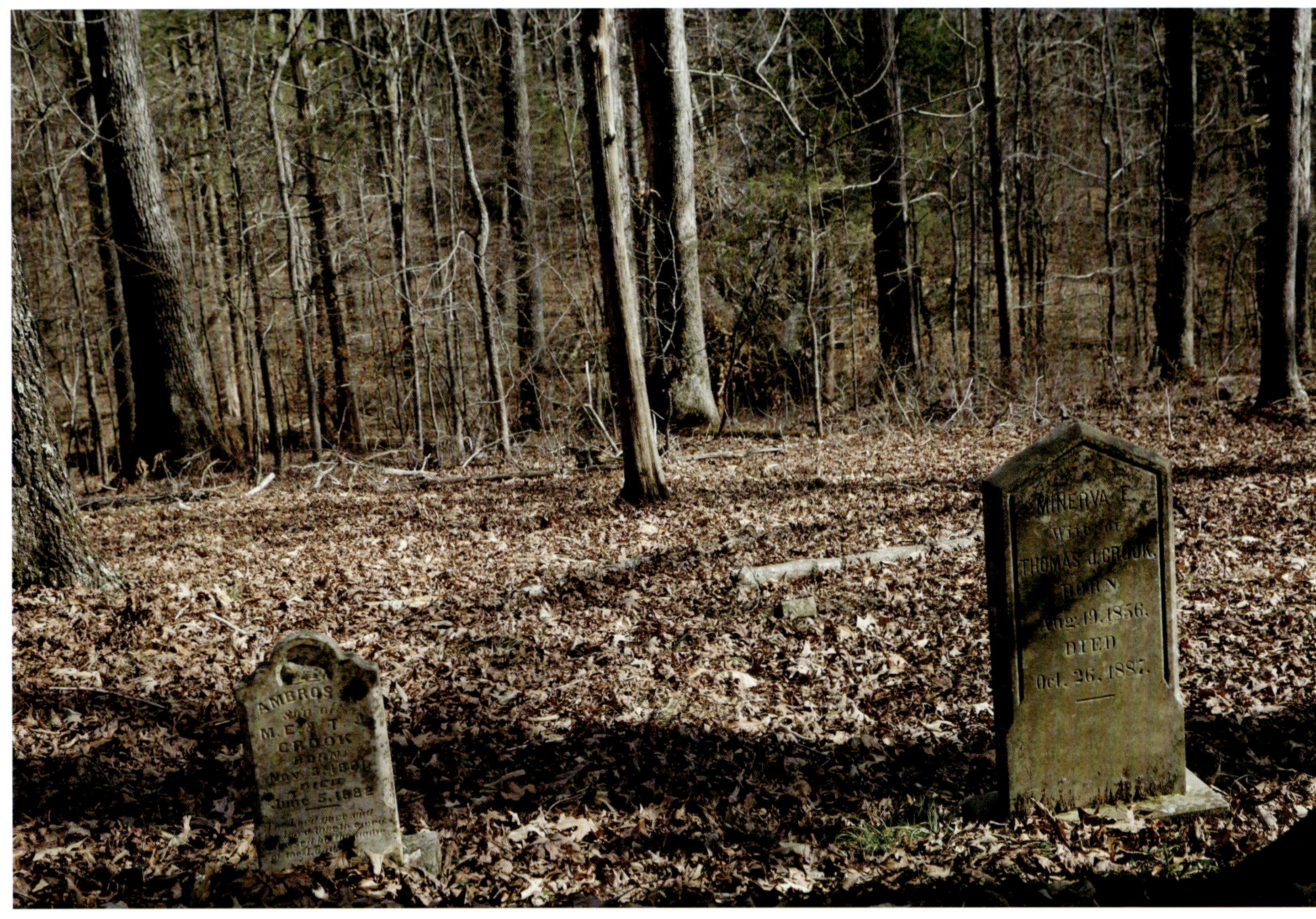

TENNESSEE RIVER. Old homestead family plots annexed by the TVA, now part of the Land Between the Lakes national recreation area. At one time the threat of malaria around the impounded river was so bad that the government forbade any occupation of the land within a mile of the banks.

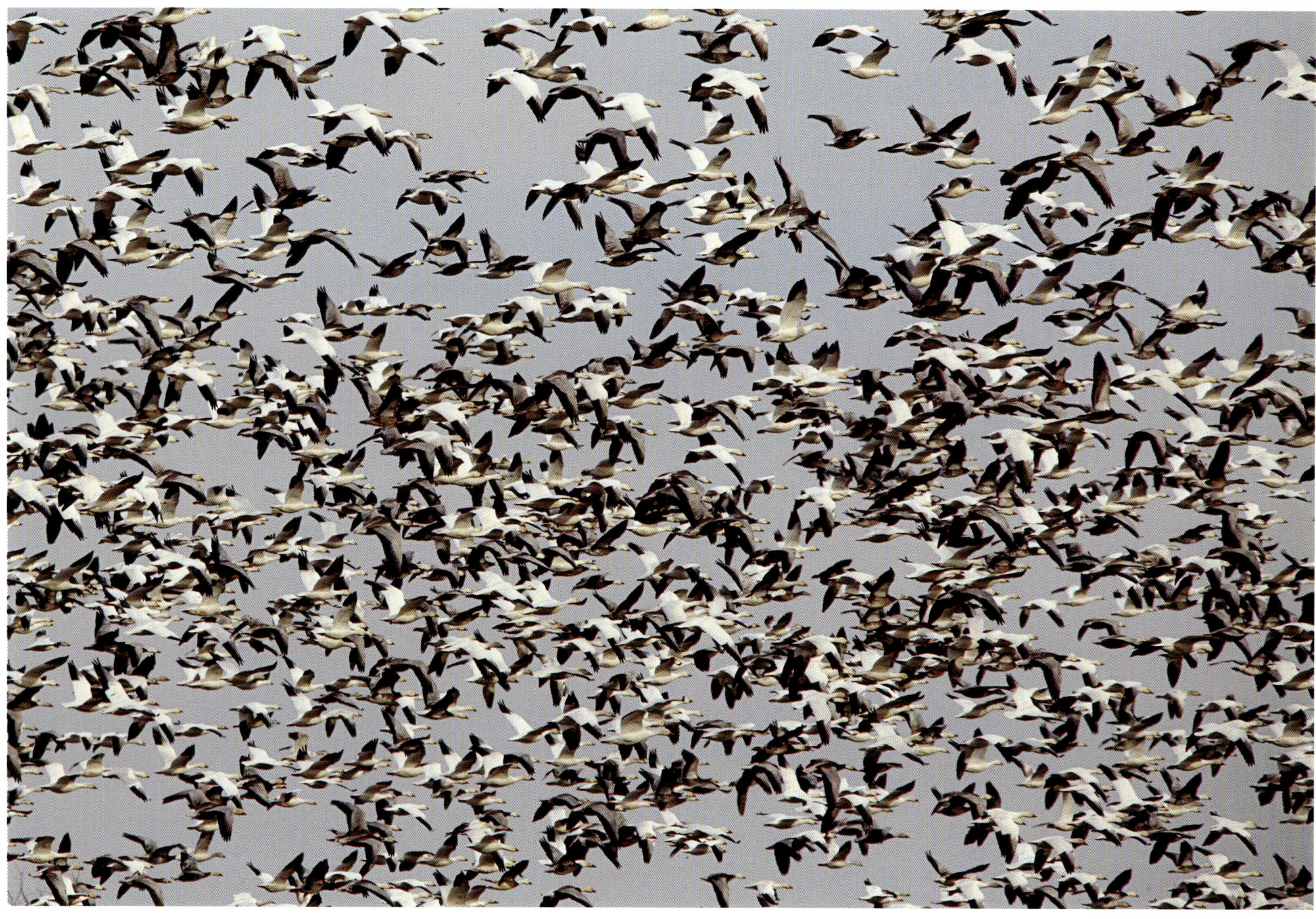

TENNESSEE RIVER NEAR THE DUCK RIVER. Goose migration.

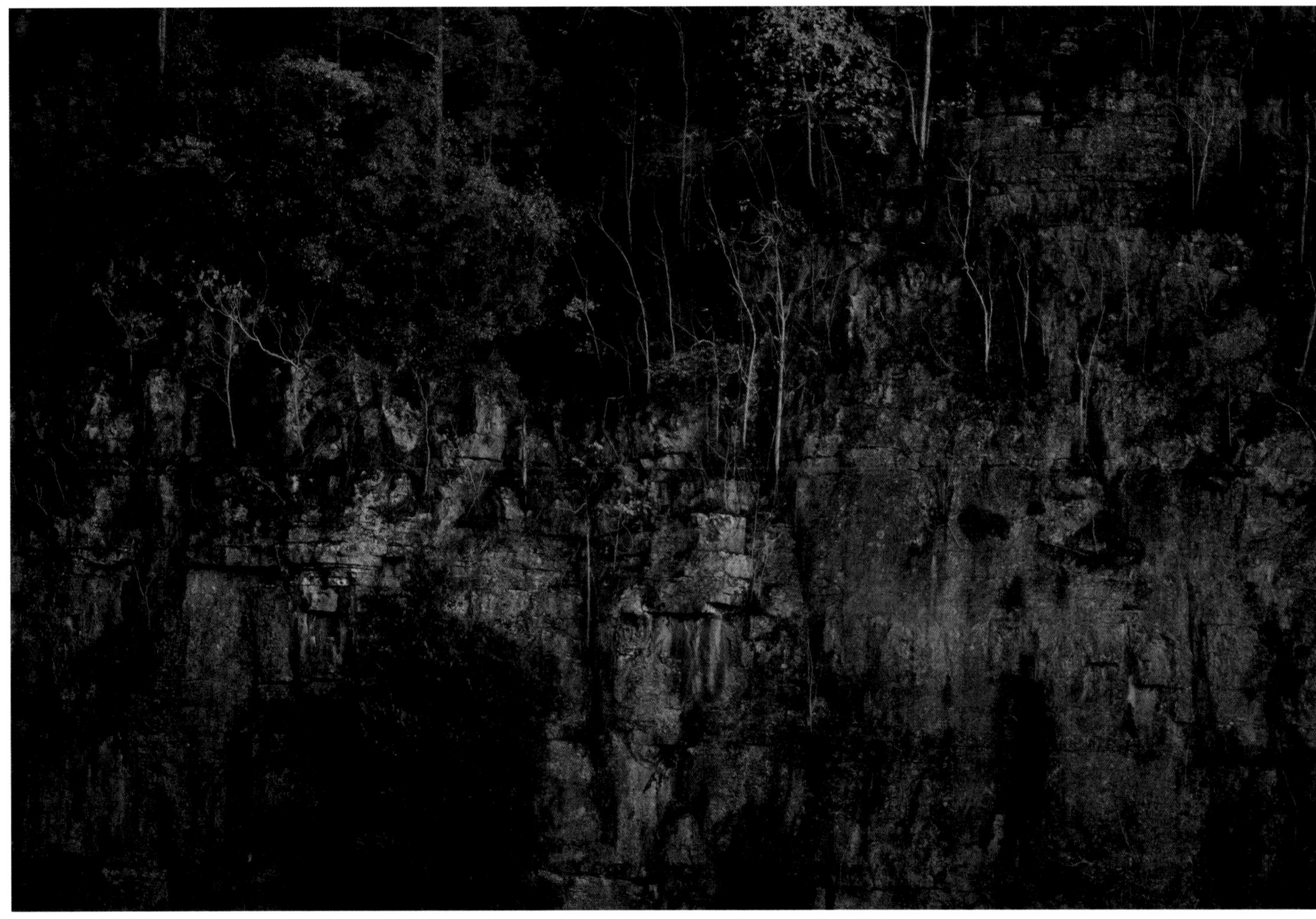

TENNESSEE RIVER. Fortress-like cliffs define the landscape. Soon the Ohio would be in reach. The Donelson party was running out of food and starvation was a concern. Plus they had no idea how they were going to wrestle the heavy flatboats up the wild currents of the powerful river. Many of the party opted to head south to farm along the Illinois or venture down the Mississippi to Natchez.

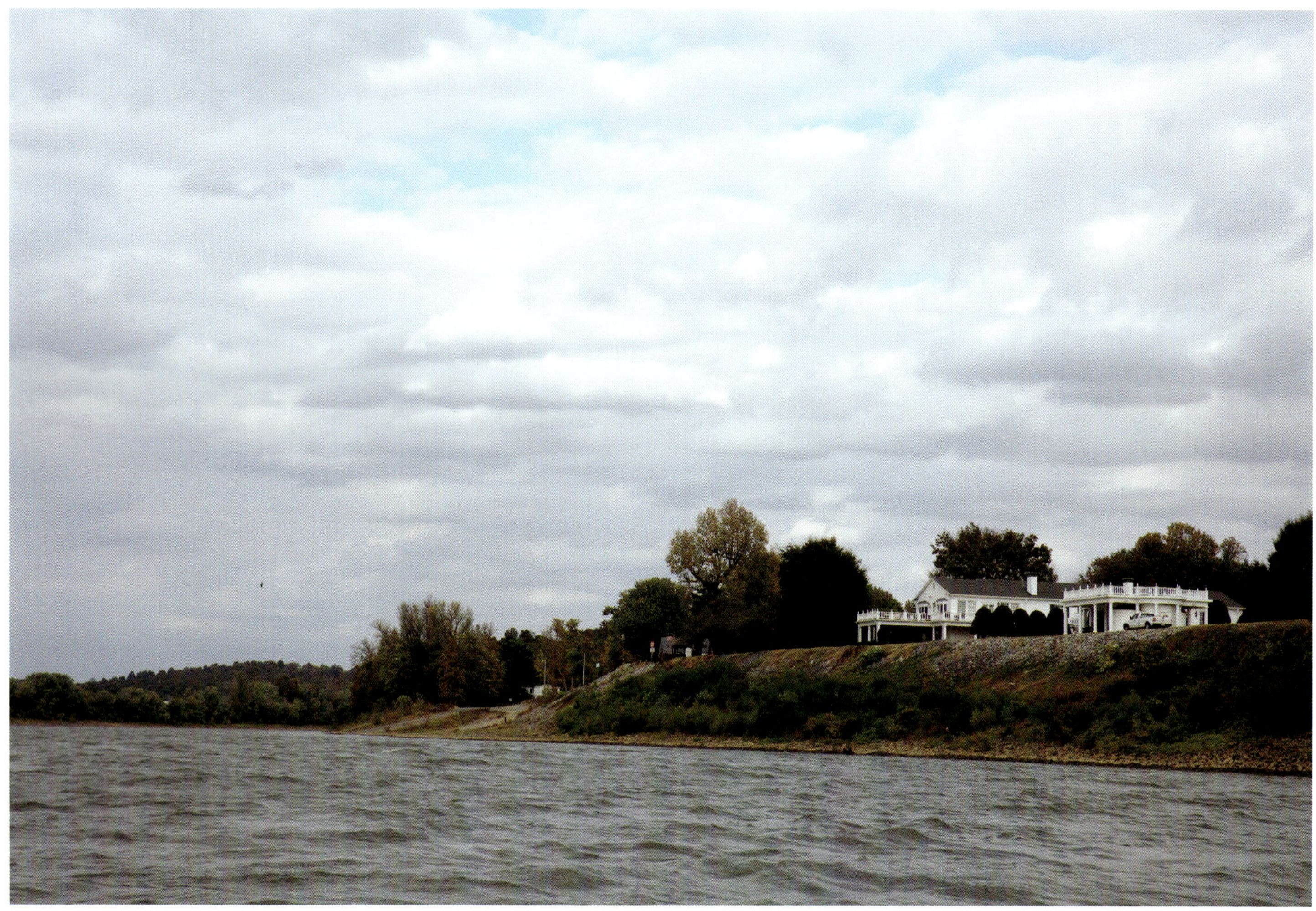

OHIO RIVER, SMITHLAND, KENTUCKY, OCTOBER 18. First view of the mouth of the Cumberland River. It took five days for the Donelson flotilla to make the twelve-mile passage up the Ohio. When they came to the confluence of the Cumberland, the river seemed so small they were unsure if it was the right one.

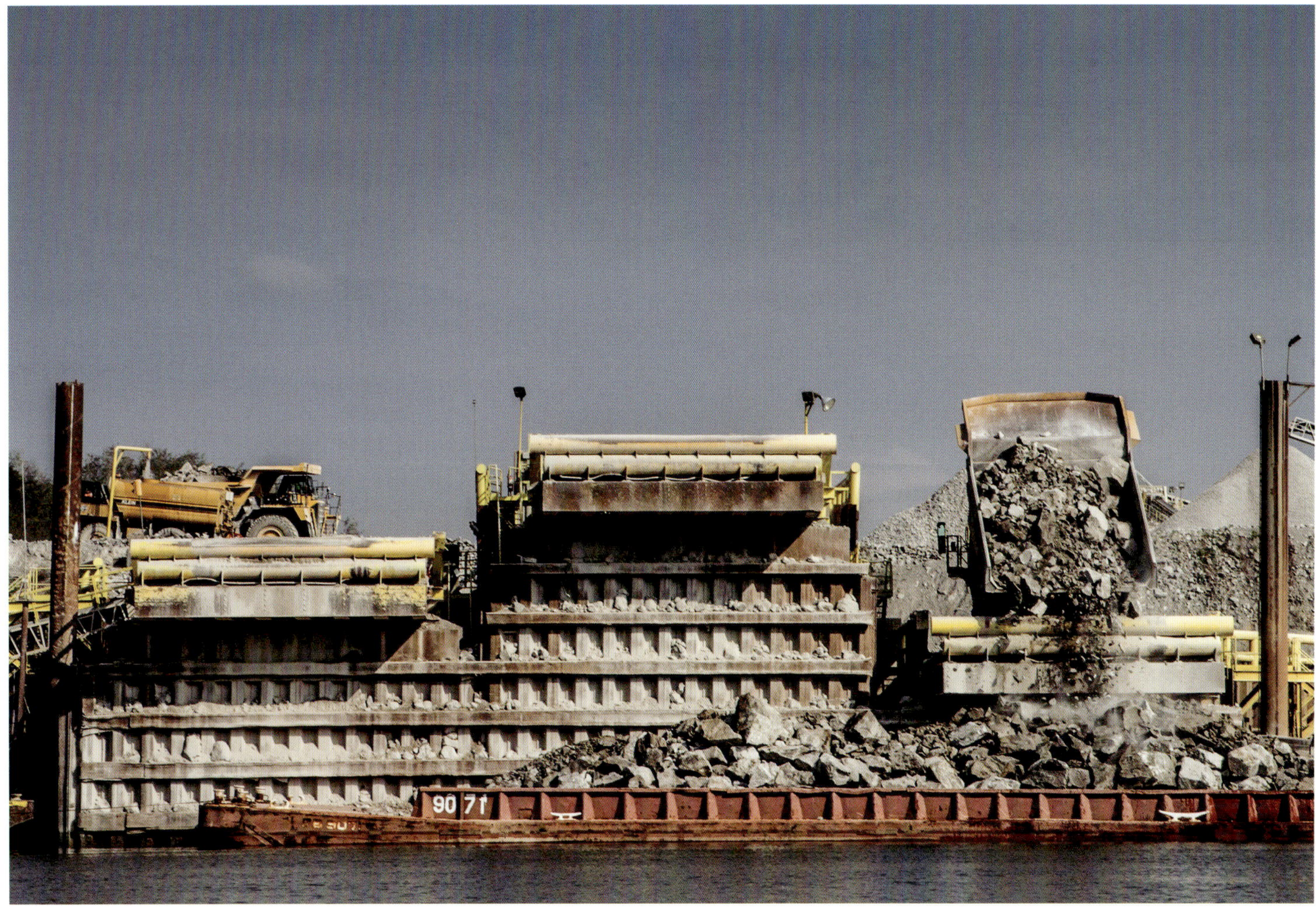

CUMBERLAND RIVER, SMITHLAND, KENTUCKY, OCTOBER 19. Large quarry operation along the river. Barges are an inexpensive way to ship bulk materials. One barge holds the same amount as eighty semitrailers or thirty-five railroad cars.

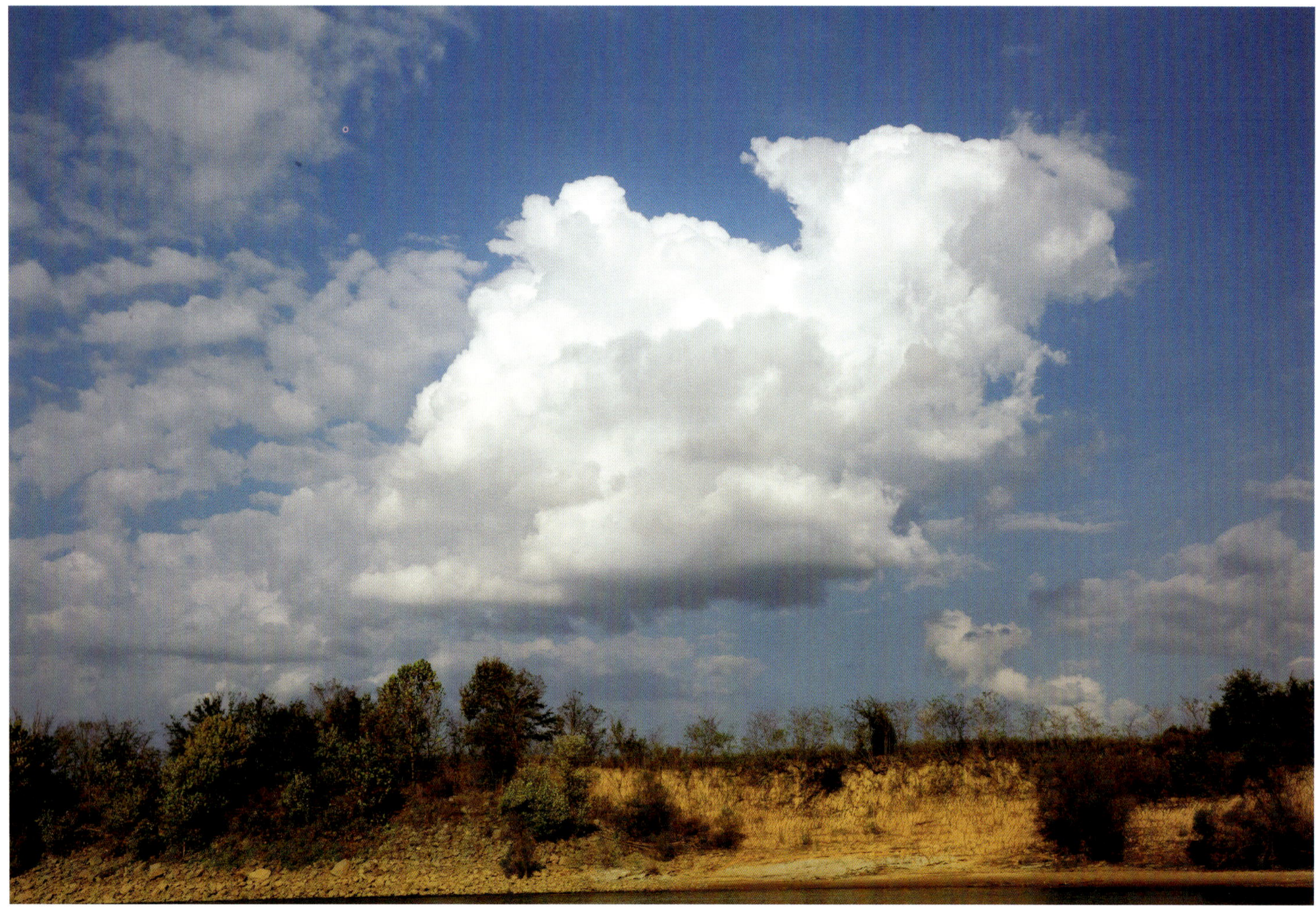

CUMBERLAND RIVER, DYERSBURG, TENNESSEE, OCTOBER 19. Lower Cumberland River landscape. Most likely one of the few parts of the river unchanged since Donelson passed by. The current on the Cumberland wasn't so strong and Donelson's flatboat even had a sail, which he raised to capture the winds blowing from the southwest.

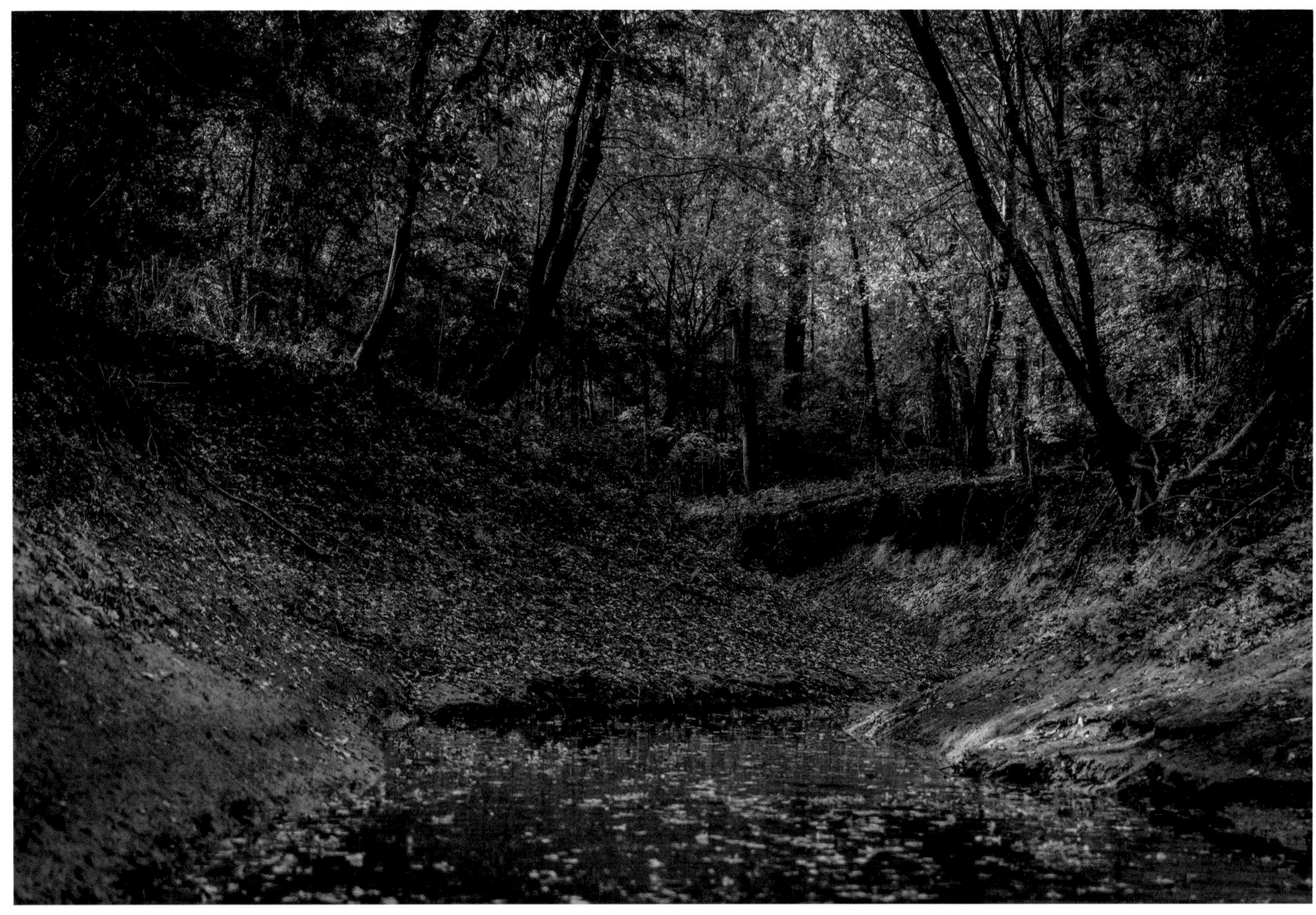

CUMBERLAND RIVER. Little coves continually line the rivers begging for exploration. If only time on earth were infinite!

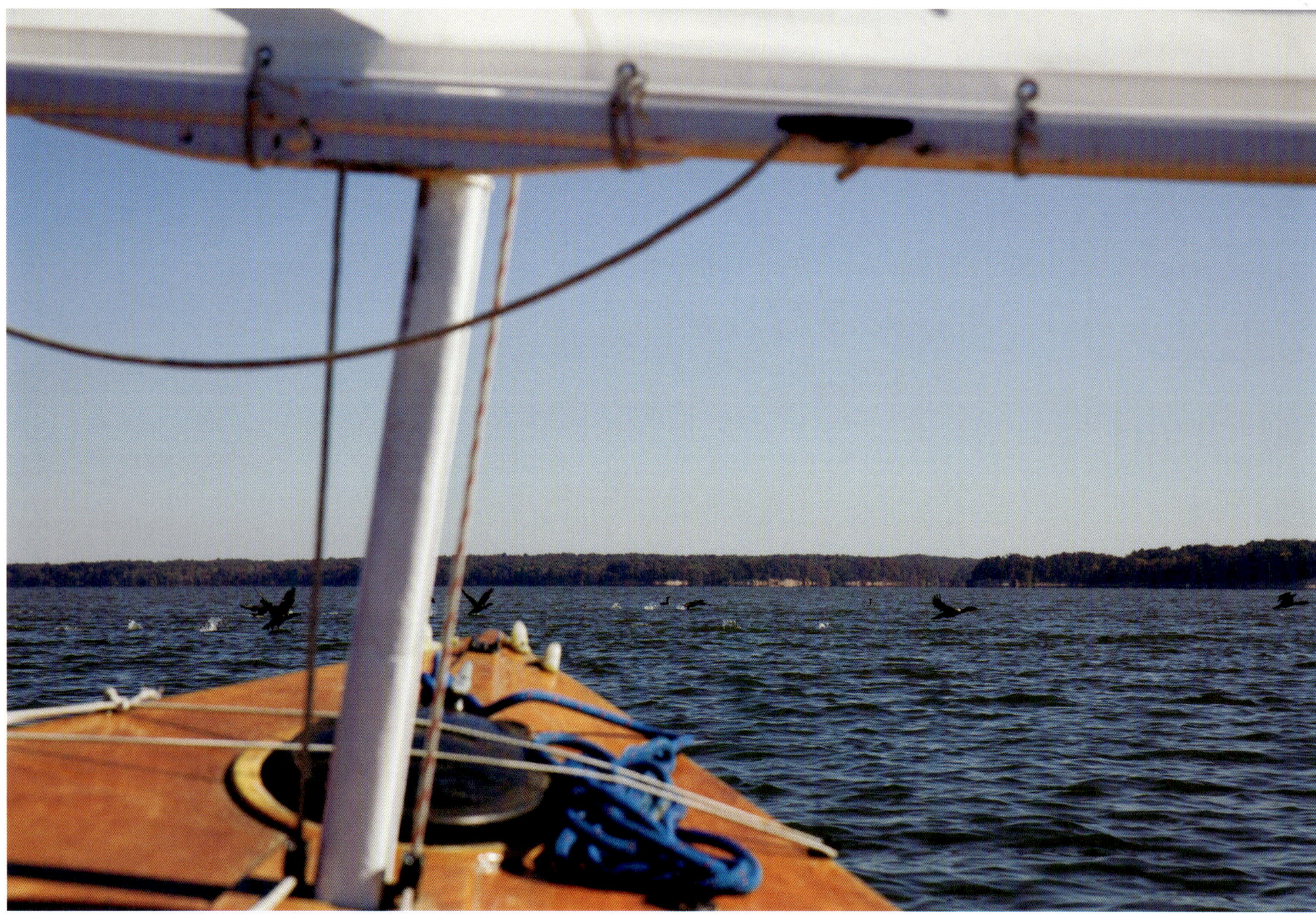

CUMBERLAND RIVER, LAKE BARKLEY, OCTOBER 22. Chasing the coots across the wide expanse of the lake.

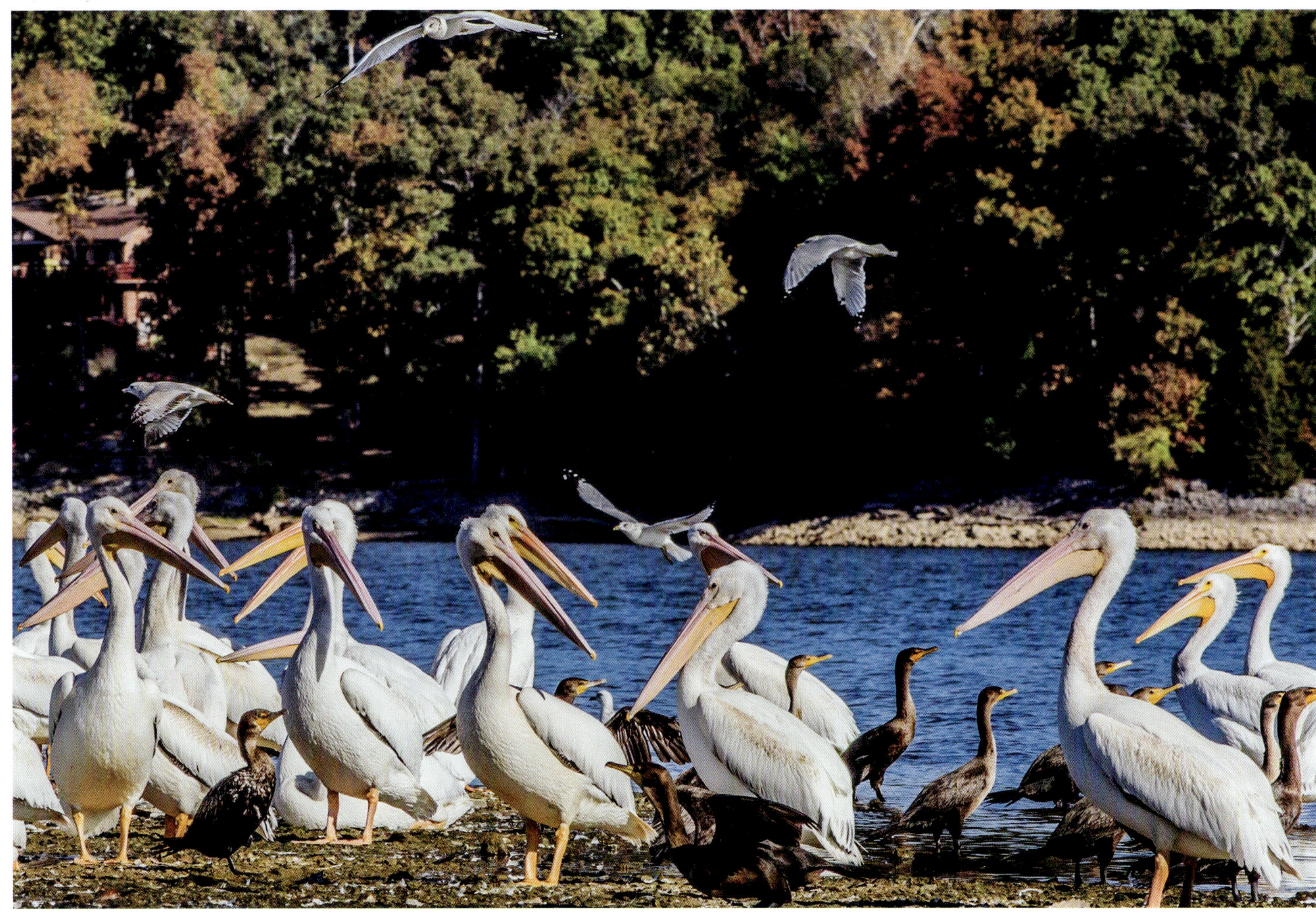

CUMBERLAND RIVER, LAKE BARKLEY, OCTOBER 23. White pelicans placidly line the shoals, unfazed by my presence.

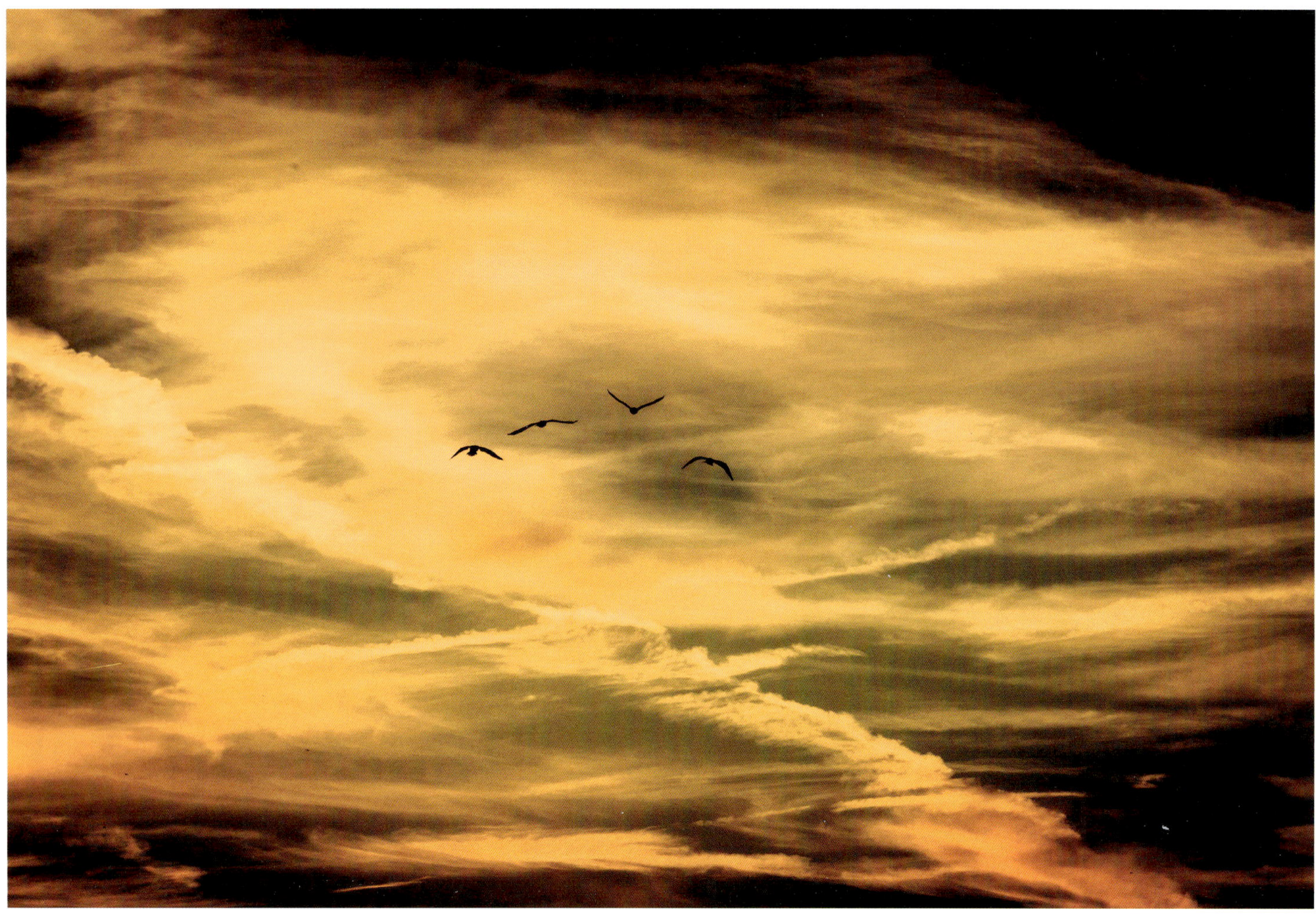

CUMBERLAND RIVER, LAKE BARKLEY, OCTOBER 23. Migrating birds continually fill the evening sky with their silhouettes.

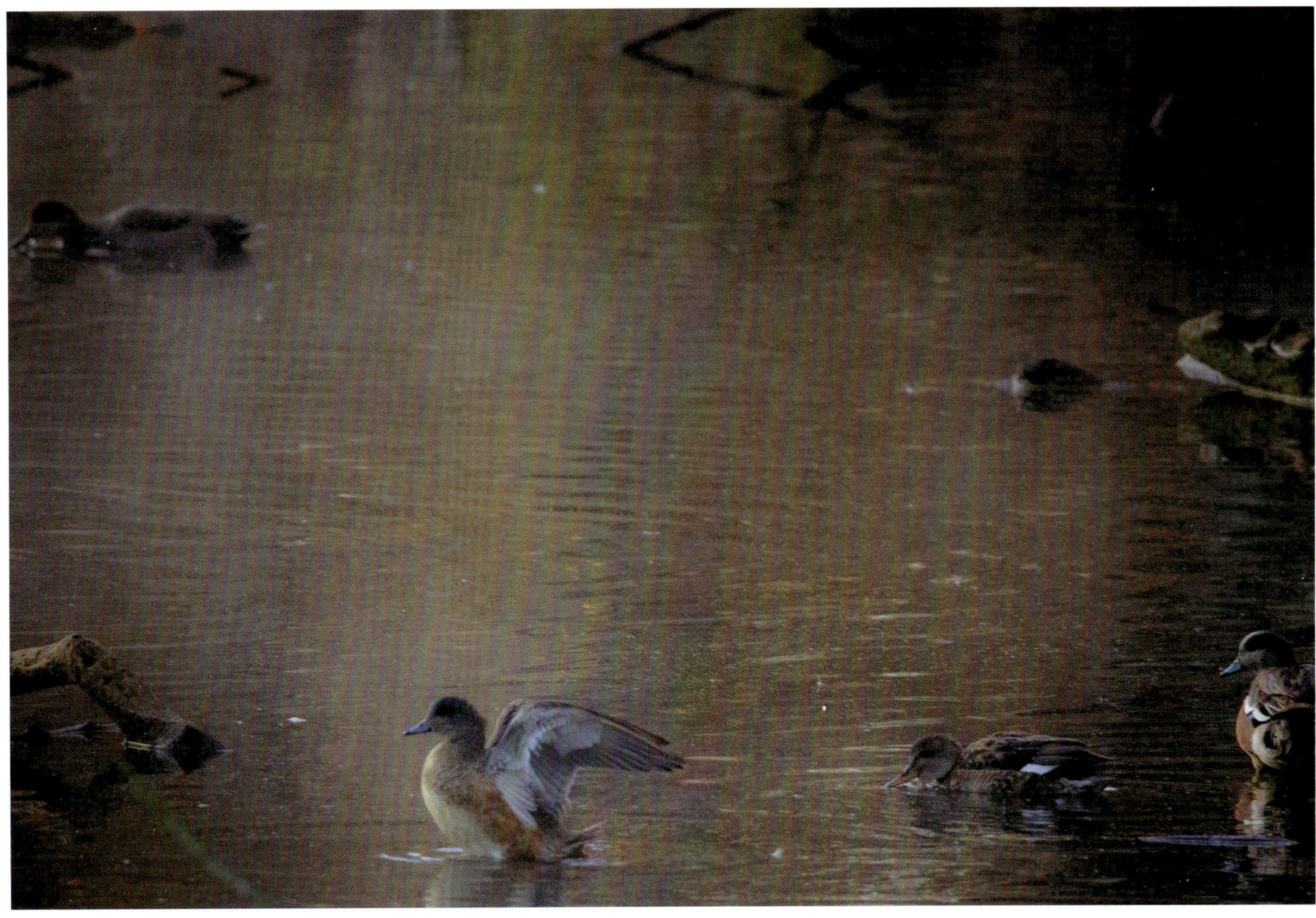

CUMBERLAND RIVER. Waterfowl enjoying the calm of the morning in the backwater bays.

CUMBERLAND RIVER. Stumps and driftwood line the river.

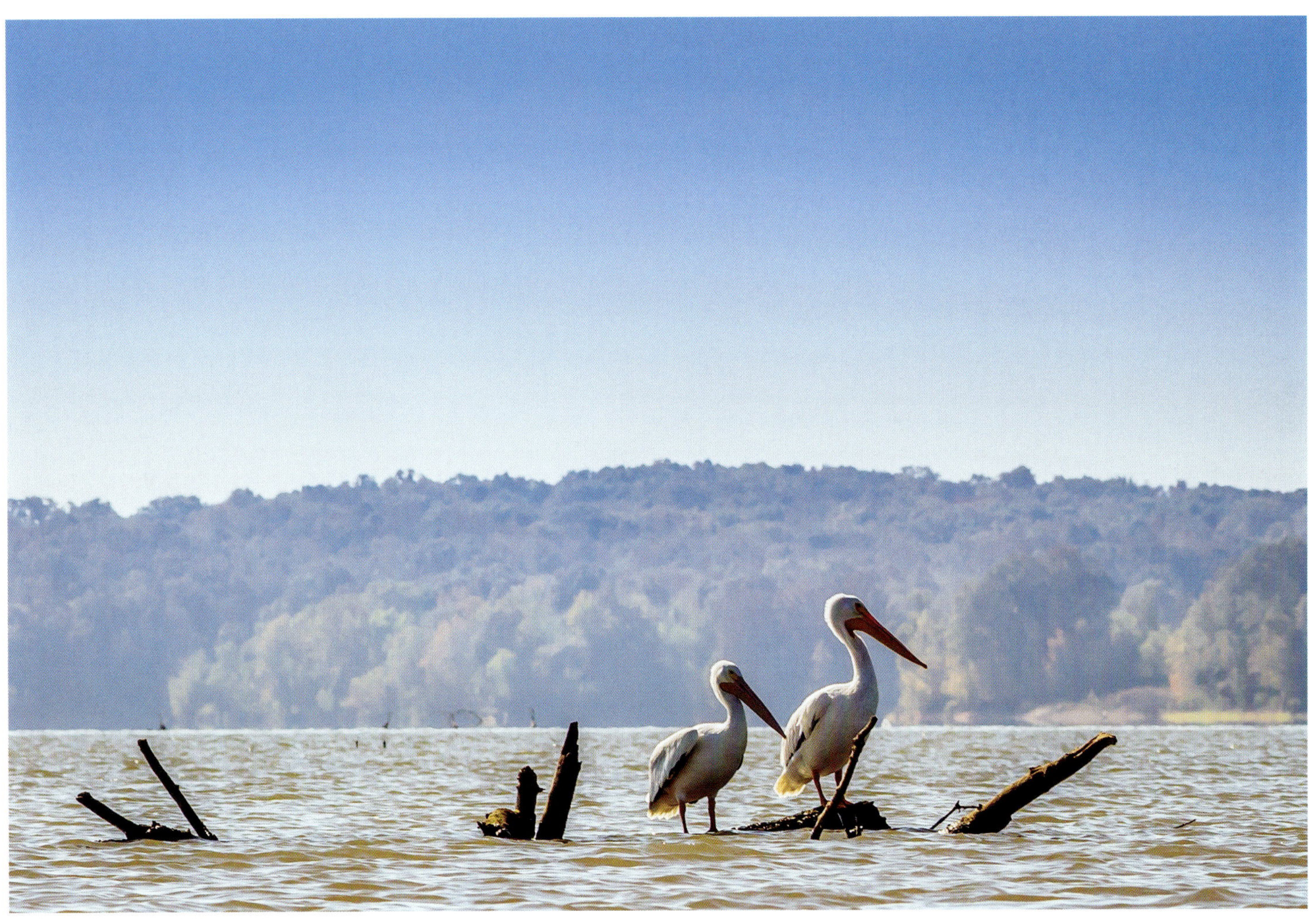

CUMBERLAND RIVER, LAKE BARKLEY, OCTOBER 24. White pelicans sunning in the shallows of the lake.

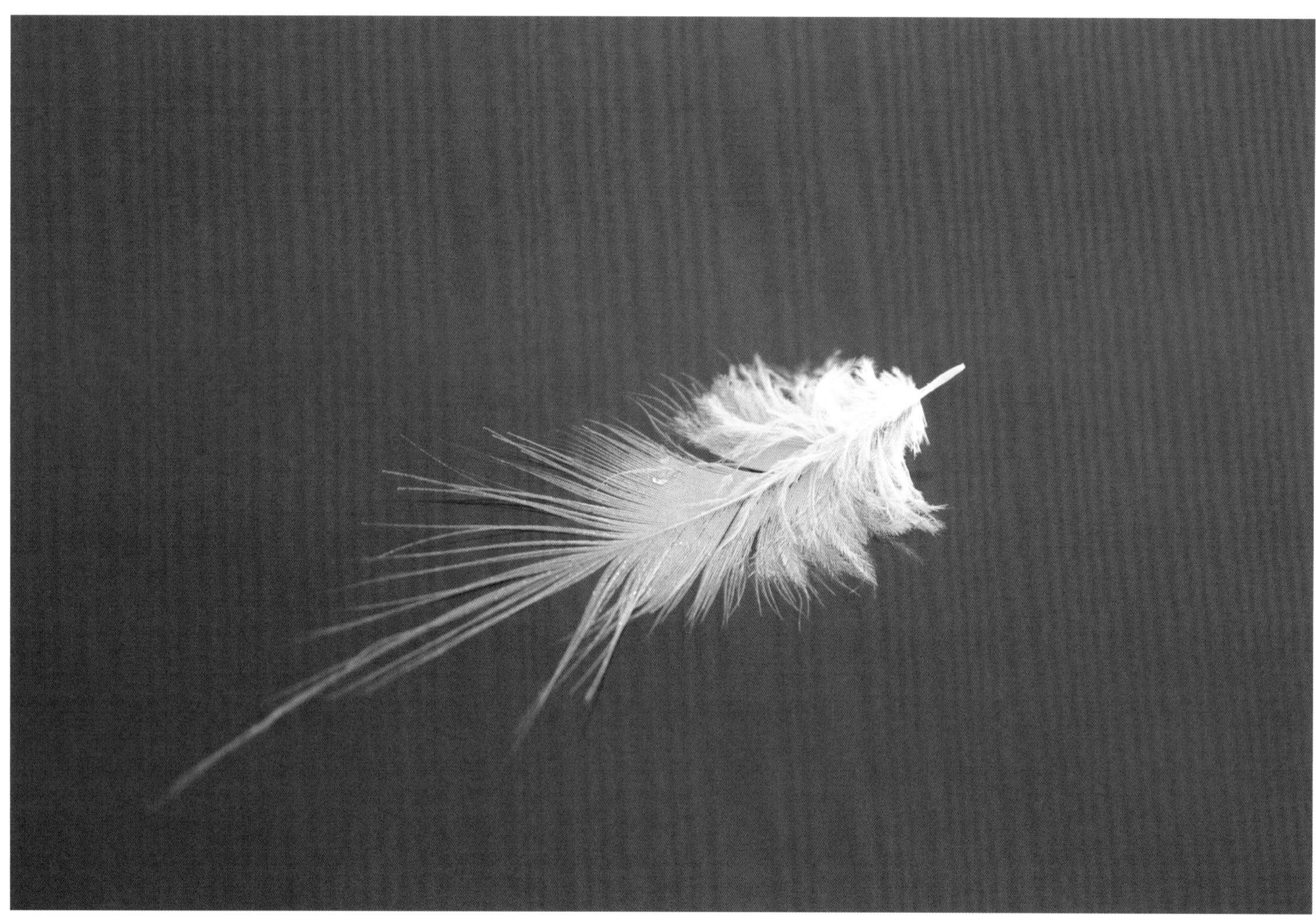

CUMBERLAND RIVER, LAKE BARKLEY, OCTOBER 25. Lone feather adrift on the water.

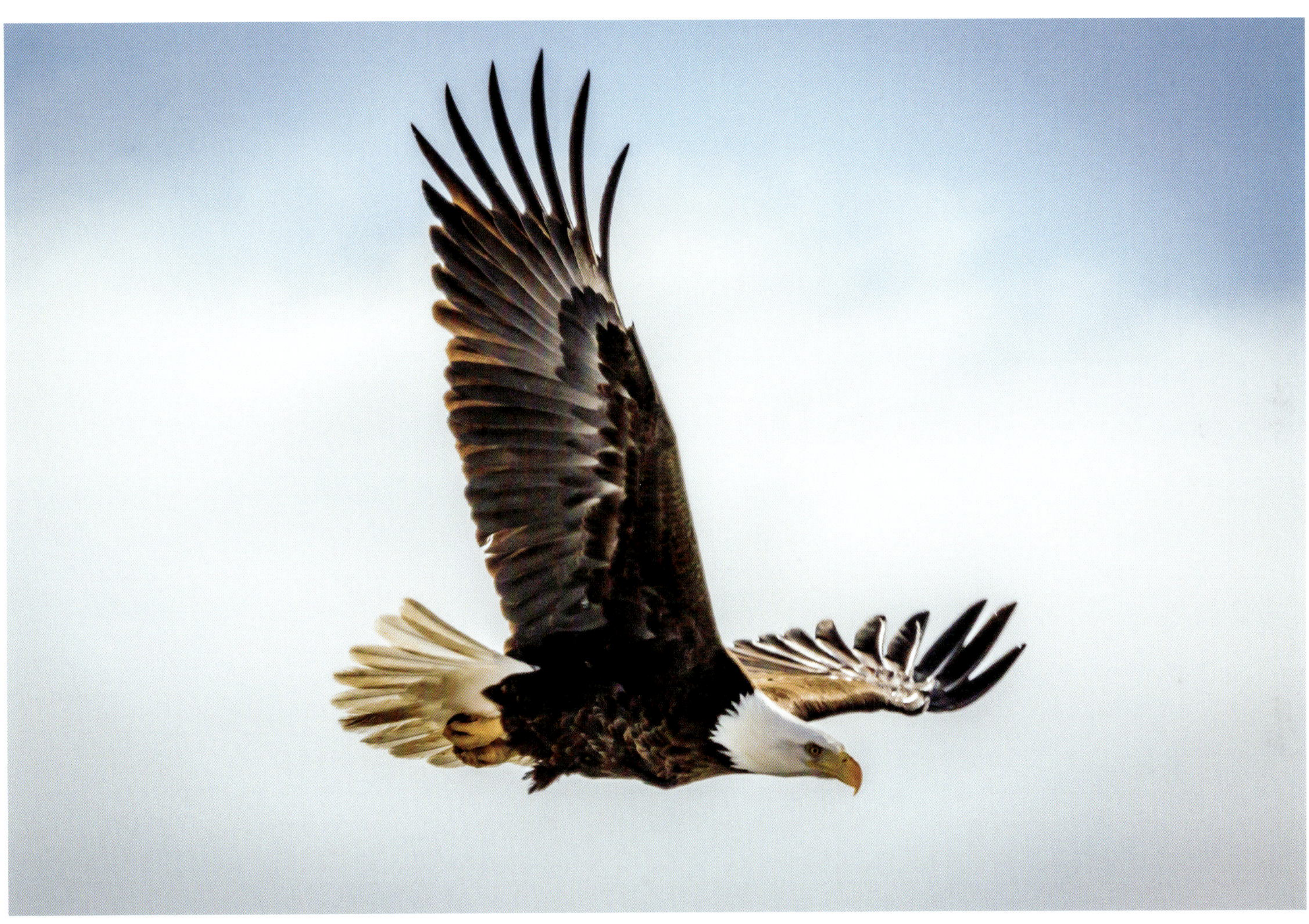

CUMBERLAND RIVER. An eagle flies overhead.

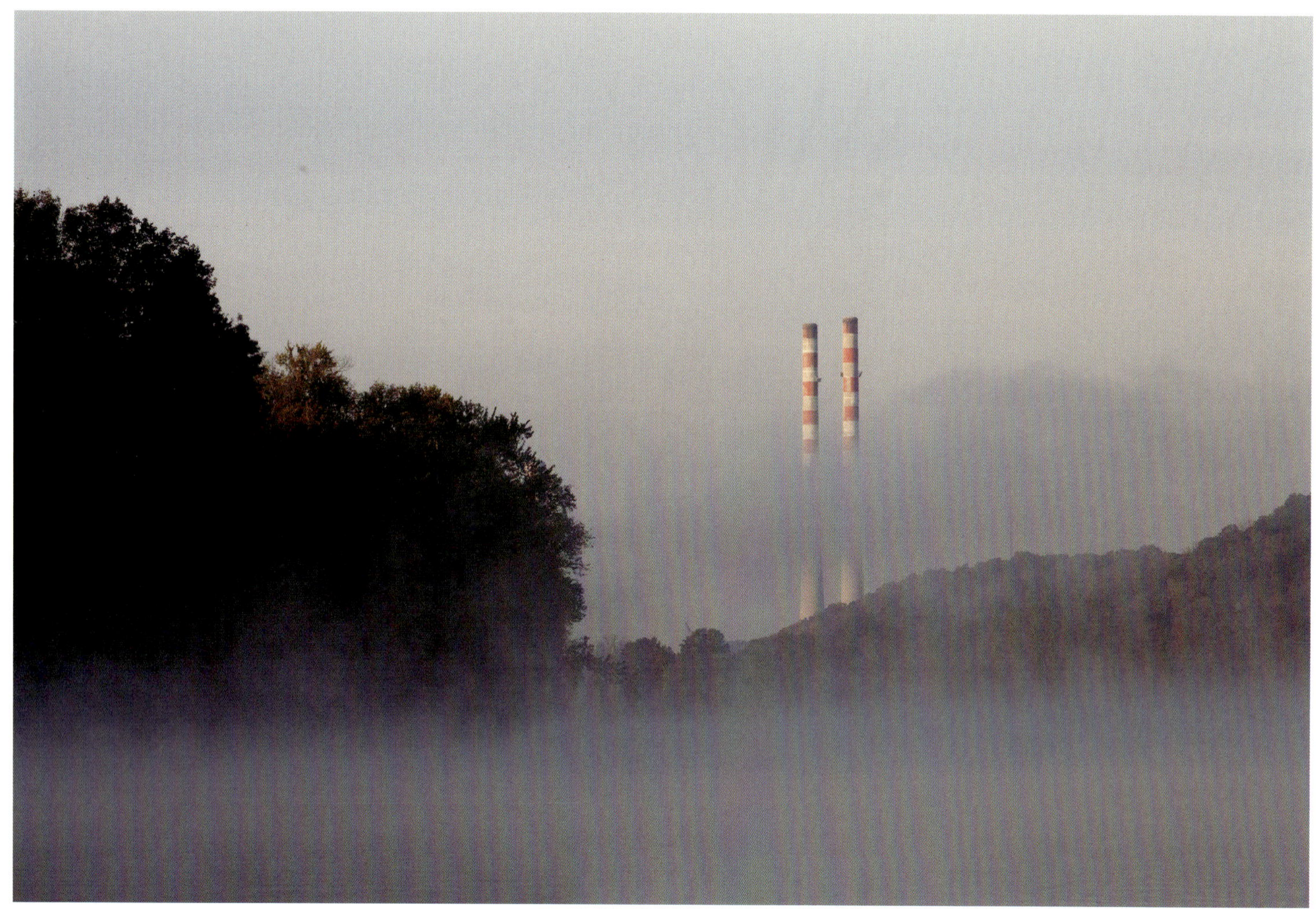

CUMBERLAND RIVER, NEAR CUMBERLAND CITY, TENNESSEE, OCTOBER 26. Smoke stacks from the Cumberland City fossil fuel plant rising out of the mist.

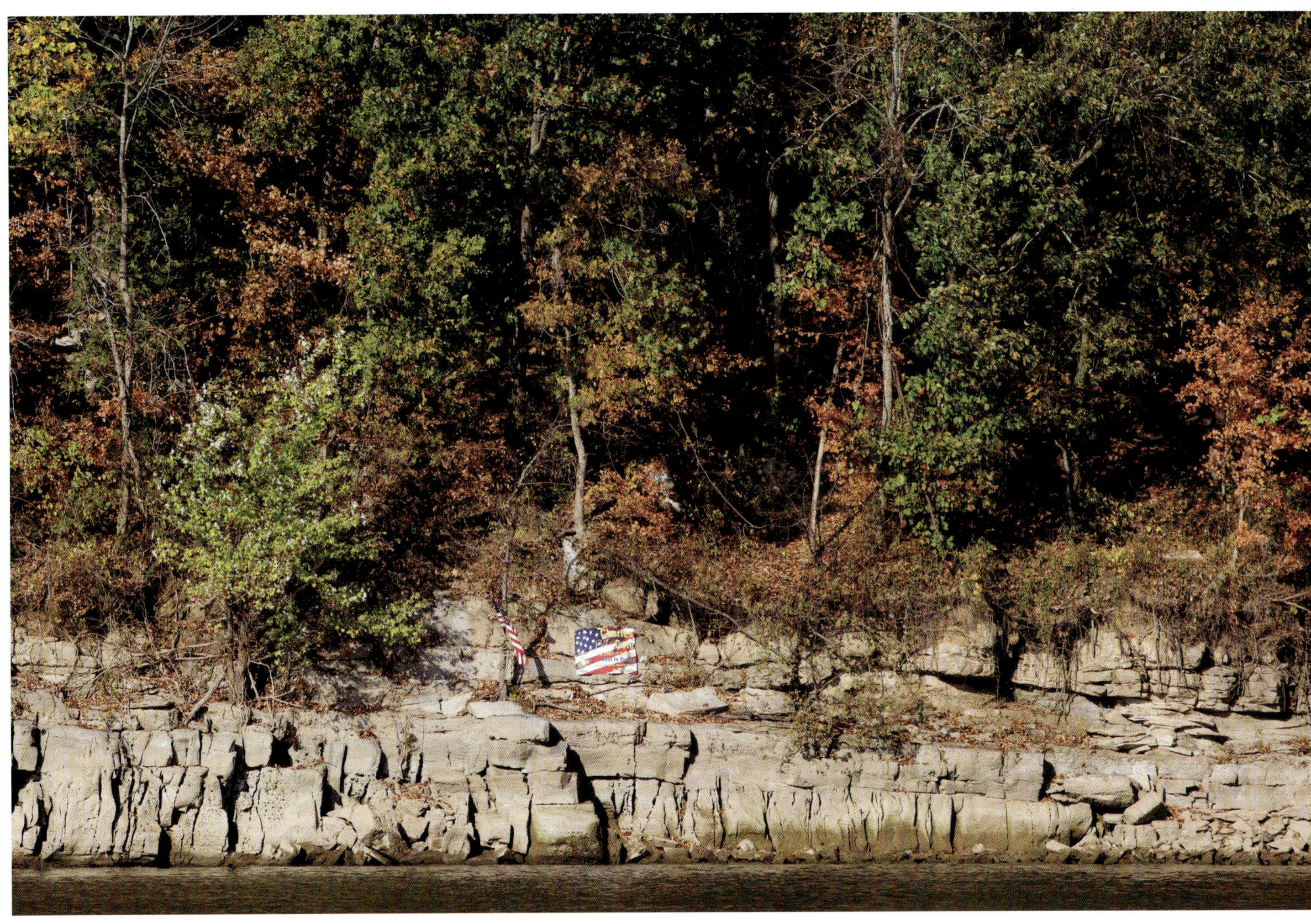

CUMBERLAND RIVER, CLARKSVILLE, TENNESSEE, OCTOBER 27. Patriotism runs high at the home of the 101st Airborne. It was around here that a party led by Moses Renfoe left the flotilla to form their own settlement along the shores of the Red River. It was short lived. Attacks from the tribes were severe, forcing the few survivors to take shelter at the newly formed Bluff Station, which would come to be called Nashville.

Modern Times for the Tennessee and Cumberland Rivers

CARROLL VAN WEST

Director of the Center for Historic Preservation at Middle Tennessee State University

The Tennessee River explored by John Guider in 2016 was not the same river traversed by generations of Native Americans and later white settlers beginning with those led by John Donelson in 1779. Guider did as well as anyone could today in retracing the general river course, and he experienced many moments of floating in the wild. But almost everywhere he rowed, he also encountered the heavy hand of modern times.

In the journal of his 1779–1780 trip down the Tennessee River and Cumberland River to the settlements of present-day Nashville, John Donelson speaks of a very different Tennessee River experience. His words are sparse. He writes mostly about the deaths and casualties of the journey, some caused by inexperience and mistakes, other from expected river currents and impediments, and most from the hostile reception the river travelers received from indigenous people, especially the Chickamauga groups clustered along the river as it passed through the southern Cumberlands. Invaders always seem surprised when the locals resist their presence. Donelson was no different than a generation of settlers to follow, who assumed their race and ambition made them conquerors, not interlopers.

Donelson also spoke of the river. He jotted many notes about the wildness of his journey, of moving through the "Whirl or Suck" and the "boiling Pot." Then came Muscle Shoals and "their dreadful appearance to those who had never seen them before. The water being high made a terrible roaring, which could be heard at some distance, among the drift-wood heaped frightfully upon the points of the islands; the current running in every possible direction." Once his boats pushed into the Cumberland, the settlers hunted wild game, finding the swan "very delicious" and buffalo meat plentiful. Soon enough they had arrived at what would become Nashville.[1]

The travel experience of Donelson and other early settlers lasted only a generation. By the beginning of the nineteenth century, settlers had destroyed or displaced those indigenous settlements, launching their own towns and building ferries to connect the once divided riverbanks to a rapidly multiplying system of roads and turnpikes. (One operating ferryboat still crosses the Cumberland River at Cumberland City, Tennessee.)

By the time of the Indian Removal in the 1830s, hundreds of Cherokees gathered on the banks of what had been their riverfront at Ross's Landing, later Chattanooga, and stepped onto boats acquired for the expressed purpose of taking them away to the west, forever. Today, parks and monuments record the nation's shame and the Cherokee refusal to be erased from the river that was once theirs.

Replacing the Native American presence along the Tennessee was a step toward progress—so assumed those in charge. Those ready to claim lands and properties along ago settled by the Cherokees, Chickamauga, and Creeks pounced once the Native Americans had been forced westward. The new residents in the 1840s and 1850s moved quickly to make the rivers, farms, and towns into a system of economic and social relations they recognized. New ports of landing and trade sprouted along the rivers. The Tennessee and Cumberland river valleys were far different places than sixty years earlier.

Other residents of the mid-nineteenth century looked at the rivers and saw a useful but dated system of transportation. Rivers had their value, and no one in the mid-nineteenth century was ready to jettison steamboats. But the quick ones knew that travel on rails, driven by steam-powered engines, was the mode of transportation for a nation on the move. And the South in 1850 was full of confidence, convinced that God endorsed its model of a southern republic, grounded in white male supremacy and an enslaved labor force of black men and women who created great wealth in cotton, crops, and livestock through their own backbreaking labor. If railroads could move the bounty created by the enslaved more quickly and efficiently to the international ports of call at Charleston and New Orleans, then the rivers be damned and forgotten. Build a bridge, lay the ballast, arrange the ties and rails, and let the trains do their job.

The assumption that railroads were the future drove the next transformation of the Tennessee and Cumberland rivers. The replacement of Ross's Landing with the railroad city of Chattanooga helps to tell the tale of change. When the Civil War began in 1861, Chattanooga was really just a transportation junction—the tracks of the Western and Atlantic stretched northward from the new city of Atlanta to the banks of the Tennessee River where they could meet the rails of the Nashville and Chattanooga Railroad coming from the north. The new rail link effectively ended the need for any future Donelson-like treks because now the steel corridor quickly connected the land of the Chickamauga to the capitol city of Nashville.

Then there was more. Coming east from the banks of the Mississippi River at Memphis was yet another line, the Memphis and LaGrange, which bypassed the Shoals, swooped down to claim the rich bounty of the lower Tennessee River valley in Alabama, and then threaded its way through the mountains to Chattanooga. Coming from the west was East Tennessee and Georgia Railroad, linking Knoxville to the new city on the Tennessee River banks.

Chattanooga and the rails eclipsed the river—the Tennessee was now available for other uses. But that same transportation connection ensured that the terrible swift sword of Northern retribution would use Chattanooga as a launching point to destroy the Deep South. In the aftermath of the bloody battles of Chickamauga and Chattanooga, the Union army gained control of the Chattanooga railroad junction, turning it into an occupied base for the southern invasion to follow and becoming a destination point for thousands of escaped slaves who found safety behind Union lines.

The Civil War transformation of the Tennessee River at Chattanooga came late in the fighting between North and South. From the beginning Union commanders wanted to take control of the South's inland waterways. The first three major battles in Tennessee in 1862 occurred along the rivers—Island No. 10 on the Mississippi, Fort Henry on the Tennessee, and Fort Donelson on the Cumberland. Once control over the river was ensured, the Union army located a base on the east bank of the Tennessee River at a place called Johnsonville, named for Military Governor Andrew Johnson. From that river base, mostly African American labor, escaped slaves categorized as contraband, built a railroad line to Nashville. Many of the African Americans stayed at Johnsonville and established their own community in and around the fortifications overlooking the river.

The Civil War years meant that the riverfronts at Knoxville, Chattanooga, and Nashville changed not just in military terms, but also in who lived there and who worked there once the fighting ended. All three cities gained in African American population and all three cities became larger and more industrial. A New South emerged from the ashes of war. Mills, bridges, and industrial wastelands soon defined riverbanks all along the old John Donelson route.

In the new industrial age, the US Army Corps of Engineers kept the waterways alive for river traffic through dredging and open-channel clearance and by removing snags and impediments from the main course of both the Tennessee and the Cumberland. The army engineers especially struggled to keep the Cumberland cleared once New South–era timber companies began clear-cutting thousands of acres of northern Cumberland forests and floating the logs down the Cumberland to the hungry sawmill companies in Nashville.

By the end of the nineteenth century, the army engineers concluded that the rivers themselves had to be bypassed and controlled to ensure better navigation. They called it canalization. From the 1890s to the 1920s, the corps constructed along the Cumberland River "fifteen low timbercrib dams and masonry locks" to create at least a six-foot depth for steamboats.[2]

At the Shoals of the Tennessee River in Alabama, the army engineers did much more. In 1871 Congress appropriated money for a canal that could bypass this most famous impediment to navigation along the lower Tennessee River. Construction began four years later and continued for the next fifteen years. The finished project opened to great fanfare in 1890. It produced not just an improved and wider canal than the earlier inadequate antebellum canal but it was also an engineering marvel, an aqueduct at Shoals Creek together with a fourteen-mile railroad line. The new canal system, however, did not solve the problems of silt build-up and poor navigation, not to mention flood control. The engineers understood they could not tame the river, but they could destroy it and replace it with a designed system that they could control.

The next step was finding an excuse to build a dam, replacing the uncertainty of water level and the rough water of a natural river with a smooth, calm man-made lake. The Muscle Shoals Power Company, newly formed in 1898, created the excuse—the city needed hydroelectric power for its future. In 1899 Congress and President William McKinley agreed on legislation allowing for the construction of a hydroelectric dam and power plant at Muscle Shoals. An assassin's bullet, however, took President McKinley's life and his successor, the much more conservation-minded Theodore Roosevelt, vetoed the federal plan for a Muscle Shoals dam.

The respite for the Tennessee River did not last long. During World War I, the federal government worried that its nitrate supplies—for gunpowder—might not meet the demands of the armed forces. It began to search for a place to build nitrate factories and decided that the Shoals of the Tennessee River was perfect—especially since a hydroelectric dam across the river there could produce all of

The massive dam and powerhouse replaced the wildness of the Shoals with an engineering system controlled by men and women.

the necessary power. Construction of Wilson Dam, named for President Woodrow Wilson, began in 1918. But when the war ended in November of that year, the federal interest in Muscle Shoals lagged and progress slowed. Stepping forward was the Motor King, Henry Ford, who wanted the dam finished and the federal land passed to his company so he could create a workers' wonderland in the lower Tennessee River Valley where nitrates, fertilizers, electric power, and new industrial marvels could be manufactured. Congress, encouraged by Nebraska senator George Norris, was not ready to give Ford so much so quickly and for so little in return to the federal treasury. Nor did progressives like Norris want to give up the notion of a public solution to the federal investment at Muscle Shoals. Not until 1925 would Wilson Dam be completed.

The massive dam and powerhouse replaced the wildness of the Shoals with an engineering system controlled by men and women. The concrete and steel behemoth was 137 feet high and over 4,500 feet long—nothing like it had ever been seen on the Tennessee and Cumberland Rivers. Only the most visionary saw Wilson Dam as a sign of even greater things to come.

One dam on the Tennessee at the Shoals was not enough for the federal government to meet its goals of better river navigation, power production, and flood control. In 1932, the US Army Corps of Engineers began site preparation for a second dam, named in honor of former Confederate general Joseph K. Wheeler, some sixteen miles above Wilson Dam. The next phase for hydroelectric power and modern river navigation on the Tennessee River was underway.

Prospects to actually build the second dam were not particularly promising since the Great Depression that began in 1929 was now haunting millions of Americans and getting worse as the months passed. Newly elected President Franklin D. Roosevelt was willing to try almost anything to get the nation back to work and moving forward. Once Roosevelt took office in March 1933 he and Congress soon agreed that tackling the Tennessee River Valley was among the nation's highest priorities. Thus, in May 1933 Congress created the Tennessee Valley Authority, charging it with improving river navigation, controlling river flooding, producing fertilizers, generating electric power, and uplifting the region's economy and culture in a coordinated, planned fashion.

President Roosevelt explained his vision for the Authority in remarks to the National Emergency Council on December 11, 1934. The president admitted that the Tennessee Valley Authority was

> a social experiment that is the first of its kind in the world, as far I know, covering a convenient geographical area—in other words, the watershed of

a great river. The work proceeds along two lines, both of which are intimately connected—the physical land and water and soil end of it, and the human side of it. It proceeds on the assumption that we are going to the highest mountain peak of the Tennessee Watershed and we are going to take an acre of land up there and say, "What should this land be used for, and is it being badly used at the present time?" And a few feet farther down we are going to come to a shack on the side of the mountain where there is a white man of about as fine stock as we have in this country, who, with his family of children, is completely uneducated—never had a chance, never sees twenty-five or fifty dollars in cash a year, but just keeps body and soul together—manages to do that—and is the progenitor of a large line of children for many generations to come. He certainly has been forgotten, not by the Administration, but by the American people. They are going to see that he and his children have a chance, and they are going to see that the farm he is using is classified, and if it is not proper for him to farm it, we are going to give him a chance on better land. If he should use it, we are going to try to bring him some of the things he needs, like schools, electric lights, and so on. We are going to try to prevent soil erosion, and grow trees, and try to bring in industries. It is a tremendous effort with a very great objective. As an incident to that it is necessary to build some dams. And when you build a dam as an incident to this entire program, you get probably a certain amount of water power development out of it. We are going to try to use that water power to its best advantage.[3]

For the New Dealers, generating hydroelectric power was the best way to sell the project. But the Authority was more than a power company. Its real purpose was to bring that prototypical rural valley resident "the things he needs"—better soil, better roads, better economic opportunities, and a better life for him and his children. The project represented coordinated planning by outsiders on a massive scale and the transformation of the Tennessee River on a similar massive scale.

TVA constructed or took over nine major dams on the Tennessee River system. It began with Wilson Dam in Alabama. Over the course of a generation it would finish the Wheeler Dam project in Alabama and then add Fort Loudon, Pickwick, Chickamauga, Nickajack, and Watts Bar dams to the river course in Tennessee, the Kentucky Dam in Kentucky, and the Guntersville Dam in Alabama. All together the dams and reservoirs achieved the Authority's mission, but they also destroyed the river and replaced it with a series of lakes, creating a modern river highway of some 652 miles.

By the middle of the twentieth century, the Tennessee River Valley was an engineered landscape much as if landscape architects had been given tens of thousands of acres to redesign as a nature reserve, as long as they placed huge modern machines in the middle of it. A similar fate awaited the Cumberland River. The US Army Corps of Engineers was not to be outdone. In 1949–1951 it built the Cheatham Dam and Lock west of Nashville, and then in 1966 it completed Barkley Dam, named for the Kentucky native and former vice-president Alben Barkley. The lake stretched from deep into Stewart County, Tennessee, almost to the river's confluence with the Ohio River. The Cumberland River immediately east of Nashville disappeared under the waters of Old Hickory Lake, created on the Davidson-Sumner county line by the Old Hickory Dam and Lock, which was built between 1952 and 1957, the year the hydroelectric plant went operational.

The Tennessee Valley Authority also would not be out done in the Cold War years of the 1950s and 1960s. It constructed huge coal-fired steam plants at Kingston and New Johnsonville on the Tennessee River. When the nuclear age beckoned, the Authority never looked back and installed nuclear power plants at Watts Bar and Sequoyah in Tennessee and Browns Ferry in Alabama. The immense power, potential profits, and dangers of the nuclear energy plants marked yet another transformative era for the Tennessee River.

In the 1970s, to further enhance its power production at peak times, the Authority built the innovative Raccoon Mountain Pumped Storage facility outside of Chattanooga. Its most productive hydroelectric plant, Raccoon Mountain uses huge pumps to move water from Nickajack Lake on the Tennessee River to a reservoir on top of the mountain. When demand requires it, water is then released from the reservoir, through an underground tunnel to underground hydroelectric power generators to add power to the electric grid. There is no better place to see how the river is now just a source of energy for many residents.

The Corps of Engineers and the Tennessee Valley Authority also created a system of lakes that became home to a modern recreational industry enjoyed by thousands of boaters and floaters on any given summer day. The Raccoon Mountain Reservoir is a popular hiking and nature viewing spot for Chattanooga area residents. Multiple National Wildlife Refuges, state parks, and US Forest Service reserves as well as the national battlefield parks at Shiloh, Chattanooga, and Fort Donelson help give river travelers some sense of what past travel was like.

But don't let the quiet and solitude of those handful of isolated stretches fool you. The Tennessee and Cumberland Rivers of the Native Americans and John Donelson are gone. Guider's Tennessee and Cumberland Rivers remain, still compelling, still magical, but no longer wild and of nature. They are of man, and as much machine as they are rivers of nature.

NOTES

1. John Donelson's Journal, 1779–1780, Tennessee Historical Society Collections, Tennessee State Library and Archives.

2. Leland Johnson, "U.S. Army Corps of Engineers," *Tennessee Encyclopedia of History and Culture*, edited by Carroll Van West, et al. (Nashville: Tennessee Historical Society, 1998), 1005.

3. Quoted in Carroll Van West, *Tennessee's New Deal Landscape* (Knoxville: University of Tennessee Press, 2001), 212.

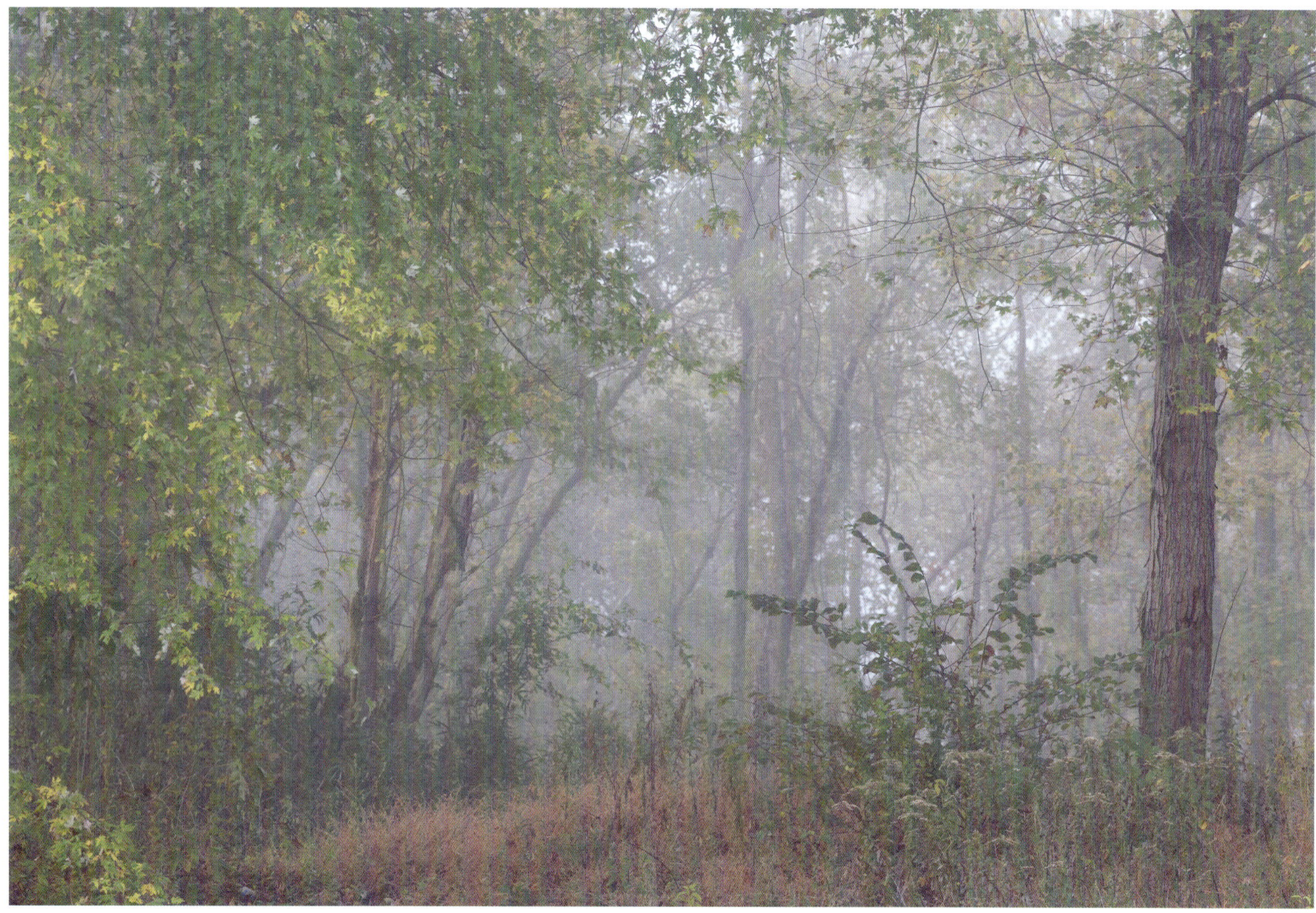

CUMBERLAND RIVER, CLOSING IN ON NASHVILLE. Lovely fall landscape with the rolling hills over a cavernous limestone base. For the Donelson flotilla, the spring colors were returning to the forest and the large animals were migrating back south to feast along the riverbanks. Food was in better supply and the settlers were able to supplement their meat with greens harvested from the riparian floor line.

CUMBERLAND RIVER. Morning mist cascading through the trees.

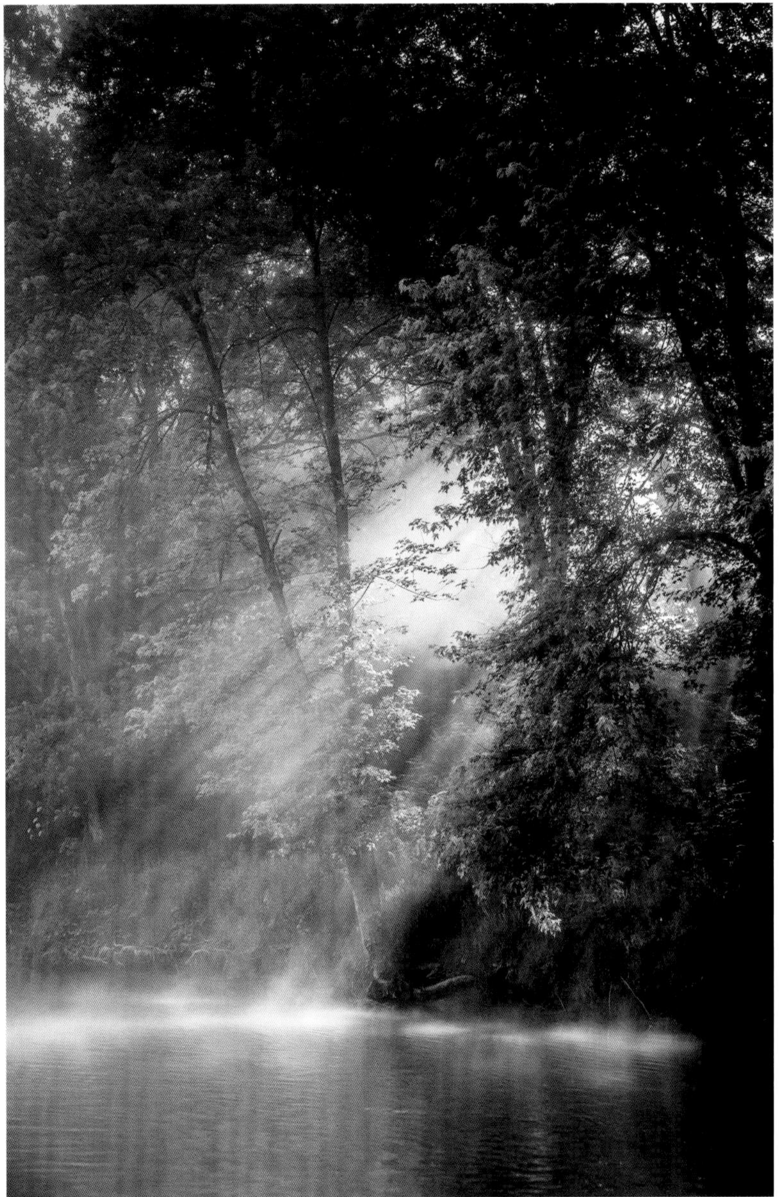

CUMBERLAND RIVER. Pleasure boat moving stealthily in the morning air. Closer to the city the river traffic picked up once more.

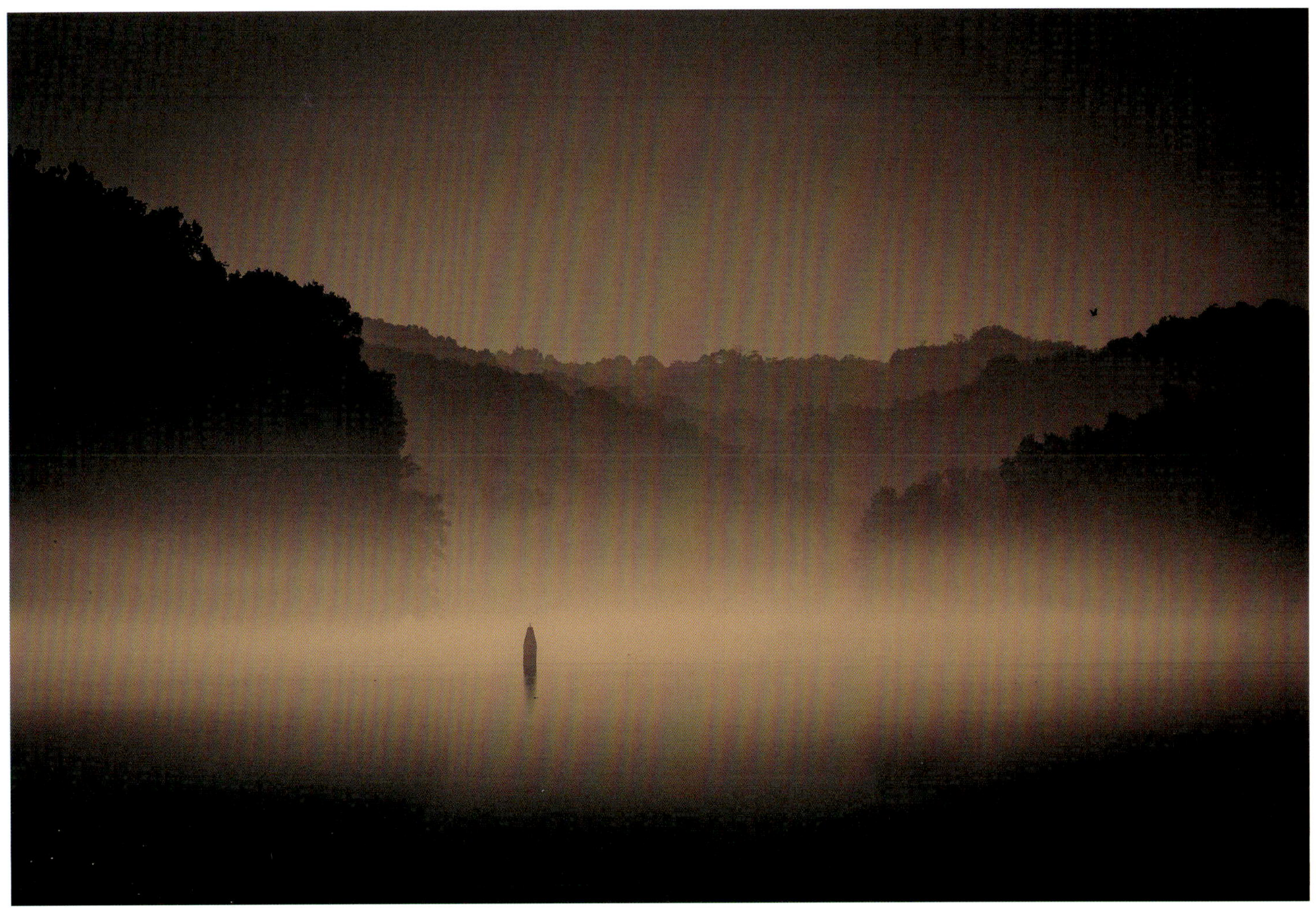

CUMBERLAND RIVER, NEAR NASHVILLE, TENNESSEE, OCTOBER 28. Channel buoys show the way home. At times I would row past midnight because there was no safe place to pull off and sleep.

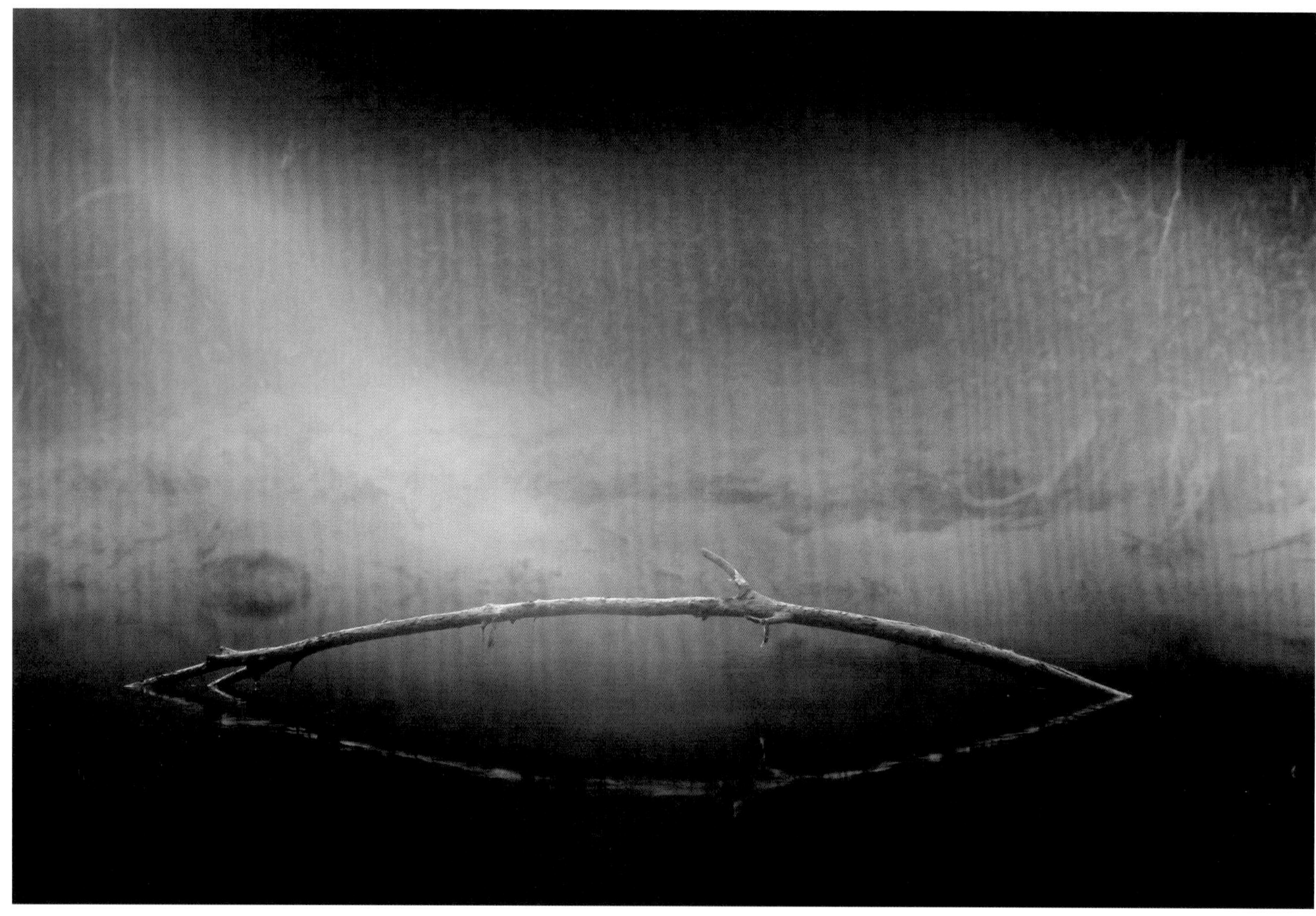

CUMBERLAND RIVER, ASHLAND CITY, TENNESSEE, OCTOBER 28. Tennessee landscape nourished by the river's presence.

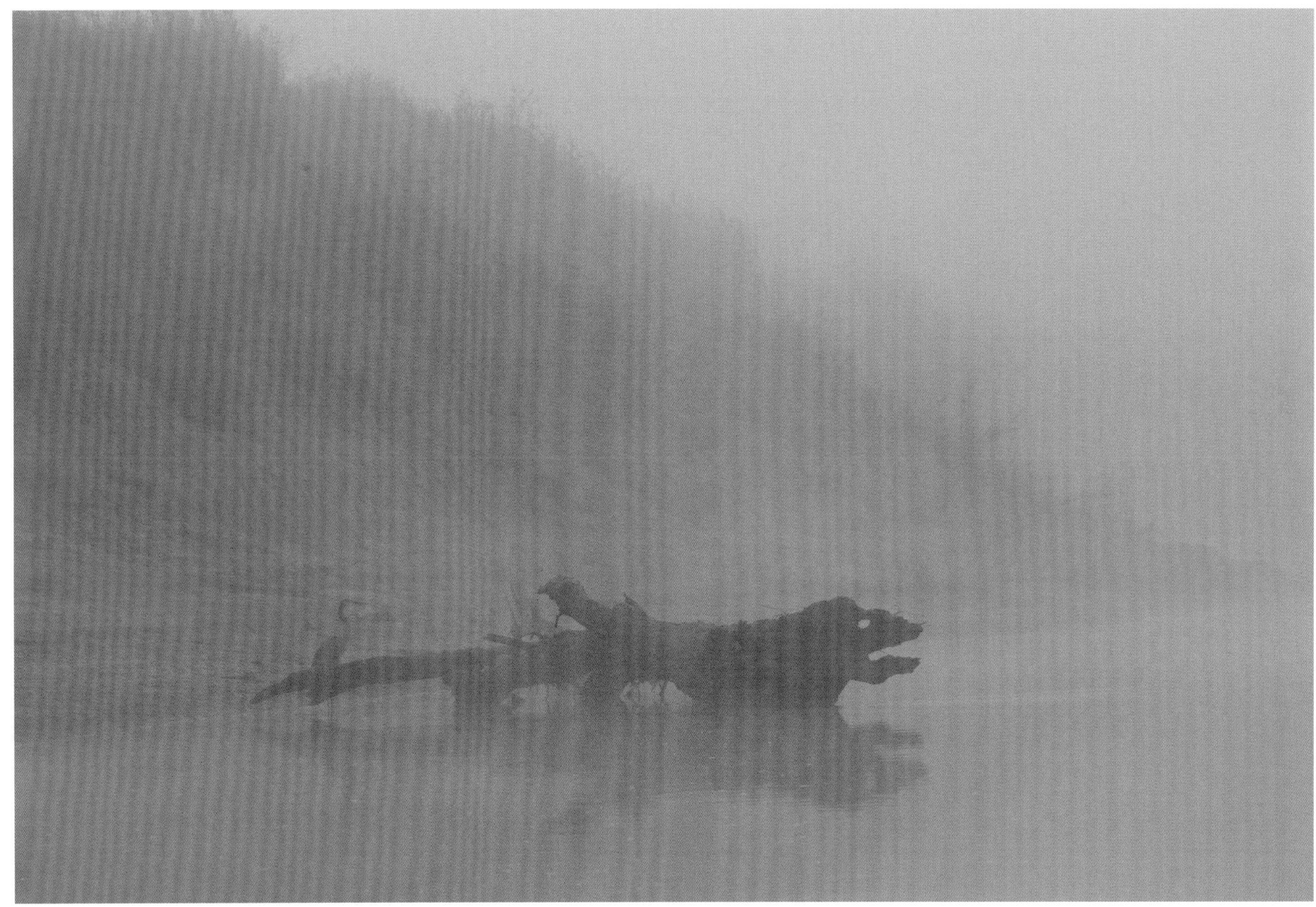

CUMBERLAND RIVER, ASHLAND CITY, TENNESSEE, OCTOBER 28. Young blue heron appears to be part of the driftwood in the water. The gauzy light created by the morning mist is a photographer's dream.

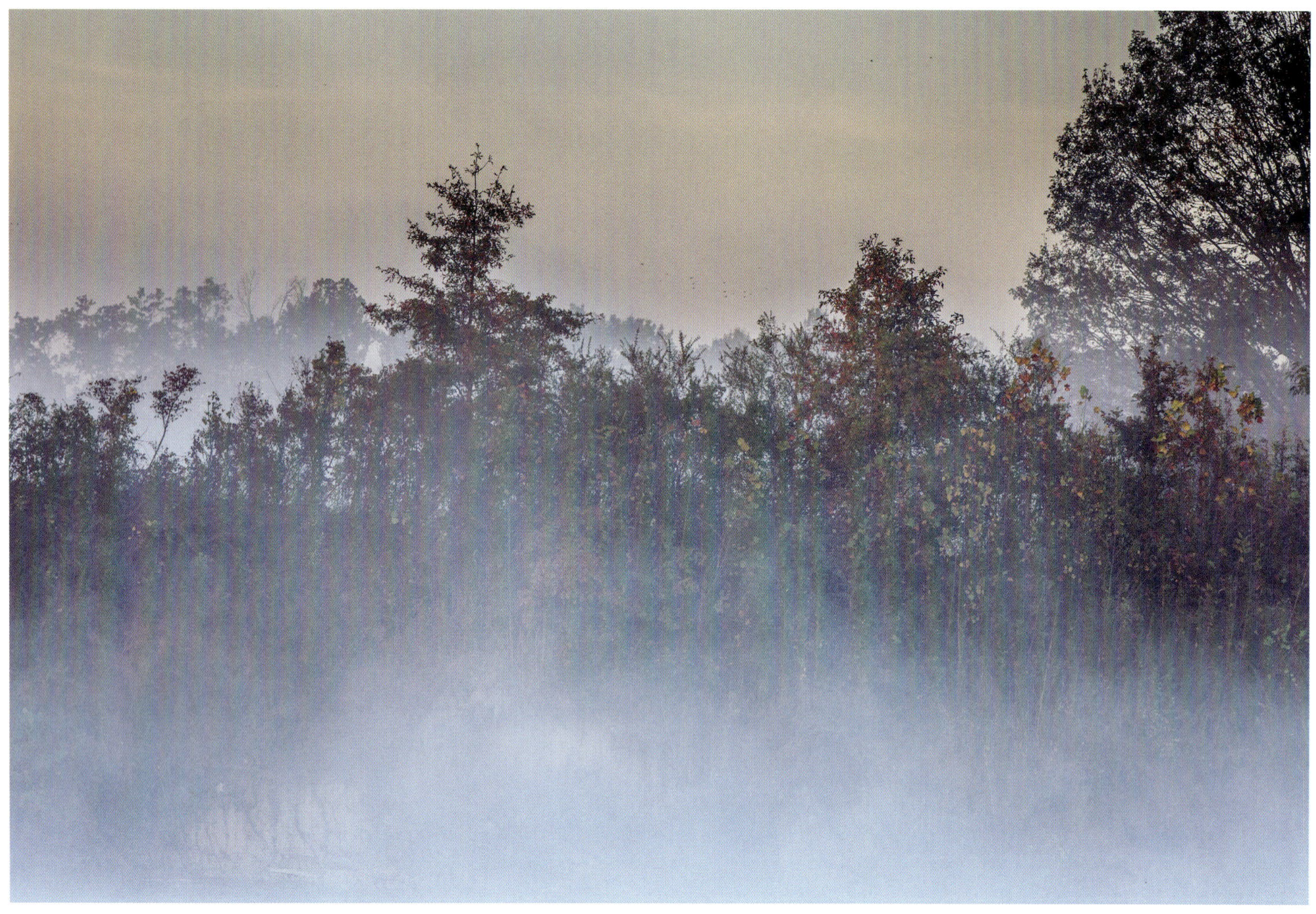

CUMBERLAND RIVER, WEST NASHVILLE, TENNESSEE, OCTOBER 29. Morning mist greets me on the last day of my journey. The young children aboard the flotilla had to be especially pleased as they neared journey's end. Among them was twelve-year-old Rachel Donelson, who would make her own lasting fame as the bride of Andrew Jackson.

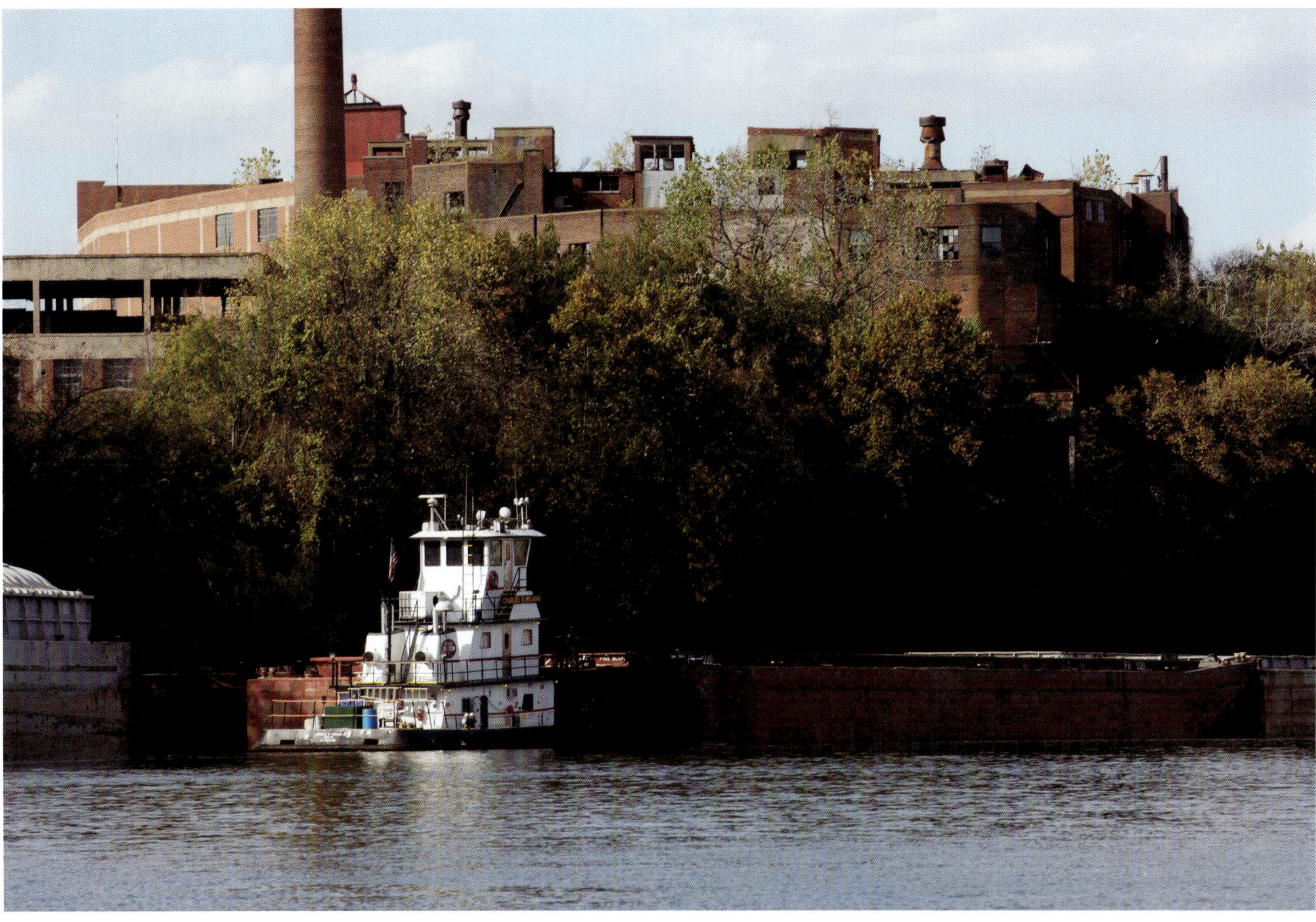

CUMBERLAND RIVER, NASHVILLE, TENNESSEE, OCTOBER 29. Harbor tug working the empty barges below the old Neuhoff slaughterhouse. Cows are no longer barged to Nashville. Germantown, where the meats were once processed, is now filled with homes and high-rise condominiums for the affluent.

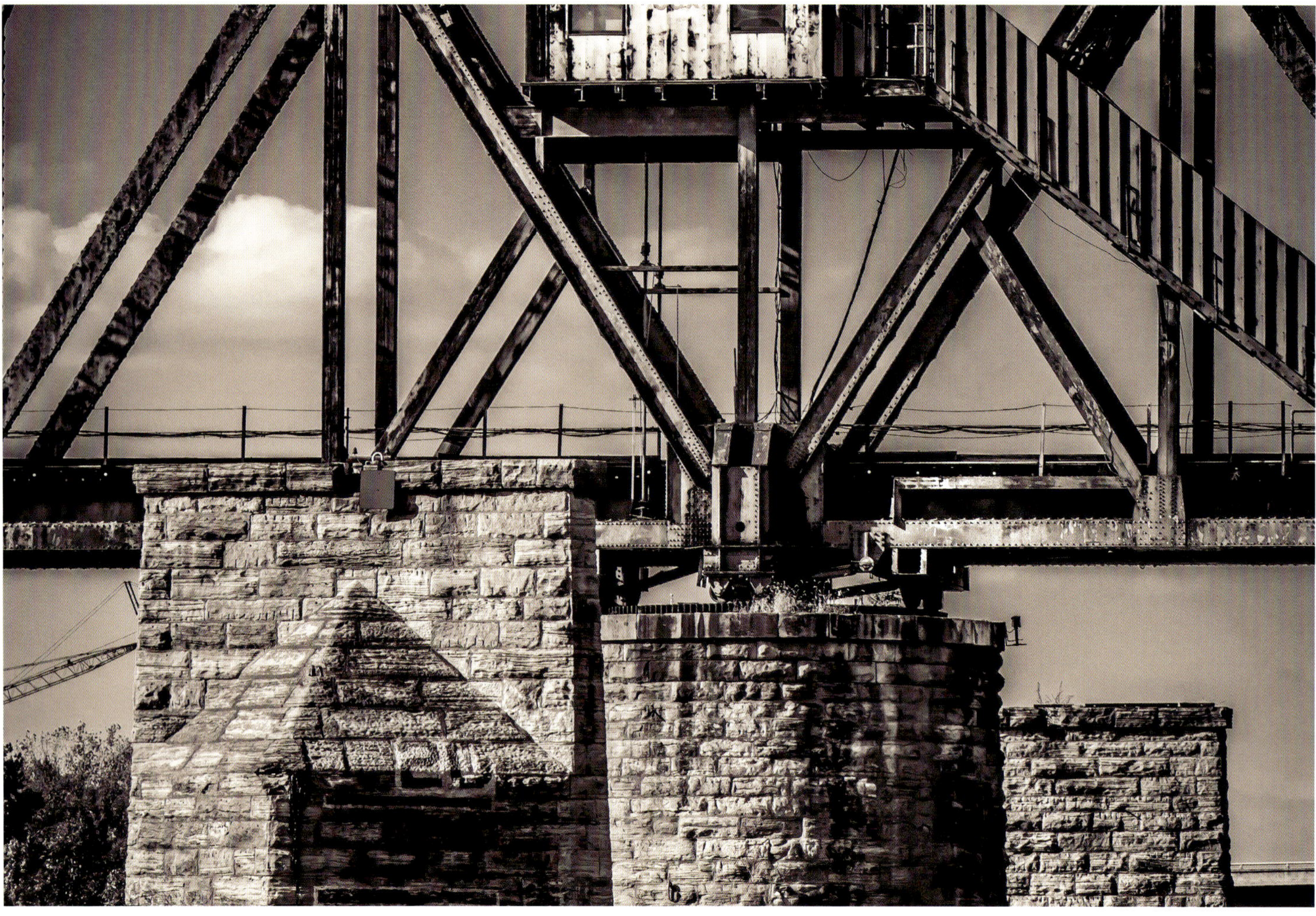

CUMBERLAND RIVER, NASHVILLE, TENNESSEE, OCTOBER 29. The L&N Railroad Bridge towers over the river. Both my goal and that of the Donelson party have been realized. Women and children on the flotilla reunited with husbands who followed James Robertson over the Wilderness Trail, shepherding the livestock as they went. But the Donelson journey does not have a storybook ending. Within a few years, a good number of the party had perished—including Donelson himself.

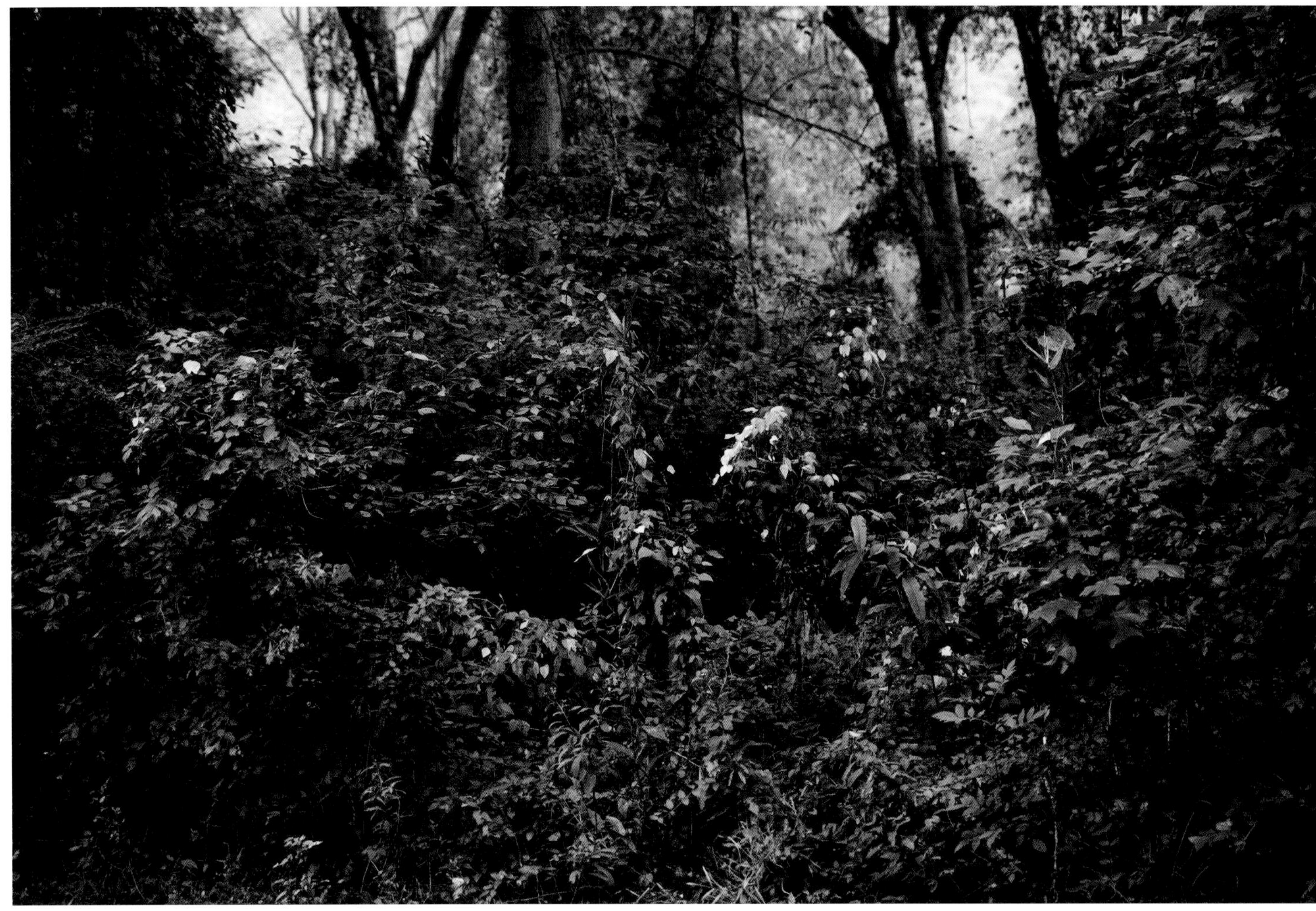

Riverbanks overgrown with shrubbery. For me the physicality of the two-month row and the spirituality of an immersion in nature away from the hubbub and stress of urban life left me fully restored and healthier than when I left.

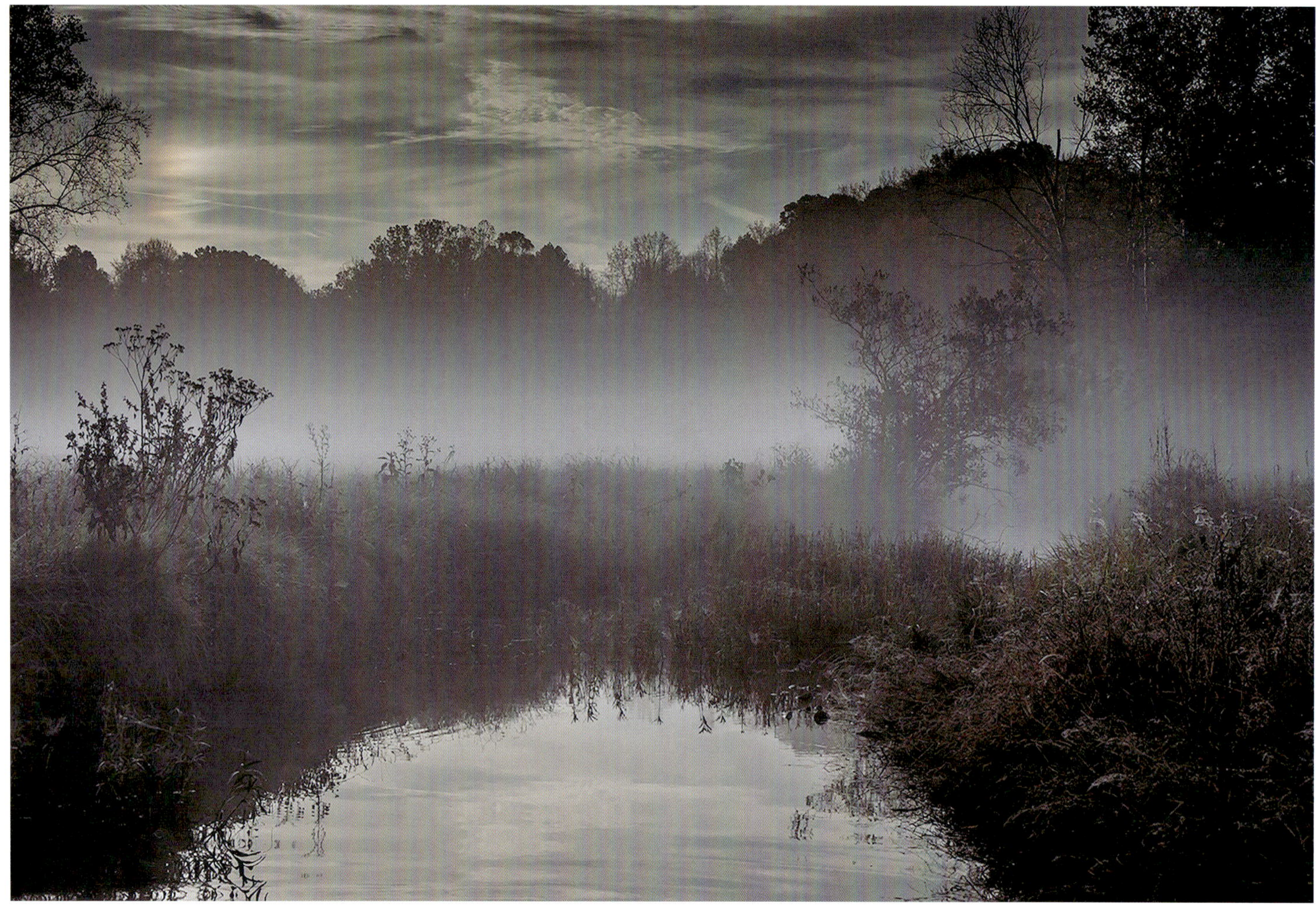

Ponding waters, part of the extensive Tennessee River watershed that continually feeds our river system.

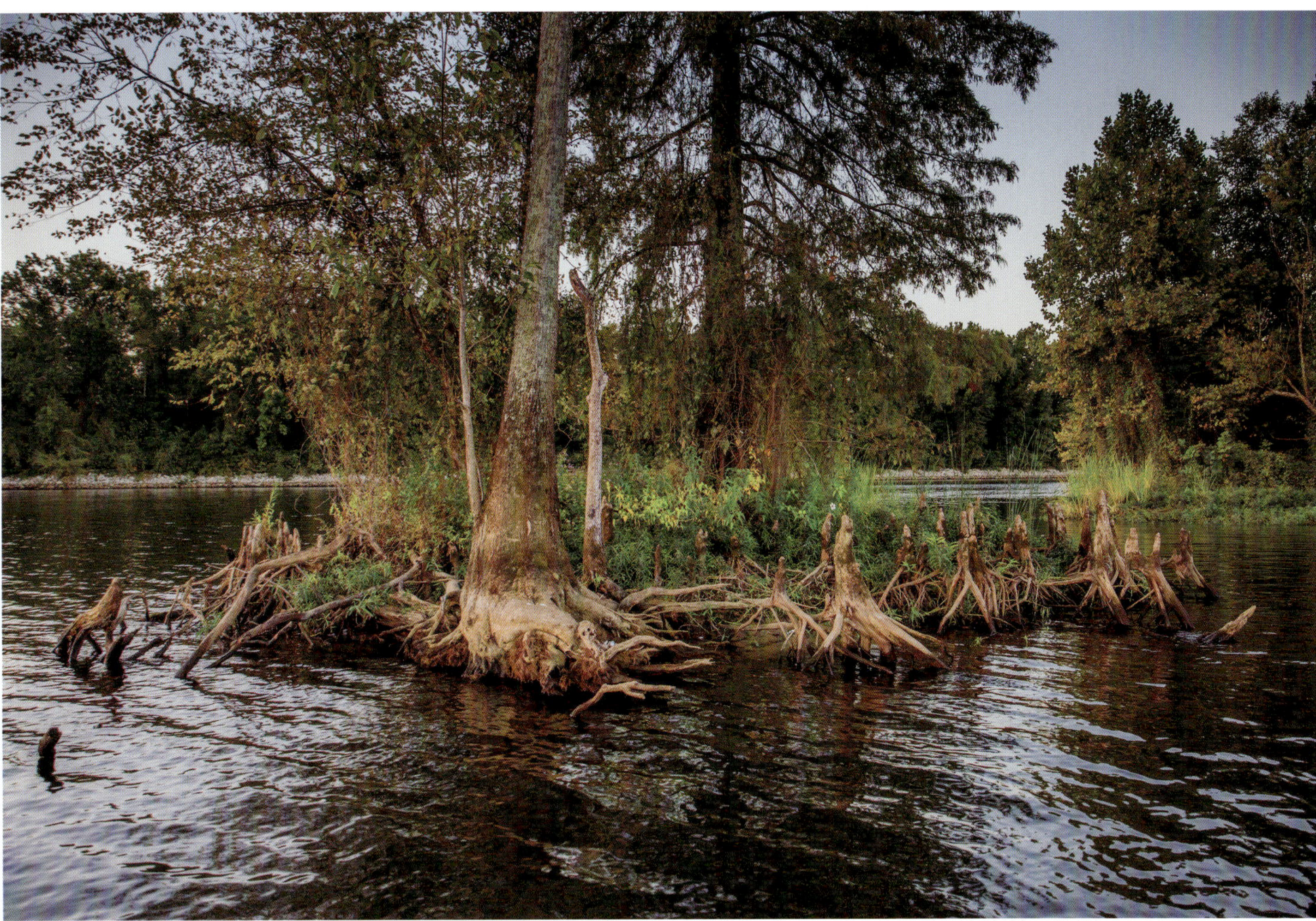

TENNESSEE RIVER, FLORENCE, ALABAMA, OCTOBER 5. I had slept close to a tall cypress and its toes reached out to the boat like ancient melted candlesticks. Wildflowers grew from the soil around its base. I took picture after picture knowing how much joy I was going to derive from revisiting the images and reliving the moment for years to come.

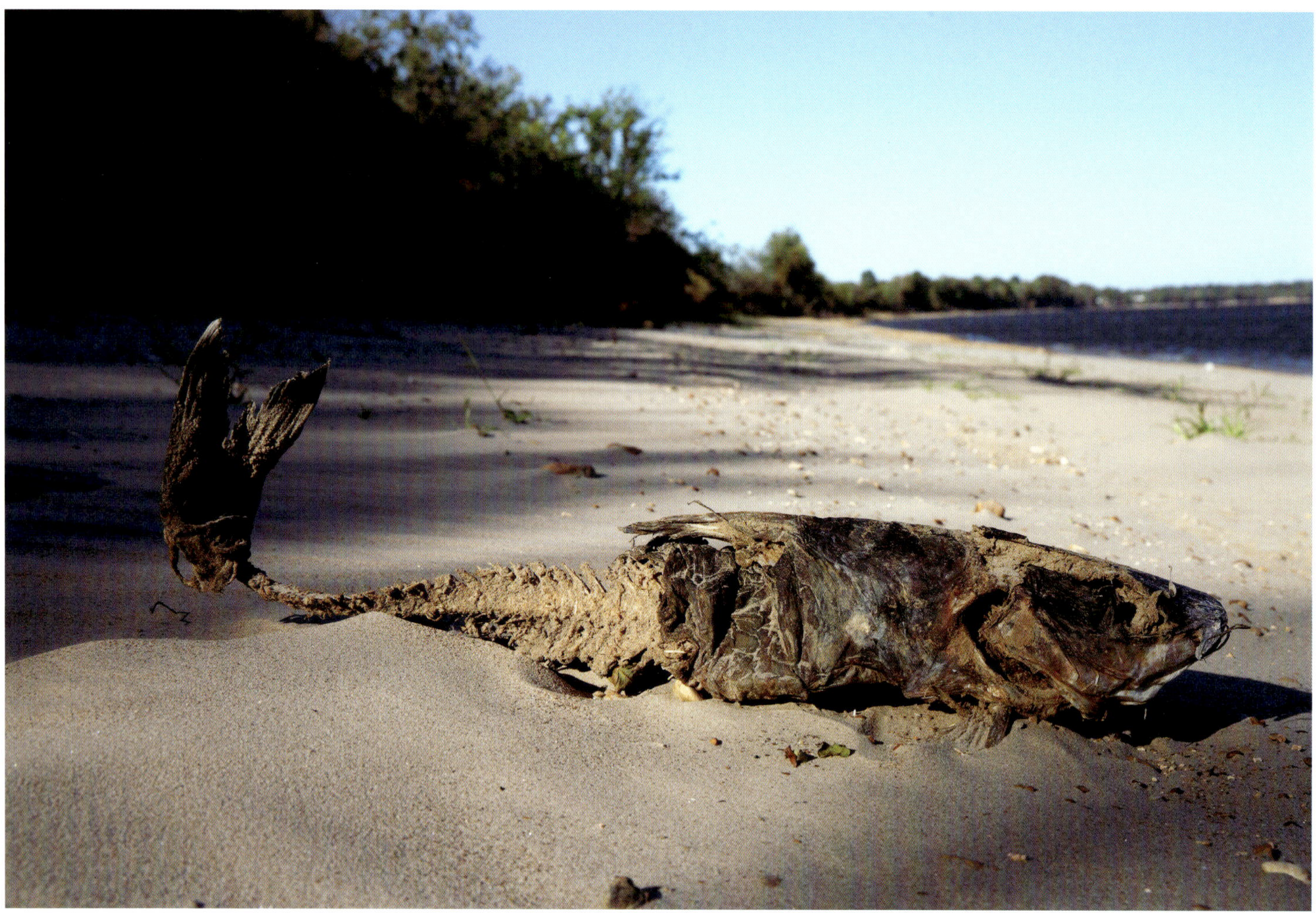

TENNESSEE RIVER, SAVANNAH, TENNESSEE, OCTOBER 10. Mummified catfish lying on the sandy shoreline. Camping along the river's edge at night, I would often hear the splash of the fish as they leapt out of the water in attempts to catch their prey. Every now and then one would misjudge its location in the darkened landscape and flop onto the riverbank next to my tent. Some made it back while an unfortunate few did not. It was in these moments that I realized what the saying "a leap of faith" truly meant. The world is full of unintended consequences, and as we strive to build our own empire, we must give careful thought to what we leave for future generations to inherit.